THE

UNMAKING

OF

ISRAEL

Also by Gershom Gorenberg

The Accidental Empire
The End of Days

THE
UNMAKING
OF
ISRAEL

Gershom Gorenberg

HARPER ● PERENNIAL

NEW YORK ● LONDON ● TORONTO ● SYDNEY ● NEW DELHI ● AUCKLAND

HARPER ● PERENNIAL

FIRST HARPER PERENNIAL EDITION PUBLISHED 2012.

The Library of Congress has catalogued the hardcover edition as follows:

Gorenberg, Gershom.
The Unmaking of Israel / Gershom Gorenberg.—1st ed.
    p.   cm.
Includes bibliographical references.
ISBN 978-0-06-198508-9
1. Land settlement—West Bank—History. 2. Land settlement—West Bank—Government policy—Israel. 3. Israelis—Colonization—West Bank—History. 4. Jews—Colonization—West Bank—History. 5. Religious Zionists—Political activity—West Bank. 6. Arab-Israeli conflict—Occupied territories. 7. Israel—Politics and government. I. Title.
HD850.5.Z63G67   2011
956.9405—dc22   2011009150

ISBN 978-0-06-198509-6 (pbk.)

12 13 14 15 16   OV/RRD   10 9 8 7 6 5 4 3 2 1

For my children
Yehonatan, Yasmin, and Shir-Raz
the rebuilders

CONTENTS

I.	The Road to Elisha	1
II.	Remember the *Altalena*	15
III.	The Capital of Lawlessness	56
IV.	Children of the Hills	97
V.	Disorderly Conduct	135
VI.	The Labor of the Righteous Is Done by Others	163
VII.	Importing the Revolution	195
VIII.	The Reestablishment of Israel	221
	Acknowledgments	249
	Notes	253
	Bibliography	299
	Index	315

THE
UNMAKING
OF
ISRAEL

I.

THE ROAD TO ELISHA

The Elisha academy doesn't look like the embodiment of three social revolutions. The dining hall facing the brick quad is prefab; the administration building is a mobile home. Only the stone-faced study hall–cum–synagogue is a permanent structure. The dorms that house several dozen students are also weather-stained mobile homes, arranged in two concentric semicircles lower on the West Bank hillside. At the compound's entrance a bored Israel Defense Forces sergeant sits in a guard booth. He glances at me through the open car window, sees that I'm Israeli, half listens to me say I have an appointment with the dean, and waves me in.

There are no colonnades, no statues of heroes in the quad. Nothing here looks monumental. Rather, the changes in Israeli society that Elisha represents are like shifts in the ground—half visible, powerful, and ongoing. They create fissures in the foundations of the state. But they are the result of human choices, not forces of nature.

I've come to Elisha because I am concerned that the state of Israel is steadily dismantling itself, and because Elisha is in several ways a marker of its undoing.

To start, Elisha is an illegal outpost, one of about a hundred small settlements established across the West Bank since the 1993 Oslo Accord committed Israel to a negotiated peace agreement with the Palestinians. Since that agreement, the Israeli government has not approved new settlements in the West Bank. Ostensibly, the settler activists who established the outposts defied the government and the laws in force in Israeli-occupied territory. In reality, multiple state agencies lent a hand, while elected officials ignored or helped the effort. The Housing Ministry spent over $300,000 on infrastructure and buildings at Elisha alone. The army provides soldiers to guard the spot. The purpose of the outpost enterprise is to fill in the gaps between larger existing settlements, to extend Jewish control over West Bank land, to fragment the territory left to Palestinians. It is actually a massive rogue operation, making a mockery of the rule of law.

At the same time, Elisha is an institution of Orthodox Jewish religious study. The students are young men at the end of their teens. The dean is a charismatic rabbi with a quiet, warm voice. By coincidence, he was born in 1967, the year of Israel's victory in the Six-Day War. Because of that perceived miracle, a new theology swept much of Israeli Judaism. It described the battlefield triumph as part of God's plan for redeeming the world, for bringing humankind into the perfected age of the messiah. The theology assigned sanctity to the state of Israel and its military. It made settling Jews in the newly conquered territory a divine commandment "as important as all the others combined." The new doctrine constricted Judaism's universal moral concerns, and made militant nationalism a pillar of faith. In his office, explaining his educational message, the dean uses the code words of that theology: his students "must understand," he says, that they are "part of the redemption of Israel." At the exclamation point of an idea, his eyes widen and a catlike quiver of pleasure runs through his shoulders. He undoubtedly assumes that the skullcap-wearing Orthodox interviewer facing him agrees with him; he has grown up in a community where his views are mainstream, taught in countless state-run religious schools.

Elisha, however, is a very particular kind of school: a pre-military academy. In principle, Israel has a universal draft at age eighteen. But the army grants deferments to high school graduates to spend a year or more at preparatory academies that combine physical training and studies that boost motivation to serve and to rise through the ranks. At Orthodox academies, one goal is to strengthen students' faith, so they can resist pressure to give up religious practice during their service. Another goal is to create a cadre of ideologically committed Orthodox officers. Despite being an illegal outpost,

Elisha appears on the Defense Ministry's Internet page of pre-military academies. The Education Ministry has provided a third or more of its budget.

During the two decades since the academies began operating, religious men have taken a growing role in the Israeli army's combat units and in its officer corps. Yet the windfall of new manpower comes with a troubling question: How much influence does a politicized clergy have in the military? This question could loom immense if Israel decides to withdraw from the West Bank—"Judea and Samaria," the biblical name for the territory used in Israeli officialese and most public discourse. In the courtyard at Elisha, I ask a young man with a dark shadow of a beard what he would do if he received orders to evacuate a settlement. "I'm not going to break religious law if all the rabbis say not to," he answers.

On the road to Elisha, no sign marked the line between Israel and occupied territory. I did not expect one. Since 1967, the government has worked to erase that line—on maps, and on the landscape. The road led eastward into the West Bank mountains, past the Palestinian village of Deir Nidham and the suburban homes at the Israeli settlement of Neveh Tzuf, until I reached the chain-link gate. For most Israelis, who rarely venture beyond the edges of occupied territory, Elisha is invisible.

Yet Elisha represents a crossroads—not on the map, but in Israeli history. The ongoing occupation, the fostering of religious extremism, the undercutting of the law by the government itself all threaten Israel's future. In particular, they place its aspiration to democracy deeply at risk. As an Israeli, I believe that the country must change direction. My questions—the questions I seek to answer in this book—are how Israel reached this point, and what path it must take from here in order to repair and rebuild itself.

There are two common ways of portraying Israel. The first stresses its successes. It has given Jews refuge and sovereignty in their own country. Six decades after its establishment, Israel is a rarity among countries that gained their independence in the era of decolonialization. It is a parliamentary democracy. Economically, Israel has climbed from the Third World to the First, from exporting fruit to exporting software.

The second portrait is of conflict—of terror attacks against Israelis, but also of roadblocks, walls, settlements, and Israeli offensives in Gaza and Lebanon. In the media and academic analysis, that picture increasingly focuses on Israel's occupation of the territory it conquered in 1967 and the plight of Palestinians living there. The regime in the West Bank—or even within Israel itself—is sometimes equated to apartheid. Zionism is cast as a colonial movement, and the displacement of the Palestinians in 1948 is seen as an inevitable consequence of Zionism's nature. The most concise criticism is that Israel is an "ethnocracy," as Israeli political geographer Oren Yiftachel argues in his 2006 book of that name. An ethnocracy, he explains, is a regime promoting "the expansion of the dominant group in contested territory while maintaining a democratic façade."

The dichotomy between these two pictures is stark—and misleading. Nations don't necessarily fit into clean categories; they are not chemical elements. Like a figure in great fiction,

Israel is better portrayed through its contradictions, through its tragic flaws and heroic aspirations.

Zionism, understood from within, is the national liberation movement of the Jews. The movement began in Eastern and Central Europe—an expanse of overlapping, entangled ethnic groups who by the late nineteenth century were all seeking political self-determination. Jewish life in that region had been precarious and fruitful, but now precariousness was winning out. Zionism defined the Jews primarily as an ethnic group, rather than a religious community. It saw the creation of a Jewish society in the Land of Israel, also known as Palestine, as the rightful repatriation of a stateless, persecuted people to its long-lost homeland. Return, Zionism posited, was the only workable solution of the world's longest-running refugee problem.

But that homeland was also home to another people— Arabs who gradually defined themselves more distinctly as Palestinians. In 1881, on the eve of European Zionist immigration, Arabs outnumbered Jews eighteen to one in Palestine. Seen from the shores of Palestine, Zionism was a movement of foreigners coming to settle the land, to colonize it. The argument between these accounts is like a debate over whether water is really oxygen or really hydrogen. That both are partly true is the starting point of the tragedy of the Israeli-Palestinian conflict.

Israel, founded in 1948, was the product of this contradictory history. More immediately, it was the child of the United Nations' November 29, 1947, decision to partition Palestine into Jewish and Arab states. For the mainstream Zionist leadership, partition meant international recognition of the Jews' right to statehood. For Palestinian Arabs, the same decision meant that foreign powers were imposing a "Jewish State in Arab territory" in "an act of aggression." So Israel was born in war—first with Palestinian Arabs, then with neighboring Arab states. For Palestinians, that war was the Nakba, the Catastrophe, in which most Arabs fled or were expelled from what became Israel; for Israeli Jews, it was a traumatic war of survival. Again, both descriptions are true.

At birth, Israel was heir to Zionism's own divisions—between political factions that covered the spectrum from the pro-Soviet left to the radical right, and between a secular majority and a religious minority. The new country's declaration of independence said that it expressed the "natural right of the Jewish people" to sovereignty, and also promised "complete equality of social and political rights to all its inhabitants irrespective of religion, race or sex."

These were the starting conditions. They limited the political choices that shaped the state of Israel, but they did not predetermine the outcome. From the same beginnings, Israel could have become a pro-Soviet or right-wing dictatorship, or could have collapsed in internecine fighting. Instead, as I'll describe in the next chapter, Israel's founders managed to create a stable state. It was a democracy, albeit a deeply flawed one—most obviously, in its treatment of the Palestinian Arab minority that remained in Israel after the Nakba. Other flaws were far more subtle, such as early decisions that over decades would reshape ultra-Orthodox Judaism in Israel, making it economically dependent on the democratic society it rejects. Nonetheless, during the period I'll call the First Israeli Republic, the country made uneven and sometimes remarkable progress toward a more liberal democracy.

Ironically, the Six-Day War of June 1967 was a turning point—a military victory that led to political folly. It marked the beginning of what I like to call the Accidental Empire. The war took Israel by surprise; the conquests of the West Bank, Gaza Strip, Golan Heights, and Sinai Peninsula were unexpected. But afterward, an Israeli government suffering from paralysis and hubris was unable to make hard political choices, especially about the West Bank and Gaza. Instead, it kept the Palestinians who lived in those territories disenfranchised, under military occupation, while settling Israeli citizens in the occupied land.

So at the moment of its triumph, Israel began to take itself apart. Long-term rule of Palestinians was a retreat from the ideal of democracy, a retreat that governments denied by describing the occupation as temporary. The settlement enterprise was a multipronged assault on the rule of law. Contrary to a common portrayal, secular politicians initiated settlement in the occupied territories and have continued to back it ever since. But the most ideologically committed settlers have been religious Zionists—and the government's support for settlement has fostered the transformation of religious Zionism into a movement of the radical right.

A country, as I said, can be best understood through its contradictions. In some ways, Israel has continued to become more democratic. The 1977 election proved that power could change hands peacefully in Israel, even as it gave the right-wing Likud the keys to government and the opportunity to escalate settlement. The Supreme Court has taken a larger role in protecting civil rights. The elected leadership of Israel's Palestinian citizens has become more assertive, more independent. The 1993 Oslo Accord signaled recognition—at least by half of the Israeli public—that Israel would have to give up the West Bank and Gaza to remain democratic.

Yet with the Oslo Accord, Israel became the Ambivalent Empire. It turned over the Gaza Strip and fragments of the West Bank to limited Palestinian self-rule, in a seeming down payment on the end of occupation. Advocating a Palestinian state alongside Israel became a centrist political position, instead of a subversive one. Even rightist prime ministers Ariel Sharon and Benjamin Netanyahu eventually paid lip service to a two-state solution. Culturally, the debate in academia and the media about the country's present and past policies became more open than ever.

At the same time, Israel's entanglement in the West Bank has only deepened. Since 1993, the number of settlers in the West Bank—outside annexed East Jerusalem—has risen from 116,000 to 300,000. The lawbreaking that was always intrinsic to the settlement enterprise is more open in the post-Oslo outposts; the religious radicalism has become more extreme. Leaving the West Bank is all the more difficult because the military cannot be certain its officers and soldiers would carry out orders to do so.

In parallel, the government continues to subsidize the ultra-Orthodox community, fostering another form of religious extremism. Over 20 percent of Israeli Jewish schoolchildren are now in ultra-Orthodox schools. Ultra-Orthodox parties, with their theocratic agenda, have grown more powerful. They not only prevent separation of religion and state but pose a threat to Israel's economic future. They are also essential members of the political alliance backing West Bank settlement.

The occupied territories are not overseas colonies. The lawlessness, the hypernationalist politics, and the struggle between Jews and Palestinians for control of the land cannot be fenced off beyond an invisible border. Settlers are targeting shared Jewish-Arab cities within Israel; rightist politicians portray Palestinian citizens as Israel's misfortune. This is one more blow to Israel's founding commitment to equality for "all its inhabitants," one more way of dismantling the state.

Let me stress: the trends I've introduced here did not grow out of one carefully premeditated policy. Some resulted from ignoring commonsense warnings about long-term rule of another people. Some are the completely unintended consequences of seemingly safe decisions, or of choices made to solve immediate problems. Many are the product of continuing to sanctify values that made sense before 1948, when Jews were seeking self-determination—and that make no sense in an independent state.

But these trends now threaten Israel's democratic aspirations and its existence. The country must and can choose a new direction. To complete this story, I will explain what Israel must do to put itself back together, to resolve the tension between Jewish independence and liberal democracy, to create the Second Israeli Republic.

Israel is not South Africa; the West Bank is not Algeria. To paraphrase Tolstoy, each troubled country is troubled in its own way. Parallels with the history of others can teach us lessons—as long as we remember that the similarity is incomplete. With that in mind, I'll mention two historic parallels that shed light on Israel's situation.

The first is with America. The newborn United States was "a settling ethnocracy," to use Oren Yiftachel's term. It enslaved black people and steadily pushed Native Americans from their land. Indeed, Israeli philosopher Avishai Margalit describes the compromise struck by the framers of the U.S. Constitution, which allowed slavery to continue, as a cardinal example of a morally indefensible "rotten compromise," one that establishes or maintains "an inhuman regime, a regime of cruelty and humiliation . . . a regime that does not treat humans as humans."

Yet the United States was also a revolutionary experiment in democracy that inspired revolutionaries elsewhere. It seems that a polity can be born as both democracy and ethnocracy, its politics built forever after around the contradiction between the two.

Inevitably, we base our judgment of which side of a country's personality is its real, underlying character on what happens later—just as the meaning of a novel's first chapter changes with each successive chapter one reads. Judged in March 1857, after the Supreme Court ruled in the *Dred Scott* decision that a black person could not be a citizen, the United States looked like a country created as an ethnocracy with a democratic false front. Judged on November 5, 2008, the day after it elected its first African American president, it looked like a fundamentally democratic nation. As much as history helps us make sense of the present, the present constantly alters the meaning of the past. As Israeli rule over the Palestinians has dragged on, academic and popular evaluations of Israel's genesis have grown harsher. If Israel ends the occupation and enhances its democracy, it will redeem not only its future but its past.

The second, very partial parallel is with Pakistan: in that country a series of policies, often adopted for short-term political reasons, has strengthened fundamentalist education, expanded the constituency for theocracy, and given religious radicals a powerful role in the military. More moderate forms of religion, conducive to a modern secular state, have suffered.

Israel certainly has not gone as far down that road. But Pakistan's experience should serve as a warning. When a country's leaders act as the patrons of religious movements opposed to an open society, they do double damage: to the state and to the religion. Israeli government sponsorship of the religious settlement movement and of ultra-Orthodoxy has enabled both to become more influential, more unbending, and more intolerant. Judaism has been terribly distorted in the process.

I make this critique not as an opponent of religion, but as a religious Jew. Since this book is not a treatise on Jewish belief, I will only briefly state what appears to me self-evident: the first lessons of Judaism's sacred texts, in the books of Genesis and Exodus, are that all human beings are created in the divine image and deserve freedom. The reason that the Bible describes humanity as beginning from a single person, as the Talmud explains, is to teach that "whoever destroys one life, it is as if he destroyed an entire world, and whoever sustains one life, it is as if he sustained an entire world." The purpose of Jews living together in their land, and the condition for them to do so, is to "pursue justice" as a society, and not just as individuals.

One of the most outspoken critics of state-linked religion in Israel was Orthodox scientist and theologian Yeshayahu

Leibowitz. "There is no greater degradation of religion than the maintenance of its institutions by a secular state," he wrote in 1959. After the conquests of June 1967, Leibowitz was also among the first critics of holding on to the occupied territories. The religious right's view of the Land of Israel and the state of Israel as inherently sacred was idolatrous, Leibowitz argued. Holiness, he said, could not be imputed to soil or to human institutions. Leibowitz, who died in 1994 at the age of ninety-one, is remembered as a strident, raging man—a rationalist philosopher with the impatient fury of a prophet. Going back to his early writings against the occupation, it seems clear to me that he feared not only the corruption of the state but also the corruption of Judaism. Time has shown that his fear was well founded.

One more personal note: I am an Israeli by choice. I came here as a student, and decided thirty years ago to stay as a citizen. My three children were born here. Two are currently serving in the Israel Defense Forces. I am writing this book because I am concerned about my country's future.

I did not think Israel was a utopia when I chose to live here. I did think it was a society in which average people were unusually engaged politically, and I hoped that this increased the potential for change. I thought there was a chance of fully realizing liberal democracy together with Zionism: of creating a society in which Jews are the majority, in which Jewish arguments are the arguments of the general society—but also a society with full rights for non-Jews, a democracy in the deepest sense. I still believe that is possible and necessary, even if much time has been wasted.

What follows is not intended as a history of Israel, nor as a diplomatic plan for Israeli-Palestinian peace. Rather, it is a selective and personal journey through Israel's past and present, for the purpose of presenting an argument: that Israel is unmaking itself, and must put itself back together.

II.

REMEMBER THE *ALTALENA*

"The units have begun moving toward the beach. The separatists have mined the bridge to Kfar Vitkin and set up machine guns. All roads have been blocked by our units," said the note to Prime Minister David Ben-Gurion from his top military aide, Yisrael Galili. "We are concentrating more forces. . . . There is no doubt that our forces will face fire when they approach the beach. We shall act decisively."

Galili was writing from Camp Dorah, an army base on the Mediterranean coast near the Jewish farming village of Kfar Vitkin. It was early on the morning of June 21, 1948.

Five weeks earlier, on May 14, Israel had formally declared its independence, at the end of the British Mandate. In late June, a UN-imposed cease-fire was providing a temporary respite from war with the neighboring Arab countries. Yet Galili was sending troops into action—against Jews. And in a very practical sense, the events of the next day and a half, at Kfar Vitkin and at the Tel Aviv seafront, would mark the actual birth of Israel as a sovereign state, with the government possessing the "monopoly [on] the legitimate use of force."

By "separatists," Galili meant the Irgun Tzva'i Le'umi, the National Military Organization, a militant right-wing Jewish underground. Hundreds of Irgun members—some of whom had deserted the new Israeli army—held the beach at Kfar Vitkin. Through the night, they had unloaded crates of grease-covered rifles, machine guns, and other arms from a ship called the *Altalena*, anchored just offshore. By the time Galili wrote to Ben-Gurion, Irgun leader Menachem Begin had already rejected an ultimatum to turn the arms over to the army. That rejection was one step in the Irgun's escalating defiance of the young government.

Defiance was an Irgun tradition, the organization's pride. The group was born under British mandatory rule of Palestine. It was a breakaway from the Haganah, the militia of the autonomous, elected Jewish institutions in Palestine. Those institutions—the Va'ad Le'umi (National Council) and the Jewish Agency—were dominated by socialist Zionist groups, led by Ben-Gurion's Mapai party. The Irgun became the military wing of the rightist Revisionist Zionist movement—which itself had bolted the mainstream Zionist Organization in 1935. The splits were predictable; splits and violent rivalries are part of the normal life cycle of national movements.

Revisionist founder Ze'ev Jabotinsky, a Russian-born, Italian-educated writer, rejected the Zionist mainstream's policy of gradual expansion of Jewish numbers, settlements, and institutions in Palestine. He stressed national pride and military power, and demanded immediate creation of a Jewish state in the entire Jewish homeland, the Land of Israel, which, he stressed, included both sides of the Jordan River— taking in all of the present-day kingdom of Jordan. Jabotinsky, who'd written under the pen name Altalena, died in 1940. In 1943, the Polish-born Begin became the Irgun's commander. Besides Jabotinsky, the formative influence on Begin and his comrades was the Polish radical right, and more widely the European far right, with its belief in the nation as ultimate value, its trust in iron will over pragmatism, and its equal willingness to take power by the vote or the gun. The next year, the Irgun declared an armed revolt against the British, who ruled Palestine under a League of Nations mandate. (The Lehi, an even more extreme break-off from the Irgun, sporadically attacked the British throughout the war; in 1940 and 1941, it sent emissaries to seek an alliance with Nazi Germany against Britain.) While World War II continued, the Haganah tried to crack down on the Irgun; afterward, the groups cooperated for a time in a wider rebellion.

The Irgun would grandiosely give itself sole credit for driving the British from Palestine. But it rejected the UN partition plan. Irgun leaders referred to the government that the Jewish Agency was preparing to establish as a treasonous "government of partition." The organization's overseas headquarters in Paris proposed setting up a rival government. Begin decided against trying to seize power, because it would lead to both a bloody civil war and "the defeat of the Irgun." He did order the Paris HQ to raise a division of volunteers in Europe, arm it, and send it to Palestine aboard a war-surplus American landing ship that the Irgun had bought and renamed the *Altalena*. In Begin's imagination, the Irgun force would land on May 15, just after the British left, and conquer the parts of Palestine that partition assigned to an Arab state. From all of Europe, though, the Paris activists managed to recruit only a hundred untrained would-be soldiers. Their arms-buying efforts also failed. The ship did not sail.

On May 14, Israel declared independence, with Ben-Gurion as prime minister and defense minister of the provisional government. Less than two weeks later, in the midst of war, the government declared the formation of the Israel Defense Forces (IDF), based on the Haganah, as the country's army. Nationwide conscription began. Separate military forces were banned. On June 1, Galili signed an agreement with Begin to dissolve the Irgun and integrate its 3,600 fighters into the IDF. The Irgun leader had demanded that Irgun soldiers join as a single brigade. Galili wanted them drafted as individuals—but agreed to separate Irgun battalions within IDF brigades. The Irgun would cease its overseas efforts to acquire arms, the accord said.

But it didn't. On June 13, Begin informed Galili that the *Altalena* was en route from Marseilles. It was loaded with arms that the Paris office had mysteriously received from the

French government—over 5,000 rifles, at least 4 million bullets, hundreds of machine guns, bazookas, mortar shells, and more. It also carried 900 immigrants, Irgun supporters from among the homeless Jews of Europe. Begin had known of plans to send the ship, but the affair had gotten out of hand: the weapons and immigrants were set to arrive in violation of the UN-supervised cease-fire, which had begun two days before, the same day the ship sailed. In return for help, Begin appeared ready to turn over the arms to the government. The IDF's arms-acquisition chief chose Kfar Vitkin as the spot for nighttime unloading, out of sight of the UN inspectors. The village, north of the coastal town of Netanyah, had been used for arms smuggling in the past.

The Irgun, however, began upping its demands, perhaps encouraged by Galili's concession on separate battalions. It wanted to unload the weapons itself. It wanted to store them in Irgun warehouses. Most important, it wanted the arms to be allocated to its own battalions. On June 18, Galili informed Begin of Ben-Gurion's response: "The arms must be turned over to the government of Israel on the beach." Begin consulted his comrades, and said no. In a summary of the contacts, Galili stressed that the Irgun HQ was still operating in Israel, and sought "a relation of equals" with the state.

After nightfall on June 20, the *Altalena* approached the shore at Kfar Vitkin. In Tel Aviv, Ben-Gurion brought the crisis before the provisional government. "There cannot be two armies and there cannot be two states," he told his eight fellow ministers. "We have to decide whether to turn power over to Begin and dissolve our army or to tell him to stop his rebellious actions." The unanimous decision was that the army should bring in enough forces to Kfar Vitkin that the Irgun would capitulate—if possible, without a fight. Ben-Gurion feared that the government might have waited too long to act. If the Irgun gained 5,000 rifles and 250 machine guns, he warned, "what they are doing now is child's play compared to what they will do tomorrow."

By then, Begin was on the beach, along with other Irgun commanders and hundreds of members and supporters of the organization. Some dug foxholes in preparation for an attack. The ship's landing boat and two rowboats from a nearby fishing village brought the immigrants ashore first, then crates of guns and ammunition. The atmosphere was festive; Begin was apparently euphoric. During the night, he rejected Galili's final ultimatum, which gave him ten minutes to surrender the arms and warned him that the IDF had encircled the beach. The unloading stretched into the next morning and afternoon.

So, actually, did the IDF's effort to bring troops to surround the Irgun bridgehead, despite what Galili told Begin. The Alexandroni Brigade, based close to Kfar Vitkin, included one of the new battalions drawn from the Irgun. The battalion had deserted, led by its commander, to join the forces on the beach. In another battalion, the 71st, many of the soldiers were unwilling to take part in an operation against Jews. In the morning, the commander of the 89th Battalion, Moshe Dayan, got orders to bring his troops from a base outside Tel Aviv. He left behind a company made up of former Lehi men.

By late afternoon, the army was finally encircling the beach. To the south, beyond a low hill, Dayan's battalion was approaching on foot and in half-tracks. Begin and his top commanders met. They decided that Begin should take the landing craft back to the *Altalena*, sail to Tel Aviv, and unload the arms there. The Irgun had more support in the city, people would come to help, the government would have to compromise. Daylight was fading. Begin, a man of ceremony, ordered his forces to line up in formation so he could address them. As he began to speak, a fusillade of gunfire began. The formation unraveled into men running for cover.

According to the best reconstruction of events, Dayan's mechanized column had come under fire several times from Irgun positions south of the hill. Finally, Dayan's column opened up for several minutes with heavy machine guns, firing mostly in the air. Begin's review of the troops was actually hidden beyond the hill. The effect of the shooting was panic, not casualties. Begin left for the *Altalena*, which sailed south. At Kfar Vitkin, Irgun men hastily unpacked guns from crates. A standoff lasted through the night. In the morning, when Dayan again advanced, the Irgun commander on the beach began negotiating surrender.

Meanwhile, though, the climactic act of Irgun defiance had begun. Just after midnight on June 22, the *Altalena* either anchored or ran aground a hundred meters off the Tel Aviv shore. It faced the heart of the city, making it easier for supporters to gather. It also faced the Kate Dan hotel, where the UN cease-fire inspectors were based; the Home Guard headquarters of the Kiryati Brigade, the army unit responsible for the city; and the Ritz Hotel. The Ritz, it happened, was the headquarters of the Palmah, formerly the elite fighting force of the Haganah and now part of the IDF. The Palmah had its own political character: it was closely tied to the left-wing United Kibbutz Movement and the pro-Soviet Mapam (United Workers Party); its military models included the Spanish Republican army and the Soviet Red Army. United Kibbutz ideological leader Yitzhak Tabenkin had once described the Palmah as "strengthening proletarian hegemony in Zionism."

In the morning, the overage Kiryati guardsmen did nothing to keep the *Altalena*'s boat from landing and unloading arms. Nor could Kiryati roadblocks stop the mixed mob of local Irgun members, army deserters who'd flowed into the city, and Irgun supporters from reaching the beach. When the boat returned to the shore a second time, the small Palmah contingent at the Ritz opened fire. Yitzhak Rabin, the twenty-six-year-old deputy commander of the Palmah, showed up at headquarters and took charge there. An intermittent gun battle with the Irgun forces on the beach and the ship continued through the day. In the meantime, the IDF general staff ordered artillery to deploy at Camp Yonah, a base just to the north on the coast. When an *Altalena* crew member swam ashore to seek a cease-fire, Palmah commander Yigal Allon gave orders to send him back with an ultimatum and a promise: surrender the arms within half an hour, and no one will be arrested. The ultimatum ran out at 4:00 p.m. The cannon at Camp Yonah fired several shells. One hit the *Altalena*. A column of smoke rose, and people began jumping overboard.

Altogether, sixteen Irgun fighters and three IDF soldiers were killed in the fighting. The shell that hit the *Altalena* did not quite end the affair. Troops under Allon's command mopped up in Tel Aviv. The Irgun issued a statement calling Ben-Gurion a dictator, and warning that his government would rule "by means of concentration camps, torture cellars, and hangings." At the same time, it labeled the provisional government a "Judenrat." To avoid "terrible bloodshed between Jews in the hour of danger," however, it ordered its fighters not to use their weapons. Only in September did the Irgun accept a final ultimatum to disband. Yet the shell that hit the *Altalena*—Ben-Gurion's willingness to order it fired, the extremely reluctant willingness of the cannon's crew to fire it—effectively ended the Irgun's challenge to the government.

To this, I must add a postscript. The following week, Yisrael Galili resigned his post. Before independence, he had been the head of the civilian staff appointed by political parties that directed the Haganah. He himself was a member of Mapam and the United Kibbutz. Ben-Gurion did not want a tie between parties and the army, and had been working for months to push Galili out. The next step came at the end of September: overcoming intense resistance from Mapam, Ben-Gurion dissolved the Palmah command and completed integration of its units in the IDF. In the early months of independence, he also rejected requests from rabbis and from the religious Hapoel Hamizrahi party to allow Orthodox soldiers to serve in separate units.

Since 1948, there have been two ways of remembering the *Altalena* in Israel. The political camp created by Begin and other Irgun veterans has nurtured one memory, in which the affair stands for perfidy, tyranny, and inexcusable violence by Jew against fellow Jew. In the other memory, the *Altalena* represents resolute decision making that established the government's authority and averted wider civil war.

Underlying these two versions and the clash itself is a half-political, half-psychological issue: the transition from revolution to institution, from movement to state, is hard for people to make. It is not accomplished merely by proclaiming independence or appointing a government. There is greater romance in being a rebel than in being a bureaucrat.

Before the revolution succeeds, the law belongs to a foreign or illegitimate regime. Breaking it for the cause is heroic. When they ruled Palestine, the British restricted Jewish immigration— before, during, and after the Holocaust. Both the Haganah and the Irgun illegally brought shiploads of immigrants as a means of getting Jews from Europe to their homeland and as a way to challenge British rule. Illegal immigration gained mythic status in Zionist memory, as did illegal use of arms.

Ideally, after the revolution, the ex-rebels should aspire to the rule of law, legitimated by popular consent, applied equally even to acts committed in the name of ideology or patriotism. The ideal is likely to be achieved slowly at best.

Before May 14, 1948, the Zionist movement sought the liberation of territory from foreign rule, but also the liberation of Jews through control of that territory. The Palestinian Arabs were a problem, not a responsibility. Within the mainstream—the Zionist Organization, the Jewish Agency, and the Va'ad Le'umi—relations between political factions were determined by elections. But a disgruntled minority group could bolt, as the Revisionists had, so a broad consensus was vital. Between the Irgun and the mainstream, the relation was one of rivalry, suspicion, and sometimes partnership. Cooperation, when it happened, was based on agreements colored by the fact that both sides had guns.

The Irgun saw itself as representing the purest Zionism, unwilling to concede any part of the Land of Israel and un-adulterated by other ideologies, such as socialism. It asserted that liberation could come only by the gun. In its statement after the sinking of the *Altalena*, it referred to weaponry as "precious beyond all value." That love of "iron," as Begin called weapons, came from emotional as well as pragmatic need. The Zionist right carried a small stick and loved to speak very loudly. The mainstream, meanwhile, saw the Irgun as separatists and terrorists.

In the *Altalena* affair, the Irgun showed how hard the adjustment to independence could be. Begin and his colleagues treated the provisional government as a rival movement. Before May 14, Begin dreamed of conducting his own military campaign. After independence, the Irgun consented to join forces with the government, but when its guns belatedly arrived, it wanted them for its own units. Ben-Gurion's mark of Cain—or Rabin's, in the extreme right's version in the 1990s—was that he was responsible for killing Jews.

For Ben-Gurion, on the other hand, statehood meant that the civilian government alone could possess military power. To be sure, the Israeli army was never quarantined from politics. The political leanings of top officers were known, especially in the state's first years. Ex-generals dominate Israeli politics to this day. The military's analysis and policy proposals, biased toward force, have strongly influenced government decisions.

What Ben-Gurion did accomplish, though, was to ensure that political factions neither had their own military forces nor controlled parts of the country's army. Disarming parties created the space for real politics. It made way for groups to negotiate and compromise based on their ability to sway public support, not their ability to fight. It was a necessary though not sufficient condition for democracy.

Given experience elsewhere, I'd argue, this was no small accomplishment. In Europe, as Tony Judt has written, World War II included "a whole series of local, civil wars," some between rival partisan movements, some continuing well after Germany's defeat. The Greek Civil War, a legacy of liberation, was still burning when Israel became independent. The retreat of European colonial empires opened up more conflicts between rival liberation groups backed by outside patrons. In Angola, civil war lasted from 1975 to 1991. In the Palestinian Authority, even without independence, elections were held in 2006 between armed parties, which then fought and split their meager territory. The outcome of the *Altalena* affair headed off such a breakdown in Israel. What helped limit the clash was that both sides knew that it was a sideshow to the real postcolonial struggle: the one that started as a communal war with the Palestinian Arabs and continued as war with the neighboring Arab countries.

Because of that conflict, a second condition for both statehood and democracy took longer to achieve. According to Max Weber's classic description of the state, it has a "monopoly on the legitimate use of force *within a given territory*" (emphasis added). To rule by the consent of the governed, a state must have borders that define who is being governed. What was Israel's territory?

The Arab leadership within Palestine and in the neighboring countries had rejected the UN partition. Soon after the General Assembly's November 29, 1947, approval of partition, the British cabinet secretly decided to prevent the United Nations from implementing the plan, apparently in deference to Britain's Arab allies. Israel's declaration of independence did not describe borders. When it was issued, Jewish forces did not hold all the land that the partition plan had assigned to the Jewish state—but they did control some land beyond the partition lines, including a besieged piece of Jerusalem and other isolated enclaves. As the fighting continued, the IDF took more land outside the UN map.

At first, Israeli officials still thought in terms of the partition lines, and were entirely uncertain about how to treat the additional territory. In the Jewish coastal town of Nahariyah, the Interior Ministry's district administrator—a Jew who had formerly been the British district officer—reported that he initially kept a low profile. The western Galilee—the northwest corner of Palestine—was not officially part of the state. However, he decided to keep the public health service running, collect Israeli income tax, and try to reconstruct the British land registry documents, which had gone missing in the wartime change of power. In September he was told that the government had applied Israeli law to Israeli-held territory outside the partition lines. He was charged with overseeing Jewish towns in his area. A military government had responsibility for Arab ones.

Finally, between February and July 1949, Israel signed armistice agreements with Egypt, Lebanon, Transjordan, and Syria. The accord with Transjordan angered Israeli hard-liners on the left and right. Yigal Allon, now the commander of the southern front, sent a note to Ben-Gurion just before the agreement was signed, asking permission for a lightning operation to shatter Transjordan's army and take the land it held on the West Bank of the Jordan River. Allon gave reasons of military necessity, but was really expressing the ideology of his Ahdut Ha'avodah (Unity of Labor) party, a wing of Mapam. Despite their hostility on other issues, Ahdut Ha'avodah shared with the Revisionists a belief in the Jewish right to the Whole Land of Israel. One of Allon's acolytes, the poet Haim Gouri, has described him as "the armed prophet of the Whole Land."

Ben-Gurion rejected Allon's proposal. In the newly elected parliament, that decision was the basis for the first motion of no confidence in the government—submitted by Menachem Begin, now head of the Herut (Freedom) party. Ben-Gurion's response was that ruling the Whole Land, with its large Arab population, meant either giving up democracy or not having a Jewish state. The motion failed. The armistice lines—standardly printed in green on maps except where they matched the international borders of former British Palestine—became Israel's de facto borders.

If the *Altalena* episode marked the actual beginning of statehood, parliamentary democracy began with the elections of January 25, 1949. Electing a legislature, I should note, was not the announced purpose of the balloting. Officially, voters were choosing the Constituent Assembly, which, in accordance with the UN's instructions in the partition plan, would write a constitution. But it was already obvious that disputes over the country's political direction and the state's relation to religion would prevent quick agreement on a constitution.

Two days after the assembly convened, it voted to turn itself into the Knesset, or parliament. It gave itself the power to approve a government and to dismiss it by voting no confidence.

The election was proportional: the entire country was one district, voters cast ballots for parties, and the parties divided up 120 seats based on their percentage of the vote. That was the system used in Zionist organizations before independence. But it still made sense afterward; the divisions that mattered were not regional. Israel, at its birth, was not a federation of colonies or principalities. It was a confederation of political factions, of ideological tribes, some of which functioned nearly as states in themselves. The Histadrut labor union, dominated by Mapai and Mapam, ran its own school system, health-care organization, bank, building company, and more. Other parties controlled similar bodies, usually on a smaller scale. There were two other Jewish school systems—a "general" one, which was actually tied to the procapitalist General Zionist Party, and an Orthodox system, linked to two religious Zionist factions, the bourgeois Mizrahi party and the proletarian Hapoel Hamizrahi. Soccer clubs and other sports teams were ideologically identified—labor, religious, rightist. The electoral system had to give representation even to small ideological tribes so that they could conduct gritty democratic politics—compete for votes, bicker, dicker, and strike deals—rather than leave them no place to press their demands except the streets.

The parties represented in the first Knesset ranged from the Communists to the far-right Fighters List, founded by Lehi veterans. One of the Communist legislators was a young

Arab, Tawfiq Toubi. Two other Arabs represented the Democratic List of Nazareth, which was actually a Mapai auxiliary. Mapai, led by Ben-Gurion, won a plurality but not a majority. Creating majority backing in the Knesset for a government required building a coalition of several parties—as has been the case ever since.

On paper, Ben-Gurion's simplest choice in early 1949 was an alliance with Mapam, the other party of the Zionist left. But Ben-Gurion was tilting toward the United States. Mapam favored "the world of revolution." It sought to nationalize industry; Mapai tolerated a mixed economy. Mapam demanded control of the Defense Ministry, the last thing Ben-Gurion wanted to give it. On the other hand, Mapam wanted a written constitution to restrain the ruling party's power, and Ben-Gurion did not.

Not only did Mapam remain in opposition but Ben-Gurion used the security services to spy on its leaders and bug their offices. In late 1949 he dismissed thirty-one-year-old general Yigal Allon as commander of the IDF's southern front. Allon said that Ben-Gurion made clear to him that "my movement and ideological comrades were suspected of disloyalty to the state's security and independence." As its main coalition partner, Mapai took the United Religious Front, an alliance of four Orthodox parties. The Orthodox parties tended to keep their demands to issues of religion and state, leaving Mapai to run everything else. At the time, this seemed like a low-priced political bargain.

Domestically, Ben-Gurion pursued a policy called *mamlakhtiut*, which translates very roughly as "statism." Practically, it meant that the state rather than the party fiefdoms should provide services. The consolidation of the military was to be only the first step. The goal was to replace the pre-state confederation of parties with the shared, neutral framework of the state. Then again, as ruling party, Mapai ran the state. Opposing parties on both the right and left charged, with some justification, that the prime minister's real motive was to put all power in Mapai's hands. Another criticism of *mamlakhtiut* is that as a slogan and philosophy, it presented the state of Israel as a value in itself, the ultimate expression of Jewish identity and the fulfillment of Jewish history. In the long run, it seems to me, the deification of the state was even more dangerous than the potential concentration of power.

The practical policy, in any case, was hard to implement. In September 1949, the Knesset enacted free, compulsory education through age thirteen. But it left the schools in the hands of four party-run systems—the three existing ones plus a new one set up by Agudat Yisrael, an ultra-Orthodox party that opposed Zionism. Furious competition began over who would educate the children of Jewish immigrants pouring in from Europe and Middle Eastern countries. Ben-Gurion's coalition with the Orthodox parties collapsed over the issue. New elections were held just two and a half years after the first ones.

In the meantime, the Knesset decided not to write a constitution, or at least not all at once. Instead, it would pass "basic laws" from time to time that would eventually add up to a constitution. That job has never been completed. The parliamentary system remained in place. In principle, the majority in parliament held nearly unlimited power.

• • •

Yet if democracy means more than elections and majority rule—if it also means protection of individual and minority rights, if it guarantees free debate and prevents arbitrary government action—then the actual birth of Israeli democracy might be dated to October 16, 1953. On that day, the Supreme Court handed down its judgment in the case of the Communist Party's Hebrew newspaper *Kol Ha'am* (Voice of the People) and its Arabic sister paper, *Al-Ittihad* (The Union).

The case actually began with a report published in the privately owned, quite capitalist *Ha'aretz* daily in March of that year. The news item quoted Israel's ambassador to the United States, Abba Eban, as saying that "Israel could deploy 200,000 soldiers on the United States' side in case of war" with the Soviet Union. At the time, that would have meant deploying one out of every eight Israelis in the hypothetical conflict. Two weeks later, speaking in the Knesset, Prime Minister Ben-Gurion dismissed the story as a "journalistic fabrication."

By then, both of the Communist newspapers had published editorials denouncing Ben-Gurion and Eban of "trafficking in the blood" of young Israelis to satisfy their American masters. The Hebrew version pledged to "escalate the struggle" for Israel's independence; the Arabic version also promised struggle, but for "bread, work, independence and peace." The government was not happy with that rhetoric. The Interior Ministry issued orders closing *Kol Ha'am* for ten days and *Al-Ittihad* for fifteen. Both immediately went to court to block the orders.

The legal fight pitted two legacies of British rule against each other. One was the 1933 Press Ordinance, a routinely repressive colonial decree that empowered the British high commissioner—now replaced by the interior minister—to close a newspaper for as long as he saw fit if he believed it was "likely to endanger the public peace." The ordinance was typical of Israeli laws, especially those inherited from the British, in the immense latitude it gave government officials.

The other legacy was the Supreme Court's function as the High Court of Justice, a role in which it heard requests by individuals for the redress of alleged injustices by the government. Such requests went directly to the High Court. The original reason for that arrangement was also colonial: under British rule, most judges on lower courts were Jewish or Arab. But Palestine's highest court had only one token Jew and one Arab; the other justices were British—and the law channeled any challenges to official actions directly to the tribunal that could be trusted to protect British interests. With independence, the institution remained, but was now composed of Israeli justices. The common citizen could go straight to the highest court in the land to challenge an executive action.

A three-justice panel was (and still is) assigned to High Court cases. The panel in the *Kol Ha'am* case was headed by the American-born and -educated Shimon Agranat, who also wrote the unanimous opinion. Agranat had neither a written constitution nor a bill of rights on which to rely. But—as legal scholar Pnina Lahav has shown in her biography of Agranat—he used daring legal reasoning to overturn the orders to close the papers.

Agranat opened with a philosophical argument that freedom of expression is fundamental to democracy. To prove that a free market of ideas serves the common good by "clarifying the truth so that a country might choose the wisest goal," he cited American legal thinkers, including Judge Learned Hand. To demonstrate that free speech is "the condition for the realization of almost all other freedoms," he reached back to John Milton's classic *Areopagitica* and John Stuart Mill's *On Liberty*.

The ruling then cited the promise in Israel's declaration of independence that the state would be "based on freedom." Though the declaration was not a constitution, he said, it still "expressed the people's vision and creed" that Israel should be a democracy. The court was obligated to interpret laws, including those inherited from the British, in that light. In doing so, it could learn from the experience of other democracies, Agranat wrote. With that, he introduced American precedents based on First Amendment law. Before closing a newspaper, the minister had to conclude that the danger to public order was "close to certain." Moreover, the court could review and overturn the minister's decision. The *Kol Ha'am* and *Al-Ittihad* editorials did not meet the probable-danger test, Agranat concluded. The High Court overturned the closure orders.

The *Kol Ha'am* ruling was both a modest beginning and a breakthrough. The Press Ordinance remained on the books. The Israeli media remained subject to military censorship, also a product of British regulations. It would take nearly forty more years before the Supreme Court asserted its authority to overturn laws. Nonetheless, *Kol Ha'am* established freedom of speech as a principle of Israeli law. As Lahav has written, the decision also became "the model for judicial review" of the executive's discretionary powers. The government was bound by legal standards; it could not rule by whim.

Besides Agranat's courageous judicial activism, what's striking in the *Kol Ha'am* case is the behavior of Ben-Gurion's government. There is an endless Israeli debate about whether Ben-Gurion was an autocrat or a democrat, a dispute unlikely to be resolved because it originally took place within him. In this drama, he played the autocrat in the first act, the democrat in the last. Suspending publication of the newspapers, the government was unabashedly ready to stifle dissent. Yet it accepted the court's intervention. Since the judiciary's power exists only to the extent that the executive obeys its decisions, the government empowered the court. It acceded to a first, fragile set of checks and balances.

Israel "was founded as a democracy and is still a democracy, which makes it something of an exception," wrote political scientist Peter Medding in 1990. As of 1980, he noted, only twenty-one countries in the world had remained continuously democratic since World War II, or since their founding if that came later. In fact, Israel was the only country on the list founded after 1945. The military had not taken over (though General Ariel Sharon did suggest a coup to other generals just before the Six-Day War); a single party had not banned the rest.

Democracy is a relative term, though. There were flaws in the system—some whose full significance would not be seen for years, some that were already easily noticed. To start, state and synagogue were entangled—even though much of the secular majority wanted to toss religion on the ash heap of history.

To make sense of this, I must first dispense with the myth that present-day Orthodox Judaism is old-time religion as once practiced by all Jews, and that today's ultra-Orthodox Jews in particular, the black-hatted men and wig-wearing women whom tourists see in parts of Jerusalem and New York, have preserved intact the pristine Jewish lifestyle of Eastern Europe. As the preeminent Jewish historian Jacob Katz wrote, "The claim of the Orthodox to be no more than the guardians of the pure Judaism of the past is a fiction."

Like Zionism, Reform Judaism, and secular Yiddish culture, Orthodoxy is a product of the earthquake of modernity that began shaking Western Europe's Jews in the eighteenth century and Eastern Europe's in the nineteenth. The shockwaves included access to modern education, the half-fulfilled promise of acceptance into Christian society, drastic economic shifts, migration from villages to cities and from Eastern Europe westward, a population explosion, and modern anti-Semitism. Beforehand, Jewish religious tradition was simply how Jews lived; children learned more about it from parents than from books; Jews' observance of religious laws ranged from strict to merely socially acceptable. Modernity turned religion from an assumption into a question. Particularly in Protestant countries, some Jews began reforming religious practices to fit the aesthetics of the surrounding culture. New ideologies, including secular Zionism, saw the Jews as a nationality—and Judaism as obsolete. Secular Zionism claimed the Bible as a national epic that portrayed the golden age when Jews were fighters and farmers in their own land, an era that Zionism would restore.

Orthodoxy was the movement of people who held on to traditional belief and practice—in a way "both more self-conscious and less self-confident" than in the past, as Katz writes. To keep the dietary laws, avoid work on the Sabbath, pray thrice daily in Hebrew, was now a statement, an ideology.

One form of Orthodoxy advocated keeping religious law while integrating into non-Jewish society and putting positive value on secular education. The alternative that would largely shape ultra-Orthodoxy was postulated by Central European rabbi Moshe Sofer: "Anything new is forbidden by the Torah," the Five Books of Moses, the original revelation on which Jewish tradition is based. Ironically, that rigid rejection of change to fit new circumstances was new in Judaism. The ultra-Orthodox foreswore secular studies, made an ideal of observing Jewish law in the strictest possible way, and made a point of dressing distinctly as a visible sign of separation from other Jews as well as non-Jews. Reacting against the intellectual openness of the Enlightenment, against modernity's vertiginous option of questioning faith, ultra-Orthodoxy posited "belief in the sages" as the new foundation of Jewish life: truly religious Jews must accept the authority of the leading rabbis of their time to make decisions for them in all areas of life—not just in religious practice, but in politics and personal affairs as well. That, too, was a radical innovation masquerading as conservatism.

An Orthodox minority endorsed Zionism, and founded the Mizrahi movement. Most Orthodox rabbis, and especially ultra-Orthodox ones, denounced Zionism as a secular rebellion against God. They formed Agudat Yisrael in opposition to Mizrahi. In the nineteenth century, a few ultra-Orthodox Jews came to Jerusalem to devote themselves to a life of religious study far from the heresies of Europe. During the British Mandate, more came to escape rising anti-Semitism, especially in Poland and Germany. (Beginning in the 1930s, the Hebrew term *haredi*, "God-fearing," came to refer specifically to the ultra-Orthodox.) But Palestine, like America, was a place where young people left the fold under the influence of secular surroundings. Ultra-Orthodox rabbis discouraged emigration from Eastern Europe—with catastrophic consequences during the Holocaust. When Israel became independent, *haredim* comprised 5 to 7 percent of the Jewish population, according to sociologist Menachem Friedman, who pioneered the study of *haredi* society. The European center of their culture was gone. In Palestine, their schools were few and starved for funds; teachers could go for months without getting paid. Many ultra-Orthodox Jews felt "that they represented a Jewish identity that would vanish in the foreseeable future," Friedman writes. While a few zealots wanted no dealings with the secular state, Agudat Yisrael saw little alternative but to enter Israeli politics, and for a brief time even formed the United Religious Front in alliance with the rival religious Zionists and joined Ben-Gurion's coalition.

The compromises that the Orthodox parties wrung from Mapai were intended partly to protect their constituents from secular coercion, and partly to impose their own view that a "Jewish state" meant one governed by religion. The army's kitchens were kept kosher so that Orthodox Jews could serve. During the war of independence, about 400 men studying at ultra-Orthodox yeshivot—Talmudic academies—in Jerusalem were exempted from the universal draft, though other *haredi* men were conscripted. Jerusalem was outside the partition lines, and the government apparently wanted to avoid the spectacle of a conflict with extreme anti-Zionist groups in a place where its rule was tenuous. Yet the precedent stuck, and after the war the army continued to give several hundred deferments to yeshivah students. The concession seemed negligible.

More glaringly, the state left marriage and divorce in the hands of the religious authorities of each religion, as had been the case since the Ottoman Empire ruled Palestine. For Jews, that meant it was only possible to marry through the state-run chief rabbinate and to get a divorce through rabbinic courts, also an arm of the government. The only way for a Jew to marry a non-Jew was to go abroad. The arrangement created a rabbinic bureaucracy, with jobs parceled out as patronage by Orthodox parties. This impinged on the freedom of religious Jews as well as secular ones: for important parts of their religious life, they were obligated to turn to clergy that the state chose for them.

In 1953, the fight between the parties over educating immigrant children finally ended with a law creating a state school system. The time of the party-run school was over, it seemed. Yet the state system had two parts—one secular, and one "state religious." De facto, the latter was controlled by functionaries of the religious Zionist parties, which merged soon after to create the National Religious Party. The ultra-

Orthodox Agudat Yisrael party was allowed to keep the school system it had recently established, with state funding but with minimal state supervision. Those schools taught children religious law and sacred texts, along with basic math, perhaps a bit of English. Civics was not part of the curriculum. Their job was to protect children from modern society, not to prepare them for it.

One explanation for why Ben-Gurion accepted these compromises is that they were the cost of coalition making. Another is that he did not want to deepen the secular-religious split. Dissident Orthodox philosopher Yeshayahu Leibowitz quoted Ben-Gurion as telling him explicitly, "I will never agree to the separation of state and religion. I want the state to hold religion in the palm of its hand."

But the expectations of the era must be remembered—as captured in novelist Amos Oz's memoir, *A Tale of Love and Darkness*. In the mid-1940s, when it was time for Oz to start first grade, his father was in a bind. Two schools were within walking distance in their Jerusalem neighborhood—one belonging to the labor system, the other religious Zionist. Oz's father was a right-wing secularist. He chose the Orthodox school because the "red tide was on the upsurge in our land" and the socialist school might turn the boy into a Bolshevik. The religious school posed no parallel risk because "religious Jews . . . with their synagogues would disappear off the face of the earth in a few years."

A few years later, after independence, secular politicians could make the same assumption, especially about ultra-Orthodoxy. The profound consequences of those early arrangements for both state and religion were entirely unexpected. No one imagined, for instance, that by funding *haredi* schools, the state would transform ultra-Orthodox society and risk ending up in the palm of *its* hand.

The politics of religion also played a role in the Knesset's 1950 vote not to frame a written constitution for Israel. Ben-Gurion's opposition was more significant. In any case, this is one early decision that deserves less blame for hobbling democracy than is usually assigned to it.

Strikingly, the strongest advocates of a constitution in the Knesset debate came from Mapam and the Communists on the left, and from Menachem Begin's Herut on the right. "There is one thing that you wish to prevent," said Begin, railing at the ruling Mapai party, "a law of freedom, of justice, that takes precedence over other laws, and that you cannot rescind one fine morning with a mechanical majority." A Mapam legislator, Yisrael Bar-Yehudah, made the classic argument that a constitution was needed to protect "the rights of the individual in relation to the government—what is the minimum that the legislative, executive and judicial powers cannot harm."

The Religious Front's stated objection to a constitution was that the Torah had been the constitution of Jews throughout history, and a Jewish state needed no other. One function of a constitution was educational, said Agudat Yisrael's Meir David Levenstein; its preamble would be used to teach children the nation's "spiritual profile"—and for precisely that reason no religious school could teach a secular constitution. A *kulturkampf* would ensue, he said. The Orthodox politicians' more practical fear may have been that a constitution would separate synagogue and state, or even impose restrictions on the practice of religion. The left's militant secularism and the example of the East Bloc—including the infamous Yevsektsia, the Jewish Sections of the Communist Party in Russia, responsible for suppressing Judaism—frightened them.

The real danger to democracy, argued Mapai's Yosef Lam, came from the very parties that demanded a constitution. Neither Herut nor Mapam understood democracy, he said. "In a democratic regime you don't change the direction of the majority with threats that its leaders will be brought to trial," he said, referring to Herut's rhetoric. As for Mapam, it believed in "people's democracy," in protecting the rights of the minority only until the next "revolutionary moment," when it could take power. With those parties in parliament, no consensus wide enough to frame a constitution could be reached, he said. Ben-Gurion, concluding the debate, took a similar line: normal laws could protect civil rights, but the majority should not be straitjacketed. Unlike the United States, the pioneer of modern constitutionalism, Israel did not need to resolve the relations between a federal government and individual states. Most important, it could not afford to restrict the power of a democratic government to defend itself against antidemocratic minorities. Turning to Mapam leader Meir Ya'ari, he said, "It cannot be that Knesset Member Ya'ari does not know that there are people in the Knesset and in the country who want to destroy the democratic regime in Israel and who aspire to a totalitarian regime."

It may be true that in the name of protecting democracy,

Ben-Gurion was really resisting restrictions on his own pow-
ers. It may also be true that an ideal constitution could have
guaranteed basic freedoms, the equality of non-Jewish citi-
zens, the power of the courts to overturn repressive laws.
Then again, Mapai's Lam was right when, speaking at the
Knesset lectern, he said that the constitutions adopted after
World War I had not saved democracy in Poland, Latvia,
Italy, or Germany.

Besides that, a real—rather than ideal—constitution can
set in stone the unjust compromises that are necessary at the
time of its passage. The U.S. Constitution originally obligated free states to return fugitive slaves to slave states. To this
day, it grants disproportionate power in the Senate to the
citizens of states with tiny populations, defying the principle
of majority rule.

An Israeli constitution ratified in 1950 could well have
stood in the way of progress toward a more liberal democracy. In the Knesset debate, Mapam wanted the constitution
to require turning shopkeepers into workers. Menachem Begin attacked Ben-Gurion's willingness to cede Jewish claims
to Bethlehem, Hebron, and the rest of the West Bank, imply-
ing that he would want a constitution to declare Israel's ever-
lasting right to that territory. To satisfy the Orthodox parties,
a constitution would have married Judaism and the state, not
divorced them. In 1950, it would almost certainly have established the inequality of Jewish and Arab citizens.

Here we come to the most basic question about the condition
of Israeli democracy, the question that existed not only from
its birth but from its gestation: what the status of Arabs

would be in a Jewish state. The answer is riddled with contradictions.

On the surface, the partition plan approved by the United Nations in November 1947 offered a straightforward way to deal with two national groups claiming the same territory: each would get part of the land. The problem with that solution was the same one faced in drawing borders between nation-states in Europe after both world wars, or in partitioning the Punjab between India and Pakistan in 1947. No clean geographic line separated the groups that were to be divided. They lived among each other. The UN plan for Palestine gave 55 percent of its territory to the Jewish state and 40 percent to the Arab state, with Jerusalem as an international enclave. In the area designated for the Jewish state lived 500,000 Jews and 450,000 Arabs. Another 100,000 Jews lived in Jerusalem, and a small number in scattered communities in the land assigned to the Arab state.

Given those numbers, and given what happened to the Palestinian Arabs in 1948, it is easy to conclude that the founders of the Jewish state adopted a policy of expulsion and proceeded to carry it out. Zionist leaders, asserts Palestinian historian Rashid Khalidi, "understood the well-established demographic calculus of Palestine" and therefore planned to "clear as much of the country as they could of its Palestinian population." The conclusion, however, is too neat. It suffers from the fallacy of intent—assuming that if things turned out a certain way, someone planned it that way. More subtly, it fails to distinguish between political mood and explicit policy.

The partition map was based not only on the 1947 population of Palestine. It assumed that the Jewish state would absorb up to half a million European Jewish refugees, who did not want to return to their pre-Holocaust homes and were not wanted there. In this sense, the argument that the Palestinians paid for Europe's crimes is correct. Nor were the European refugees the only prospective immigrants; the founders of Israel hoped to "ingather" Jews from around the world. Their most basic belief was that the proper place for Jews was their homeland. Practically speaking, they expected immigration to create the necessary Jewish majority.

Even so, Zionist leaders were concerned about the expected size of the Arab minority. A good example of that concern is a telegram from the Jewish Agency's "foreign minister," Moshe Shertok, to Ben-Gurion, then head of the agency, in October 1947. Shertok (later Sharett) was in New York, where the final version of the partition plan was being hammered out. The plan allowed Arabs living in the Jewish state to opt for citizenship in the Arab state, and vice versa. (Jerusalem residents could also choose to be citizens of one of the states.) Shertok told Ben-Gurion of a U.S. proposal requiring anyone who chose citizenship in the other state to move there within a set time. Shertok opposed the idea because it would "not result [in] transfer but discourage Arabs [from] opting out." The Zionist interest was to "reduce [the] Arab political minority even if [the] economic minority [is] irreducible." Were the UN plan to include a population transfer, that would be ideal, Shertok implies, but this was not in the cards. Since the Arabs would stay put, it would be best if they chose citizenship in the Arab state, so that they would not be able to vote in the Jewish one. Meanwhile, the

Jewish political majority would be boosted by Jews living outside the state.

It should be no surprise that Zionist leaders thought about transfer. Population transfer—less politely, the forced uprooting of men, women, and children in order to create ethnically homogenous states—was part of the zeitgeist. The original British proposal for dividing Palestine, submitted by the Peel Commission in 1937, included the transfer of Arabs from the Jewish state, and cited the forced exchange of 1.3 million Greeks and 400,000 Turks in 1923 as a positive precedent. After World War II, that precedent became the brutal norm in Europe, as Tony Judt writes: 160,000 Turks expelled from Bulgaria to Turkey; 120,000 Slovaks sent from Hungary to Slovakia in exchange for the same number of Hungarians going the opposite way; nearly 3 million Germans expelled from the Sudetenland in Czechoslovakia, with the approval of Britain, Russia, and the United States. The full list is much longer. "The term 'ethnic cleansing' did not yet exist, but the reality surely did," Judt writes. It was a crime against humanity, described as such at the time by morally awake observers, yet accepted by "pragmatic" statesmen as a necessity.

All the same, the evidence is missing to back up the claim that the Jewish leadership planned from the start to expel the Arabs. In fact, there is strong evidence for the opposite: that the leaders of the state-to-be expected and planned for the Arab population to stay put. That evidence comes from the report of the opaquely named body known as the Situation Committee.

In October 1947, even before the UN partition vote, it was

clear to the heads of the Jewish Agency and Va'ad Le'umi that the British Mandate would soon end. They needed to plan how to run a country—build roads, deliver mail, provide health care, maintain sewage lines. The Situation Committee was created in order to draw up a blueprint. Ben-Gurion chaired it. Other senior politicians, including Golda Meir and Jewish Agency treasurer Eliezer Kaplan, headed subcommittees that designed ministries, down to the number of district veterinarian officers and school inspectors, and the precise budget needed to pay them.

In the Situation Committee's final report, the chapter on education notes that the state will be responsible for the eleven existing Arab schools in the partly or completely Arab towns of Haifa, Tiberias, Safed, and Beit Shean, and the ninety-two schools serving the 248 Arab villages in the area of the Jewish state. The health chapter states that government clinics established by the British in Arab villages will keep operating; villages without clinics will be served by the Histadrut labor union's clinics in neighboring Jewish communities, under government contract. The Interior Ministry, in charge of local administration, will have twenty-four district officers—sixteen Jewish and eight Arab. The report is in Hebrew. It is not intended to impress outsiders; it is intended for use.

The pre-independence musings among Zionist leaders about population transfer represented one political inclination. The Situation Committee report represented an opposing inclination, among the same people, for integrating a large Arab minority into the Jewish state. Events on the ground tipped the balance.

The committee completed its report sometime between April 10 and April 30, 1948, though most of the work was obviously done earlier. By then, the sections referring to the Arab population were already dated, rendered obsolete by gunfire. Fighting between Arabs and Jews in Palestine had broken out the day after the United Nations approved partition and steadily escalated. It was a war of communities, not of states. Both sides believed their survival was at stake. In the first months, the Arab middle and upper classes began fleeing their homes. Local Arab village militias cut the road to Jerusalem; starvation loomed in Jewish areas of the city.

In April—perhaps while a typist in Tel Aviv was working on the mimeograph stencils of the Situation Committee report—the Haganah went on the offensive. It aimed at taking control of the land assigned to the Jewish state, opening the road to Jerusalem, and preparing for defense against the coming Arab invasion. In some places, Jewish commanders expelled Arabs from conquered villages. In many more, panic led to mass flight, especially after Irgun and Lehi fighters perpetrated a massacre in the village of Deir Yassin outside Jerusalem.

By early May, Shertok was speaking of the "astounding" and "unforeseen" Arab exodus, as if describing an unexpected inheritance. Going back to the status quo ante was unthinkable, he said. When the provisional government discussed the issue in June, the consensus—supported by Ben-Gurion—was to keep the refugees from returning. A later cabinet decision said that "a solution to the refugee problem" would have to be part of a formal peace agreement. The policy was partly defensive, to avoid a fifth column. But in the June cabinet meeting, Shertok also described all "the lands and the houses" as "spoils of war," and as compensation for what Jews had lost in a war forced on them.

Afterward, as the fighting continued, cases of the IDF expelling Arabs grew more common. The decision to prevent return was the turning point, transforming what began in the chaos of war into a choice.

To understand later events, it's worth noting that Arab forces also expelled or massacred Jews or prevented their return to places they had fled. But they could do so rarely, because the Arabs were losing on the battlefield. Nonetheless, Transjordan's Arab Legion emptied the Jewish Quarter of Jerusalem's Old City; Arab fighters massacred about 150 Jewish defenders of Kfar Etzion, a religious kibbutz south of Bethlehem, after they surrendered. Several other isolated Jewish farming communities were abandoned. Though relatively small, those losses would help shape Israeli policy nineteen years afterward.

With the war's end and the signing of the armistice agreements, the Situation Committee's blueprint for coexistence was less than a memory. Tiberias, Safed, and Beit Shean were empty of Arabs, as were 350 or more villages that had existed in 1947. In Haifa, only a fraction of the Arab population remained. The same was true in Jaffa, Akko, Lod, and Ramleh, towns that partition had assigned to the Arab state but were now part of Israel. About 150,000 Palestinian Arabs lived in Israel, less than a fifth of the number who had lived in the same territory beforehand. The laws and policies adopted in Israel's first years marked those who remained as citizens, and at the same time as outsiders and potential enemies. They were Israeli Arabs, or Arab citizens of Israel, or as they would be more likely to say decades later, Palestinian citizens of Israel—but not Israelis.

In 1952, the Knesset belatedly passed a law on citizenship. One section said that residents of British Palestine who had remained continuously in Israel, or who had been given legal permission to reenter the country, would be citizens. The law thereby accomplished two things. It defined citizenship in universal, liberal terms: everyone who lived in the state's territory qualified. It also defined Palestinian Arabs who had left as noncitizens.

Another section of the law granted citizenship to any Jew who immigrated to the country. That fit together with an earlier piece of legislation, the 1950 Law of Return, which gave every Jew the right to immigrate.

Together, the two laws pointed to a lasting conundrum about the meaning of statehood. For Jews, one piece of self-determination was being able to gather in one territory and create a national community. The second piece was achieving political independence. Independence made free immigration possible, but it didn't complete the job by any means. When it came to repatriation, the Israeli government's constituency was the same as the Zionist movement's: the Jews, including those who lived elsewhere, and especially those who needed refuge.

But in every other way, independence meant that the liberation movement had fulfilled its purpose. In their historical homeland, Jews now had a state in which the daily rhythms, the language and public culture, were Jewish, where their furious argument about what it meant to be Jewish was a debate of the general society, not the parochial concern of a minority. But the political community to which the democratic government rightfully owed responsibility was the citizenry of Israel, the people inside its borders, Jewish and non-Jewish.

When it came to accepting this change, Ben-Gurion and everyone around him did poorly at making the psychological and political shift from national movement to statehood, from revolution to institution. In key ways, they continued to act as if the community they led and served comprised the Jews in Israel and, more widely, the Jews in general, including the almost-citizens around the world. The borders of the polity shimmered and shifted. Seen from one angle, they were the lines on a map. Seen from another, they were the social boundaries of an ethnic group.

The policy on land ownership expressed the attitude that the state served Jews. From the start of Zionism, purchasing real estate in Palestine was central to its efforts. The goal, especially on the Zionist left, was to bring Jews back not only to their homeland but to the soil itself. So Jews needed places to live and, just as important, to cultivate. To buy land, the Zionist Organization created the Jewish National Fund, which held the property it acquired in perpetuity for the Jewish people. But British legal restrictions, an Arab nationalist campaign against selling land to Jews, and a lack of cash slowed the buying effort. At independence, the JNF owned less than 5 percent of Israel's land; total Jewish landholdings were less than a tenth of the country. Land previously owned by the British government was now the property of the Israeli government, but most of that was unusable. As for the rest of the country, the government was sovereign, but sovereignty doesn't mean holding property rights.

But there were the abandoned fields, orchards, and houses of Arabs who had fled. In 1950 the Knesset passed the Absentees' Property Law, which put such real estate in the hands of a government custodian. An "absentee," according to the law, wasn't only someone now living on the far side of the border. It was anyone who had left his home after November 29, 1947, for another country or for a part of Palestine then held by Arab forces. You were an absentee if you had been expelled and came back. You were an absentee if you had fled from your village to the nearest town, which was conquered afterward by Israel. If you had been born in the village of Taybe, moved to Jaffa to seek work, bought a house there, and returned to Taybe for refuge during the fighting, you were an absentee—even though Taybe was in a strip of land turned over to Israel under the armistice with Transjordan. If you returned to Taybe and moved into the home of your brother or cousin who had meanwhile left for Tul Karm, just across the armistice line, you were living in absentee property, and had to pay rent to the custodian, as handwritten records from the time show. An "absentee" who happened to be present in Israel was a "present absentee." By one estimate, 75,000 Arab citizens fit into that category.

The law allowed the custodian to sell absentee property to a newly created Development Authority, which under another law could sell land to the JNF. By the end of 1950, title to nearly 12 percent of the country's land had been shifted to the JNF in this way. The JNF leases rather than sells land. It does not lease to non-Jews. The state was using its considerable power to accomplish the Zionist movement's goal of acquiring land for Jews. In the process, it treated Israeli Arabs as ethnic adversaries, rather than citizens to be integrated into a new, shared civic community.

In its day-to-day functioning, the state related to Arab citizens as a suspect population. The memory of communal war was fresh. Most Arabs lived for years under military government. At first, the military government was a temporary arrangement to control areas outside the partition lines that were conquered during the war. In 1949, the decision was made to continue using military government to rule Arab-populated areas. The legal basis, again, was a draconian British-imposed law—in this case the Emergency Regulations of 1945, originally enacted to deal with the Jewish revolt. The military government was the channel for all state services. Arabs needed permits from local military governors in order to travel legally inside the country. One function of that system was to limit Arab competition with Jews for jobs at a time when the country was flooded with Jewish immigrants. The military government, the police, and the Shin Bet security agency all recruited informers to track the Arab population, control political activity, and suppress Arab nationalism. The Communist Party served as the main public opposition to military rule. The army and security agencies encouraged support of Mapai and its Arab satellite parties, offering incentives such as permits to travel and own guns. In this case, Mapai's use of the machinery of state to serve party interests was glaring.

In a dissertation harshly describing the military government, American historian Shira Nomi Robinson speaks of the "paradoxical reality" of Palestinian Arabs who remained in Israel and became both "citizens of a liberal nation-state and subjects of a colonial administration." In my view, the word *colonial* has become a blunt instrument. Used too widely, it obscures the particular tragedies of history. But it is essential to stress that in Israel's first years, Arabs were not only subjects of the military government. They were also citizens. The fact that they could vote did not mean they enjoyed anything resembling equality, but it created a slow dynamic for change. In 1950, Robinson notes, foreign minister Moshe Sharett reluctantly agreed to a family reunification program that allowed several thousand Palestinian refugees to return—in part because "he hoped to draw Arab support away from the Communists toward the ruling Mapai party."

More significant, Mapai's major political rivals—from Mapam on the left to Herut on the right—opposed the military government because the ruling party exploited it to get Arab votes. The other parties wanted a level playing field. Ben-Gurion, the strongest advocate of military government, resigned in 1963. Three years later, at the end of 1966, the military government was abolished. This change did not bring equality or a shared civic identity. It did not end expropriation of Arab-owned land or official discrimination. Yet it was a significant step toward greater democracy.

In the meantime, Israel had not become a "people's democracy." Mapam and Ahdut Ha'avodah had recovered from their romance with the Soviet Union. Even the Communist Party had split over loyalty to Moscow. On the right, Herut's last flirt with violent opposition had been in 1952, when the

Knesset debated accepting reparations from West Germany for the Holocaust and Menachem Begin threatened to resume an underground struggle against the government. By 1966, with that episode long past, Herut had found respectability in an alliance with the moderate right-wing Liberal Party. Ben-Gurion's successor, Levi Eshkol, was a conciliator. The most common criticism against him was not that he was an autocrat, but that he was indecisive. A generation of Israeli-educated Arab intellectuals was about to come of age, their Palestinian nationalism shaped by the classic Zionist poems of Haim Nahman Bialik and Shaul Tchernichovsky they had learned in school.

The Israeli republic was maturing. Today that is difficult to remember. The process of coming apart was about to begin.

III.

THE CAPITAL OF
LAWLESSNESS

"No building permits or exemptions from building permits have been issued for the structures in the settlement of Ofrah," says the fax. At the top is the coat of arms of the Civil Administration, the branch of the IDF that governs the West Bank. Dated August 12, 2007, it is a response to a human rights researcher's freedom-of-information request. The five bland bureaucratic sentences on the page are a confession of complete official disregard for the law.

At the time, Ofrah had over 2,700 residents and over 500 buildings. The fax also states that the relevant Israeli authorities have never approved a town plan for Ofrah or defined its municipal area. Those are legal preconditions for issuing building permits in an Israeli settlement. The fax does not explain why those conditions have never been met. However, an army database on settlements known as the Spiegel Report, leaked in 2009, does give the reason: most of Ofrah was built "with no legal basis" on land privately owned by Palestinians. The state never acted to stop the trespassing.

Ofrah lies north of the Palestinian city of Ramallah on the mountainous spine of the West Bank. Just past the entrance gate is a boarding school for Orthodox girls, a clinic belonging to Israel's biggest HMO, and a park where a tiny wooden bridge arches over irrigation-fed rushes. On the side streets are two-story houses faced in white stone and topped by red tile roofs. Big pines tower over the homes. Flower boxes line stone walkways. A wooden wagon wheel leans against a home in artificial rusticity.

Ofrah is the most establishment of settlements. It was the first bridgehead of Gush Emunim, the "Believers' Bloc"— the movement of the religious right that became synonymous with the settlement effort. Its founders invented a members-only form of community that served as the model for dozens of other settlements. Its prominent residents include Yisrael Harel, founder of the Council of Settlements in Judea, Samaria, and Gaza; Pinchas Wallerstein, for decades the head of the municipal authority for settlements north of Jerusalem; and Moti Sklar, director-general of the Israeli equivalent of the BBC, the Israel Broadcasting Authority.

Ofrah is also the embodiment of lawlessness. Like other Israeli settlements in occupied territory, it was built in violation of international law. It was established in 1975 without government permission, with the express goal of undermining the foreign policy of prime minister Yitzhak Rabin—but with the help of Rabin's defense minister and rival, Shimon Peres. Its founder, Yehudah Etzion, was a leader of the Jewish terror underground that carried out attacks on Palestinians in the early 1980s. The first proposal for building private homes at Ofrah notes a minor complication: "the strange act of building without permission of the owner of the land," which the settlers mistakenly believed to be the government of Israel. Ofrah epitomizes casual disregard for property rights and for the land-use laws of Israel's military government in occupied territory. Yet like other settlements, it has benefited from the authorities' support. One piece of that support is a legal system that mocks equality before the law, applying entirely separate rules to Israeli settlers and Palestinians in the same territory. Ofrah, the quintessential Israeli settlement in occupied territory, is where the state of Israel unthinkingly attacks its own foundations.

Behind this behavior lie both Israel's particular history and a universal human trait. The trait is best described by geographer Jared Diamond in his book *Collapse*, on the causes of ecological disasters that shatter societies. "The values to which people cling most stubbornly under inappropriate conditions," writes Diamond, "are those values that were previously the source of their greatest triumphs over adversity." The lessons of a heroic past, applied under new conditions, can lead to catastrophe.

Diamond gives numerous examples. Medieval Norse colonists in Greenland were initially sustained by their Norwegian way of life, including cattle raising and Christianity. Clinging to that lifestyle, they built extravagant churches, depleted their soil, ravaged their forests, failed to learn from the Inuit how to exploit local sources of food, and eventually starved to death. In modern times, Diamond writes, "Communist China's determination not to repeat the errors of capitalism led it to scorn environmental concerns as just one more capitalist error." White pioneers succeeded in settling Montana through a commitment to individual self-sufficiency; maintaining that commitment has stood in the way of modern Montanans' accepting government planning to solve the environmental crisis caused by mining, logging, and ranching.

In Israel, the ideal of settling the land best demonstrates Diamond's postulate at work. From the start of Zionism in the late nineteenth century, Jewish immigrants were intent on transforming themselves from the "scrawny" urban Jews of European stereotype into muscular farmers. Moreover, in the struggle between the Jews and Arabs for one territory, each piece of land acquired and settled by Jews was an additional stake in the whole of the land.

In the next stage, settlement became a means toward socialism, as Zionist pioneers established kibbutzim, farming communes on Jewish National Fund land. The early communes turned physical work into a secular sacrament. Their members were the elite of Labor Zionism, the Zionism of the left, which saw itself as the secular replacement for Judaism. "Only by making labor . . . our national ideal shall we . . .

mend the rent between ourselves and Nature," wrote A. D. Gordon, the Tolstoyan prophet of Deganyah, the first kibbutz.

After World War I, immigrants inspired by the Russian Revolution came with a vision of turning all of Jewish Palestine into a single commune. The United Kibbutz movement, born of this dream, aimed at creating large kibbutzim, often at the edge of towns, as an example to the rest of Jewish society. But the strategy changed after the Peel Commission report of 1937. The commission's map for partition delineated the proposed Jewish state according to where Jews had already settled. The plan was shelved. But afterward new settlements were spread widely, in order to prevent division of the land or at least to make sure that as much as possible ended up in the Jewish share. Settlement would quietly establish facts and set borders. Each new farming community was a tent stake marking the national homestead. The Jewish Agency's Settlement Department coordinated the entire effort. Meanwhile, a second tier of labor settlements developed—cooperative villages, or moshavim, where members sold their produce together but had family fields and houses.

During World War II, with the formation of the Palmah as a kibbutz-based guerrilla force, rural settlements took on one more role, as the foundation of a Jewish military. In the 1948 war, kibbutzim often served as frontline fortresses.

With independence and the end of the war, settlement had in fact been a source of Zionism's "greatest triumph over adversity." Jews had achieved self-determination. Yet rather than being seen as a means to that end, settling the land had metamorphosed into a sacred value.

Nonetheless, it was about to become irrelevant as a practical program. True, in the historical moment after statehood, new kibbutzim were quickly set up along the armistice lines. The Settlement Department, headed by Levi Eshkol, filled whole new regions with moshavim. But the country now had an army for its defense. Its borders were the result of war and of negotiations conducted by a sovereign government. Government policy would determine the extent that Israel would be or cease to be socialist. Most Jews wanted to live in cities, and academic education would serve as a more certain path to success than muscle in a modernizing economy. Only ten new kibbutzim and moshavim were set up between 1961 and the first half of 1967.

Rural settlement had served the Zionist revolution, but the revolution was over. The Six-Day War of June 1967 pulled the settlement ideal from the grave and gave it an unnatural new life.

"The war in '67 was forced on us as a surprise. The victory was a much greater surprise," Sini Azaryahu told me in 2003. Azaryahu was eighty-seven years old, one of the last remaining witnesses to military decision-making in Israel's early years. In 1967 he served as bureau chief to Yisrael Galili, then officially a minister without portfolio in Levi Eshkol's government, unofficially Eshkol's closest adviser on defense policy. Each day Galili received the same military reports as the prime minister. Azaryahu evaluated them. "Because the victory was so total, no one believes . . . that the government of Israel thought the war would be a disaster," Azaryahu told me.

Azaryahu's insider telling is backed up by historian Avi Shlaim, a scholar not known for deference to the accepted Israeli narrative. "Of all the Arab-Israeli wars, the June 1967 war was the only one that neither side wanted," writes Shlaim. In early 1967, Israeli military intelligence reports showed that despite Egypt's anti-Israel rhetoric, the leading Arab country was unprepared for battle. Israel did not expect that its border clashes with Syria would spur Egypt to send its army into the Sinai Peninsula and close the Straits of Tiran, blockading Israel's Red Sea port at Eilat. Egyptian president Gamal Abdel Nasser intended to "impress Arab opinion"; instead he inflamed public pressure for war. Israel's original battle plan, essentially defensive, aimed at seizing part of the Sinai to trade it for reopening the straits. Conquests were not the objective, Shlaim writes.

When Israel launched its preemptive attack on Egypt on June 5, the government expected a one-front war. But war unleashes chaos. Defense minister Moshe Dayan ordered his generals to stop twelve miles short of the Suez Canal, but when the Egyptian army collapsed, Israeli armor rolled to the waterway. Israel's offensive against Jordan began only after Jordanian artillery bombarded Israeli cities and bases. The objectives grew from seizing corners of the West Bank, to taking everything up to the mountain ridge, to conquering the entire West Bank. Dayan talked the cabinet out of attacking Syria. He then changed his mind, exceeded his authority, and ordered an invasion. In the midst of the fighting, northern front commander General David Elazar told Yigal Allon, now a cabinet minister, that he too had exceeded his orders, sending his troops farther forward than he was supposed to. In six days, Israel conquered the Sinai Peninsula and Gaza Strip, the West Bank, and the Golan Heights.

Years later, Azaryahu described the resulting political dilemma. "We had no goals for the war . . . and therefore no one knew what to do with the gains of the war." War had not been an extension of policy. The empire was an accident. A policy had to be invented after the fact.

The government of national unity set up on the war's eve was unfit to do that. It included everyone from Mapam on the left to Menachem Begin on the right. Galili and Allon represented Ahdut Ha'avodah, the socialist party with visions of the Whole Land of Israel. Within the prime minister's Mapai party were people representing almost every view on the future of the conquered land. It was a government of national confusion.

The paralysis went deeper than disagreements between parties. The national mood—to be precise, the mood of the Jewish majority—mixed prewar dread and postwar hubris. This did not foster calm judgment.

Proponents of keeping the land argued from security and history. The Sinai would protect Israel from Egypt, they asserted. The West Bank gave Israel strategic depth; keeping the Golan would prevent Syrian artillery from using the heights to bombard Israeli communities. As for history, Jerusalem's Old City and its holy sites, the Western Wall and the Temple Mount, were part of the spoils. So were Hebron, Bethlehem, and a host of other places whose biblical past intoxicated secular Jews along with Orthodox ones.

Against the celebration of conquest stood sobering concerns. America had committed itself before the war to the "territorial integrity" of all Middle Eastern countries, and wanted Israel to cooperate in a diplomatic solution. If the Arab countries were sufficiently eager to get their land back, they might sign peace treaties with Israel in return for a withdrawal.

Most important was the problem of Israel's own character. In 1967, Israel had a population of 2.7 million people, of whom 400,000 were Arabs. Annexing the West Bank and Gaza would add another 1.1 million Arabs, and the Arab birth rate was higher. If Israel remained a democracy, how long would it be a Jewish state?

Eshkol's government did reach a quick consensus to annex East Jerusalem. The city's emotional resonance overwhelmed other concerns. The area added to the state was much larger than the Jordanian municipality of Jerusalem. Among other things, it took in the former sites of Atarot and Neveh Ya'akov, Jewish farming villages north of the city that had fallen in 1948. Arabs in the annexed land were granted the status of permanent residents of Israel, but not citizenship. According to the Israeli journalist Uzi Benziman, a cabinet committee concluded that international law forbade imposing one country's citizenship on another's citizens. Concern for international law was selective. It prevented annexing East Jerusalem's residents to the Israeli electorate; it did not prevent annexing the land.

A week after the war, on June 19, 1967, the cabinet also agreed on a message to Washington that Israel would offer Egypt and Syria "a full peace treaty on the basis of the international border and Israel's security needs." That suggested a nearly complete withdrawal. By October 1968, however, the government disavowed that offer, insisting that Israel must retain a strip of the Sinai to protect the straits.

As for the West Bank, the government failed to set any policy. Eshkol was fond of saying that in the war, "we got a lovely dowry. The trouble is that with the dowry comes the bride." Politicians quickly proposed ways to keep the dowry without the bride.

In the June 1967 cabinet debate, Dayan argued for "self-government [by] the residents of the West Bank, with Israel responsible for defense and foreign policy." The residents, he stressed, "will not be citizens of Israel." Yigal Allon's proposal eventually became best known publicly. The Allon Plan called for annexing the lightly populated lowlands along the Jordan River, which Allon saw as vital for defense. Hebron and Bethlehem might also be annexed. North of Jerusalem, the heavily populated mountain ridge and its western slopes would be an enclave under "self-rule" or even a Palestinian state. Later Allon decided that the enclave should be given to Jordan. In any case, Israel would keep much of the land and few of the people.

Others suggested holding the land and figuring out later what to do about the people. "For the interim, military government will continue, along with a search for a constructive solution," Galili proposed in the June cabinet meeting. Menachem Begin agreed. In the end, the government decided not to decide. In practical terms, that was the same as accepting Galili and Begin's position.

One did not need prophecy to know this would be disastrous. Clear-sightedness was enough. In the cabinet debate, justice minister Ya'akov Shimshon Shapira warned that were Dayan's ideas adopted, "every progressive person will rise against us and say . . . 'They want to turn the West Bank . . . into an Israeli colony.'" The only acceptable way to keep the West Bank was to annex it, in which case Jews would eventually become a minority. Annexation, Shapira argued, meant that "we're done with the Zionist enterprise." In the public arena, philosopher Yeshayahu Leibowitz warned that if Israel tried to maintain its rule over another people, "the corruption characteristic of every colonial regime will also prevail in the State of Israel."

In 1968 Mapai, Ahdut Ha'avodah, and Dayan's Rafi party merged to form the Labor Party. Only in 1972 did Labor's governing secretariat get around to discussing the future of the occupied terrritories. Veteran finance minister Pinhas Sapir told fellow members that expecting West Bank Arabs to accept an improved living standard without equal rights would put Israel in a class with "countries whose names I don't even want to say in the same breath." That debate, too, ended without policy decisions. Labor leaders were more interested in avoiding a split in the party than in reaching a coherent position.

Despite the principle of Israeli politics that all members of the cabinet are collectively responsible for government actions, neither Shapira nor Sapir resigned. So they shared responsibility for an act of immense symbolism taken by Allon in October 1967. Allon was minister of labor. His ministry included the Survey Department, which produced virtually all the country's maps. Henceforth, Allon instructed the department chief, the only boundaries of Israel on maps would be the June cease-fire lines. "The mandatory borders and the armistice lines"—the prewar boundaries—"will not be printed."

Note this well: the mandatory border and the Green Line were the closest thing Israel had to an internationally recognized border. Except in annexed East Jerusalem, they still delineated the territory in which Israel itself said that its laws and sovereignty applied. Yet Allon's memo removed from the map one of the defining characteristics of a modern state and especially of a democracy—its borders. In official Hebrew, meanwhile, places got new names. The West Bank was known henceforth by the biblical names Judea and Samaria, Judea being the southern half, Samaria the northern half.

The future of the occupied territories was already the single most important political issue in Israel, but maps no longer showed where occupied territory began. Bored schoolchildren staring at the map on the classroom wall would not learn the shape of their own country. Tel Aviv and Hebron would appear to be part of the same entity. Nearly forty years later, a study conducted among students at Hebrew University, Israel's top academic institution, found that only 37 percent could draw the approximate line between Israel and the West Bank. They had grown up in a country that treated its border the way Victorians treated sex. The border shaped society, but portraying it was simply not done.

While the change in maps was symbolic, settlements would physically blur the country's border. Before describing how that happened, I should dispose of several myths. The standard Israeli telling is that settlement in the occupied territories began with religious extremists imposing their will on pragmatic Labor leaders. That story is mistaken. Nor did the secular right, led by Menachem Begin, play any measurable role in starting the settlement process—though Begin escalated it once he took power in 1977.

Abroad, defenders of Israeli policy sometimes describe settlements as mere bargaining chips, intended to last only till Arabs agreed to make peace. This is pure fiction. On the other hand, Israel's critics cite settlement as proof of a deliberate Israeli policy of conquest and colonization. As we've seen, though, the conquest was unplanned, and the government could not articulate a clear policy in its wake.

What actually happened is this: the policy vacuum allowed a cultural disposition to take control. Settlement was a Zionist value, especially a Labor Zionist value. Now there was new land to settle. Time had rolled backward; partition had never happened. Pioneers could again set borders for the Jewish state before negotiations began. They would act like members of a movement again—but a movement with the power of a state behind it.

The initiative to start settling came mainly from Labor politicians, officials, and activists. At first, religious Zionists were junior partners. Labor governments approved new settlements on a piecemeal basis. The map of what they expected Israel to keep was drawn one fact at a time. The spread of settlements roughly fit the Allon Plan. Cabinet ministers who wanted Israel to keep a maximum amount of territory were satisfied to see new settlements; those opposed to permanent rule over the Palestinians could live with settlements in lightly populated areas. Labor governments never formally approved the Allon Plan or any other coherent strategy. But indecision allowed pro-settlement ministers—led by Allon, Galili, Dayan, and Dayan's successor as defense minister, Shimon Peres—to pursue creeping expansion. Tension between Labor and Orthodox activists began in earnest only after the 1973 Yom Kippur War, when the religious settlers feared that the government might return a piece of the West Bank to Jordan.

By the time Begin came to power as head of the Likud, an alliance of the right, the internal Israeli argument was over *where* to settle, not *whether* to. Labor had provided legitimacy for settlement and a solid start. Begin, however, did not share Labor's hesitations or its nostalgia for rural, socialist communities. His belief that Israel must rule the Whole Land of Israel had not changed since his underground days. The Likud built large suburbs and small exurban bedroom communities, offering massive subsidies to attract settlers. As head of the Ministerial Settlement Committee, Ariel Sharon took a major role in drawing the map of new settlement, aimed at driving wedges between Palestinian towns and preventing the emergence of a contiguous Palestinian state. "The intent was for there to be facts before any peace negotations . . . with the idea that wherever we were living [the territory would remain ours]. Just like in the War of Independence, when most of the places where Jews lived ended up on the Jewish side," explained attorney Plia Albeck, head of the Civil Division of the State Attorney's Office, who attended every meeting of the committee under Sharon.

And each stage in the process further eroded the rule of law, among other basic principles of democracy.

The first settlement in occupied territory was a kibbutz established in the Golan Heights in mid-July 1967, less than a month after the government told Washington it was willing to retreat from the heights. The organizers were members of Galilee kibbutzim, disciples of the United Kibbutz movement's octogenarian ideologue, Yitzhak Tabenkin. They wanted the Golan to stay in Israeli hands to keep Syrian artillery from returning to the area. Tabenkin's view that the Golan was part of the Whole Land of Israel also influenced them. So did the chance to act like pre-state pioneers and stake a claim to the land through direct action.

Though settling in the Golan defied the government policy at that moment, the new kibbutz received top-level support. Civilians needed military permits to enter the Golan. General Elazar, head of the IDF's Northern Command, issued them to the settlers, again exceeding his authority. He also allowed them to stay in an abandoned Syrian army base, and sent soldiers to guard them. The Jewish Agency Settlement Department provided supplies, funneling the help through the Upper Galilee Regional Council—a kind of county government—to hide its actions. Labor Minister Allon funded the settlement—by fraudulently diverting money from a budget for creating jobs for the unemployed.

(As a pre-state administration, the Jewish Agency should have been dissolved in 1948. Instead, it kept operating as a quasi-governmental body. Unlike the state, it could accept donations from American Jews. Soon after the war, the job of handling rural settlement activity in the occupied territories was transferred to a newly established Settlement Division in the World Zionist Organization for fear of endangering the tax-exempt status of donations to the Jewish Agency in the United States. The Settlement Division received its budget from the Israeli government.)

The Golan settlement set several precedents. Individuals sought to set foreign and defense policy, preempting the government. Some of those individuals played two roles: they starred as high government officials, and as rebels. As in pre-state days, the cause took precedence over the law. Yet the government was no longer a foreign regime; the laws were no longer decreed by outsiders. As rebels, they were defying the state they had created.

Allon exemplified this contradiction. The following spring, he encouraged a group of Orthodox activists, led by Rabbi Moshe Levinger, to settle in Hebron without government permission, then quickly paid them a ministerial visit. While returning to Jerusalem, he stopped at the previously established West Bank settlement of Kfar Etzion, where he suggested to Hanan Porat, the central figure in the community, that he lend guns to the Hebron settlers. Porat answered that Kfar Etzion members had received their guns from the IDF, and signed for them personally.

"In the time of the Palmah, we knew to do things like this," Allon said, meaning outside the law. Porat sent the guns. Neither he nor Porat noticed that the era of an underground rebel army was past.

When Porat, Levinger, and other religious activists formed Gush Emunim in 1974, they followed the example of the secular Golan settlers: they saw themselves as heirs of pre-state Zionist pioneers, shaping the future borders of the Jewish state. Yet the Jewish state existed, and they were violating its laws. They, too, had help from the highest levels of government—particularly from Defense Minister Peres, the most prominent advocate in Labor for settling throughout the West Bank.

Ofrah's founders—led by Yehudah Etzion—moved into an abandoned Jordanian army base next to the Palestinian village of Ein Yabrud in April 1975. They claimed they were creating a temporary "work camp," a place to spend their nights, while subcontracting to build a fence around a new Israeli base. Though Yitzhak Rabin's government favored settlement, it barred settling on the mountain ridge north of Jerusalem. Legally, establishing a new settlement required the approval of a ministerial committee. But Peres secured Rabin's permission for the original twenty-four "workers" to "lodge" at the abandoned base, on the strict condition that the number did not increase and that the camp did not become a settlement. Peres's office files—kept classified until 2007—show he received regular reports that more settlers were moving in with their children and refurbishing the Jordanian buildings. In December 1975, Peres approved connecting the "work camp" to the Israeli electricity grid. Like Allon, Peres was happy playing two roles—a minister sworn to uphold the country's laws, and a rebel ignoring them in the name of the obsolete value of settlement.

Those were the exceptions. The vast majority of settlements did have cabinet approval. But the government itself had a similarly cavalier attitude toward legal restraints. This time, instead of a pre-independence underground hoodwinking British authorities, the Israeli government thought it could fool the international community, and particularly the United States.

Kfar Etzion was the first civilian settlement in occupied territory for which Eshkol sought cabinet approval, and the first in the West Bank. Porat had been evacuated from the original kibbutz at the site as a child, before it fell to Arab forces and the defenders were slaughtered in 1948. After the Six-Day War, he organized other children of the original members and agitated to reestablish the Orthodox kibbutz. When Eshkol gave his assent in September 1967, Porat's group—and the press—believed that the Mapai prime minister had folded under Orthodox pressure. In fact, Porat had broken down an unlocked door. The paper trail from Eshkol's office that summer shows that even without a strategy for the future of the West Bank, he too wanted to reestablish Jewish settlements that fell in 1948. Though neither Porat nor Eshkol would ever use the term, they were advocating the "right of return" of 1948 refugees—as long as the refugees were Jewish.

Before asking the cabinet to ratify his decision, Eshkol asked Foreign Ministry legal counsel Theodor Meron, the government's top authority on international law, whether civilian settlement in the "administered territories" was permitted. Meron's written response stated unequivocally, "Civilian settlement in the administered territories contravenes explicit provisions of the Fourth Geneva Convention." The specific provision he cited was Article 49, paragraph 6:

"The Occupying Power shall not deport or transfer parts of its own civilian population into the territory it occupies."

Meron left Israel's foreign service a decade later to teach at New York University. A child survivor of the Holocaust, he became one of the world's leading experts on the laws of war, and then a judge on the International Criminal Tribunal for the former Yugoslavia. Interviewed four decades later, he stood by what he had written in 1967. "I believe that I would have given the same opinion today," he told Donald Macintyre of *The Independent on Sunday*, a British paper.

Meron's memo did note that the occupier was allowed to establish temporary military bases. Speaking in the cabinet, Eshkol described the new Kfar Etzion as an "outpost," suggesting a paramilitary settlement manned by soldiers in the army's Nahal (Pioneering Fighting Youth) unit. The press and Israeli diplomats were explicitly told that Kfar Etzion would be a Nahal position.

A secret military memorandum dated September 27, 1967—the day that the new Kfar Etzion was established— tells the real story. Addressed to the IDF chief of staff's office, it is signed by Colonel Shlomo Gazit, who served as Dayan's No. 2 in the military administration of occupied land. Gazit passed on these instructions:

```
1. As a "cover" for the purposes of the
   diplomatic struggle, the outpost of the
   religious young people in the Etzion
   Bloc will appear as a Nahal military
   outpost.
```

2. Instructions on the matter will be given
   to the settlers, in case they are asked
   questions.
3. There is no intent of the IDF taking
   practical steps to implement this "cover."

This is a directive to the army to deceive the public. It shows Eshkol accepted Meron's opinion and chose to evade it by misrepresenting what he was doing. The prime minister had also decided that the cause of settlement superseded legal constraints. In his reenactment of the pre-state script, the international community filled in for the British authorities.

Further evidence that cabinet members were aware of settlement's illegality but did not see it as an impediment comes in a 1968 proposal by Dayan for building Israeli towns in the West Bank. "Settling Israelis in administered territory, as is known, contravenes international conventions, but there is nothing essentially new about that," he wrote. After Kfar Etzion, the government did set up real Nahal outposts in occupied land—as preparation for settling civilians. Sometimes, though, settlements were established as civilian communities from the outset.

Ex post facto, government and supportive jurists produced arguments for why the Geneva Convention did not apply. The difference between Meron's position and these arguments is the difference between a lawyer's response when a client asks if the law permits insider trading and the lawyer's answer when the client says he has already committed the act and needs a defense. In the latter case, we are likely to see unconventional readings of the law.

The Israeli Foreign Ministry, for instance, asserts to this day that Article 49 only bars the occupier from "forced transfer of [its] civilians." This ignores the accepted reading that the ban is much wider, forbidding establishment or promotion of settlement by the occupying power. It also ignores the resources that the Israeli government has devoted since 1967 to building settlements—thereby warping the Israeli housing market, applying economic pressure on Israelis to buy inexpensive homes in occupied territory, and steadily constricting the land resources and freedom of movement of Palestinians.

Another defense asserts that the West Bank is exempt from the Geneva rules because the world did not recognize Jordan's sovereignty there. Since there is no previous sovereign whose rights must be protected—says this reasoning— the laws of occupation do not apply. Yet the normal reading of the Geneva Convention is that it is not aimed at protecting another country's claim to sovereignty over occupied territory. Rather it protects the *people* under military occupation. It safeguards "the demographic, social status quo" from the occupier moving its citizens into the occupied area.

Still another claim is that Israel is free to assert its sovereignty anywhere in former British mandatory Palestine, and that the right of Jews to settle anywhere in Palestine under the League of Nations mandate is still in force. All these defenses are intellectual sleight of hand, directing the readers' eyes to the West Bank and Gaza Strip, though Israel also built settlements in the Sinai and Golan, where Egyptian and Syrian sovereignty was clear. They also assert technical exceptions to the Geneva Convention, evading the ethical principle expressed in the convention's legal language: people living under military occupation are subject to a regime imposed from outside, which all too easily serves the interests of the occupying power rather than the interests of those governed. Normal democratic protections are missing; the convention is meant to serve in their stead. If Israel really believed that the territorial division created by the 1949 armistice was null and void, it could have asserted its sovereignty in all of former Palestine—and granted the vote and other democratic rights to all inhabitants. It chose not to do so for the reason given by Justice Minister Shapira: this would have been the end of the Jewish state. Instead, it behaved as if the territories were part of Israel for the purpose of settlement, and under military occupation for the purpose of ruling the Palestinians.

The same dual standard was applied to the settlers themselves. Like the physical growth of the settlements, the extension of Israeli law to cover Israelis in occupied territory began immediately after the war, at first without planning or strategy. The first step was a six-month emergency regulation that Defense Minister Dayan promulgated on July 2, 1967. It was intended to cover Israelis visiting occupied land, and preceded the first settler in the Golan Heights. Israeli courts, it said, could try anyone in Israel for acts committed in "administered" territories "as if" the offense were committed inside Israel. The court would use Israeli law, rather than the local law pertaining where the act took place. In December that year, following standard Israeli procedure, the Knesset extended the emergency regulation for another twelve months, and has gone right on extending it ever since. *As if* was the critical phrase in the law. Gradually, as settlement began and expanded, Knesset legislation and military decrees broadened the realm of "as if."

A critical example: Israel does not have absentee ballots. A citizen who is out of the country on Election Day cannot vote. But from the October 1969 national election, the first held after the Six-Day War, settlers were allowed to vote in their settlements, as if they were in Israel.

The media and the public paid little attention. Each time the Knesset extended the emergency regulation, it had the chance to add more content to make sure that the growing number of settlers enjoyed rights and obligations as if they lived inside the Green Line. For instance, Israelis dwelling outside the country normally cannot receive National Insurance pensions, roughly equivalent to Social Security. A 1984 addition to the regulation, however, granted National Insurance coverage to Israelis living in occupied territory. By then, the number of settlers in the Gaza Strip and the West Bank—not counting annexed East Jerusalem—had reached 81,000. In 1994, after the Knesset enacted a national health insurance law, another bland sentence in the unnoticed extension of the emergency regulation gave settlers health insurance as well.

Meanwhile, military orders issued in 1979 began applying Israeli law to settlements as territorial enclaves. The orders empowered the IDF commander of the West Bank to set up municipal governments on the Israeli model: regional councils for groups of small communities; a local council (township) for each larger community. The commander would set the municipal limits. But even inside those limits, the councils' jurisdiction did not apply to any private Palestinian land. The enclaves were ragged, fragmented splotches on the map because the point was not to include Palestinians in the new arrangement. (Similar orders were issued for the Gaza Strip. Israel unilaterally annexed the Golan Heights in 1981, and by 1982 withdrew from the Sinai, so the issue of municipal government for settlements in those areas was moot.)

The timing for establishing local governments for the settlements was not accidental. The Likud settlement drive was gearing up. It would be much easier to attract Israelis to live in the West Bank if they could live there *as if* living in Israel. Meanwhile, under the March 1979 Egyptian-Israeli peace treaty, negotiations were about to start on a Palestinian "self-governing authority" for the West Bank and Gaza. The military orders, it seems, were aimed at preemptively marking the settlements as a realm apart. The autonomy talks failed. The Israeli local governments remained. Additions to the original order applied more and more Israeli laws to their territories, while fine-tuning the statutes. The words *as if* were helpful here, too: laws would apply to residents of settlements as if they were residents of Israel.

In the utterly formal sense, the rule of law existed in the occupied territories. Following—ironic as it sounds—international law on occupation, the military was sovereign. It governed by laws that prevailed before the Israeli conquest, modified by the military commander or, less often, the Knesset. But the concept of the rule of law also has a substantive meaning. It requires following legal basic norms that express justice in the ethical sense. One of those norms is equality before the law. In that substantive meaning, Israel sacrificed the rule of law in order to settle the land beyond the Green Line.

In June 1967, Yisrael Galili and Menachem Begin spoke of, but could not describe, a "constructive solution" that would enable Israel to hold the West Bank without making the Palestinians part of the state. Gradually, without public debate, with no formal declaration, the "constructive solution" was patched together: for practical purposes, settlers and settlements were annexed to Israel. Palestinians lived under military occupation.

In acquiring land for settlement, the state's misuse of law was particularly blatant. So was the basic dynamic of the settlement enterprise: treating occupied territory as if it were an arena where two ethnic movements struggled for supremacy, as if it were stateless land or still under the British Mandate—while one of those movements enjoyed the power of the state.

In the first years of occupation, Israel tapped several sources of land. One was property registered as belonging to the state under previous rulers. In the West Bank, that amounted to about an eighth of the total area. On the face of it, settling Israelis on that land violates the second major source of international law on occupation, the 1907 Hague Regulations. An occupying power may administer property of the hostile state, the Hague Regulations state, and act as an "usufructuary"—meaning that it can enjoy any profits from the property, but cannot permanently alter it. The explicit purpose of settlement is to create permanent change. By military order, Israel also enacted a version of the Absentees'

Property Law, allowing the state to take control of land belonging to refugees who fled during or after the Six-Day War.

But this land wasn't necessarily where the government wanted to build settlements. In some cases, Israel used the Jordanian law of eminent domain. In 1975 and 1977, it expropriated about eleven square miles east of Jerusalem for the new settlement of Ma'aleh Adumim. Today the town is home to over 35,000 Israelis, making it one of the three largest settlements in the West Bank. The expropriation was a prima facie violation of the Hague Regulations, which state that "private property cannot be confiscated" by the occupier, and a misuse of the Jordanian law, which allows expropriation only for public use.

In the early years, though, the government more often exploited the opening in the Hague Regulations that allows the occupier to "requisition" land temporarily for military purposes. The state claimed settlements served Israeli security, an argument anachronistically based on Zionist experience up to 1948. In the occupied territories after 1967, settlements have been an extra burden on the army, which has to guard them. The Syrian surprise attack at the start of the 1973 Yom Kippur War showed that the era of settlements holding off invading armies was over. While trying to hold back Syrian tanks, the IDF had to evacuate frontline Golan settlements. But the myth had a strong grip, and successive governments stood by it in requisitioning land for settlement.

That approach collided with another legal policy: early in the occupation, a few Arab residents of the occupied territories began petitioning the High Court of Justice against IDF actions. Attorney General Meir Shamgar—later chief justice of the Supreme Court—decided not to challenge the court's jurisdiction. One face of this policy is strikingly liberal: the democratic institution that guards civil rights in Israel extended its protection to noncitizens outside Israel's borders. In a 2010 interview, Shamgar told me he saw "a need for judicial supervision of military bodies." The policy's other face is that it hinted at judicial annexation and legitimized Israeli rule. As prominent Israeli legal scholar David Kretzmer wrote, "In almost all of its judgments relating to the occupied territories . . . the court has decided in favor of the authorities, often on the basis of dubious legal arguments." Yet the exceptions, in which the court ruled against the army and government, forced the state to shape its actions to stand up in court.

The best known of those exceptions dealt with land. In 1979, under pressure from Gush Emunim, Menachem Begin's government instructed the IDF to seize 175 acres of private Palestinian land near Nablus for the settlement of Elon Moreh. Some of the landowners turned to the High Court of Justice. The court had upheld land requisitions before. This time, though, the Palestinian petitioners submitted an affidavit from former IDF chief of staff Haim Bar-Lev, who wrote, "Elon Moreh . . . does not contribute to Israel's security." The settlers filed their own brief, stating that Prime Minister Begin had assured them the settlement was permanent. The justices dismissed the state's claim that the settlement served temporary military needs, overturned the requisition order, and returned the land to its owners. Finally, it seemed, the rule of law had prevailed.

The victory proved ephemeral. Elon Moreh was reestablished on state land nearby. The pace of settlement only accelerated. The government rarely risked requisitioning private land again. The new technique for acquiring land was to exploit local laws to establish that the property belonged to the state in the first place. The essential enabler was attorney Plia Albeck of the State Attorney's Office.

West Bank land law dated from 1858, when the Ottoman Empire tried to legislate a clear system of ownership. In the prime real estate around villages, anyone who had farmed land for ten years could assert possession and receive a deed. To maintain the tax base, the Ottomans wanted to make sure the land stayed cultivated—so if a farmer let fields lie fallow for three consecutive years, he could lose his rights to them. The deeds were terribly imprecise. Many people did not bother registering their land; their claim rested on cultivation and traditional ownership alone. Britain, and afterward Jordan, tried to clean up the mess by surveying land, resolving disputes, and registering permanent ownership. But by 1967 less than a third of the West Bank had been surveyed. Israel stopped the process, claiming it would be unfair to adjudicate disputes when many claimants had left the country as refugees—as it happened, refugees whom Israel barred from coming back. That left the rest of the West Bank's land without accurate registration of ownership.

After the Elon Moreh setback, Albeck oversaw a two-pronged legal offensive by a branch of the military government, the Custodian for Governmental and Abandoned Property. Officials reviewed ownership records, and used aerial photos of the West Bank to map what land was being farmed. Albeck took advantage of the fact that many Palestinian families had lost their Ottoman deeds, and she interpreted the land laws in a much harsher manner than had the British or Jordanians. Any property that was not clearly registered and did not meet the rules for cultivation—as Albeck read them—could be declared state land. Before the state proclaimed its ownership of a particular area, Albeck sometimes checked it herself on foot. Between 1979 and 1992, the Custodian designated 350 square miles—nearly one-sixth of the West Bank—as state land. The municipal boundaries of settlements were expanded to include most of that land.

If a Palestinian wanted to dispute the state's claim and assert ownership, he had to come before a military appeals committee—and the burden of proof was on him, not the state. Few appeals succeeded. Albeck explained that Israel was simply fulfilling its obligation under international law to safeguard government property. In cases of doubt, she wrote, an occupying power was obligated to protect and manage land that might belong to the state, unless and until private ownership was proven. She did not see international law as an impediment to turning state-owned land over to the Housing Ministry or to the Settlement Division of the World Zionist Organization for Jewish settlement. If she had opposed settlement, she later said, she could not have done her job. "In all my days, I've never seen anything holy about the Green Line. I haven't found it in the Bible," she told an interviewer in 2004, shortly before her death.

A secret correspondence revealed after Albeck's death sheds light on her approach to the law. In September 1990, Albeck received a letter from Moshe Glick, a lawyer representing the Fund for Redemption of the Land, a company set up by settlers to buy land from Palestinians. Glick said that the company had bought land near the Palestinian village of Bilin. However, it had not registered the purchase, as legally required for transfer of ownership. Doing so would reveal the names of the Palestinian sellers, endangering their lives. Another Palestinian who'd sold land to Jews had recently been murdered. Glick therefore suggested that Albeck arrange to have the land declared state property, and the Custodian for Governmental Property would allocate it to the Fund for Redemption of the Land. Albeck proceeded to do so. Dozens of Palestinian families from Bilin appealed the designation of their land as state property; a few even managed to prove their ownership. In 1992, with the process completed, Albeck reminded military authorities that the "state land" really belonged to the Fund for Redemption of the Land, but that this should be kept secret.

It's true that Palestinian society regarded selling land to Jews as treason. It's also true that fraud is rife in the sales that do take place. And it is terribly unlikely that dozens of Bilin families actually agreed to sell their land. Albeck accepted that the land could be sold, meaning that it was privately owned. Then, to help the purported purchasers avoid any legal scrutiny of the transaction, she arranged for the same property to be declared state land. Everything was done according to law. But the law existed to serve the cause of settlement, not the cause of justice.

And sometimes settlements simply stole privately owned Palestinian land, without pretense of purchase. Ofrah is the extreme example. The army database assembled by Brigadier

General Baruch Spiegel lists others. At Beit El, north of Ramallah, "the northern neighborhood . . . was erected mainly on private [Palestinian] land," the Spiegel Report states. The northeast neighborhood—including twenty residential buildings, a school, and an industrial park—stands entirely on stolen land. At Ma'aleh Mikhmas, east of Ramallah, Spiegel found a new development on Palestinian property. The full list is much longer. The state stood by and let the theft take place.

Theft was only one of the offenses that went unpunished. In 1981, attorney general Yitzhak Zamir appointed a high-level team headed by his deputy, Yehudit Karp, to monitor investigations of offenses by Israelis against Palestinians in the West Bank. The Likud's settlement drive was still in its early stages. Just 16,000 settlers lived in the West Bank, about one-twentieth of today's figure, but the contagion of lawlessness was already blatant. A year later, Karp wrote a strongly worded, despairing report, a window on that one early year in the occupation.

Incidents of Israeli civilians shooting and wounding Palestinians had been on the rise, Karp wrote. But the police said "they were unable to keep track" of such cases, so they did not investigate. They did little more when a Palestinian was shot dead. After an apparent murder in the village of Bani Na'im, near Hebron, a delegation of settlers, including the mayor of Kiryat Arba and one of the suspects, arrived at a police station and announced that settlers would not cooperate with the investigation. The police did not bother to detain or question the suspect. Kiryat Arba, on the edge of Hebron, had been built by the government to house the

Orthodox activists who had tried to settle inside the Palestinian city. It was known for its particularly intense mix of religion and nationalism, and appears several times in Karp's report as the apparent home of perpetrators of violence against Palestinians.

Karp detailed fifteen cases out of a much larger number of failed investigations. She attributed the "ambivalence" of the police about tracking down offenders to "the natural complexity of the situation," a polite way to describe Palestinians living under Israeli military rule while the government sponsored settlement of Jews in their midst. The police, she wrote, did not relate to suspects as "criminals in the normal sense." Worse yet, officials of the military government often interfered in investigations, ordering the police to drop cases or free suspects. The chief of investigations for the police's Judea District—the southern half of the West Bank—had reported "his impression" that someone high up in the army or Defense Ministry had let settlers understand that they were "soldiers for all practical purposes," not subject to the authority of civilian police. Karp concluded that there was no point in the team continuing to monitor the police. It would only serve as a fig leaf for a failed system that required "radical rethinking of what the rule of law means."

Even when Jews were tried for attacks against Palestinians, the justice system showed a split personality—treating the perpetrators as criminals, but also as misguided patriots and sometimes as victims of Palestinian violence. In 1988 Moshe Levinger went on a rampage after Palestinians threw rocks at his car in Hebron. Levinger walked down the street firing his pistol wildly and killed a shopkeeper standing in front of his shoe store. In a plea bargain, he was convicted of "causing death by negligence." Sentenced to five months in prison, he served three.

The Jewish terror underground of the early 1980s serves as the most extreme example of schizophrenic justice. The group's twenty-eight members, most of them settlers, crippled two Palestinian mayors and an IDF sapper with explosive booby traps, murdered three students at a Hebron college, attempted to bomb five East Jerusalem buses during rush hour—and plotted to blow up the Dome of the Rock in Jerusalem in order to shatter Israel's peace agreement with Egypt and prevent the Israeli withdrawal from the Sinai. Judges in the case noted that if carried out, the Dome of the Rock plot could have ignited war with the entire Muslim world. Three men were sentenced to life for the Hebron murders. But with repeated commutations, they walked free after less than seven years in prison. Yehudah Etzion, mastermind of the Temple Mount plot and an organizer of the attacks on the mayors, spent less than five years behind bars. Ze'ev Hever, charged with attempted murder for trying to booby-trap another Palestinian leader's car, was free on a plea bargain a year after his arrest. In a 1986 interview, he told me he was "not ashamed" of what he'd done. Involvement in terrorism did not hurt his career. As of this writing, he has been the secretary-general of Amana, a settlement-building organization with close government ties, for over twenty years.

Karp's report did not spark the rethinking of the rule of law that she sought. The "natural complexity of the situation" prevented that. As she noted many years later, the army and the police understood their role as protecting Israelis, not

Palestinians. Put differently, they were not responsible for the welfare of the governed, for equal enforcement of laws, or for preventing conflict; they were a side to the conflict. The presence of Israeli civilians in the midst of a population under military occupation made this inevitable. As for the settlers, they were "soldiers" serving the policy of creeping annexation, but were not subject to military discipline or even to consistent legal constraints. For beyond the selective attention to international law, beyond the dual legal system and the misuse of local law, the settlement project turned occupied territory into a realm where, ultimately, there was no law.

The rule of law, in its substantive sense, is essential to a democratic state. By increments, the settlement project hollowed out the rule of law. Clear borders are fundamental to democracy. Settlement erased Israel's border, or created several. For Jews, the state stretched from the Mediterranean to the Jordan, or perhaps to the Green Line plus the municipal limits of settlements. For Palestinians, the Green Line marked where government by the consent of the governed ended. Palestinians in occupied territory were only the subjects of military government. Unlike Arabs who had lived under military rule in Israel, they were not also "citizens of a liberal nation-state." No political party in Israel stood to gain votes by paying passing attention to their needs.

From July 1967, all those involved in settlement saw themselves as serving Zionism. In fact, they were doing the opposite. They were living backward, turning a state into a movement. Stone by stone, they were dismantling the state of Israel.

All of this, I must stress, spurred opposition inside Israeli society, which has grown as the occupation has stretched on and settlement has expanded. Even in the ecstasy immediately after the Six-Day War, a few sober voices warned of the consequences of ongoing occupation. Egyptian president Anwar al-Sadat's visit to Israel in 1977 catalyzed the start of the Peace Now movement, which demanded that the government show its willingness to cede land for peace. Human rights organizations have sprung up and made the abuses in the occupied territories much or all of their agenda. The perennial problem of the critics has been that while they write reports and hold marches, the coalition of state agencies and settlers has continued "creating facts" by building houses in occupied land.

The unplanned war of 1967 and the ill-considered settlement effort afterward had another consequence, entirely unintended: they transmogrified religious Zionism from a moderate political movement to a sect with Jewish control of the Whole Land of Israel as its primary principle of faith.

Before the war, Orthodox Zionism had functioned mostly as an auxiliary to the secular mainstream. Its emblematic achievement in the state's early years was establishing Bar-Ilan University, an Orthodox corner of the academic world, an artful compromise between self-segregation and full participation in modern society. Politically, the National Religious Party was a perennial coalition partner, generally dovish on foreign policy issues, in Mapai governments. Like secular Zionist parties, it had its own youth movement, Bnei Akiva, which hoped to keep its members Orthodox and make them aspire to live in religious kibbutzim.

Theologically, the oft-cited sage was Rabbi Avraham Yitzhak Hacohen Kook, who had served as chief rabbi during the British Mandate and died in 1935. Kook's teachings melded Jewish mystical doctrine and European nationalist theory. The Jews' return to their land, he had taught, was part of God's plan for redemption of the world, and secular Zionists were unconsciously doing God's will. Kook's ideas provided legitimacy for Orthodox Jews to join forces with Jews who ate pork and worked on the Sabbath, but he was quoted more than seriously studied. After his death, his only son, Rabbi Tzvi Yehudah Kook, headed a small yeshivah in Jerusalem and taught that Israel was "the state that prophets foresaw" when they spoke of the End of Days. The state's military, said Kook fils, was not an expression of human power and pride. Rather, it made possible "study and fulfillment of the Torah," since "we are learning that we must carry out the divine obligation created by that power—conquering the Land." He developed a circle of young disciples—including Porat and Levinger—but remained a marginal figure.

Until June 1967. For many religious Jews, especially younger ones, the miraculous victory demanded explanation. Tzvi Yehuda Kook provided one: the conquests were the next step in God's plan, in the process of redemption. When the government of Israel had acted as if "redemption stopped at the Green Line," God had forced the Jews to conquer the rest of the homeland. So wrote Rabbi Yaakov Filber, another Kook disciple, stressing that "there is no complete redemption without the complete Land of Israel." As reframed by the younger Kook and his followers, mystical nationalism not only justified taking part in the secular project of nation building. It taught that the world's spiritual condition was measured by Jewish military power and territorial expansion. Religion swallowed whole the hard-line nationalism of soil, power, and ethnic superiority, and took on its shape.

Settling in "redeemed" territory was a way of consciously advancing God's plan. For young religious Zionists, it also cured a double sense of inferiority. In building the state, their movement had been a very junior partner. Secularists saw them as milquetoasts. The ultra-Orthodox, meanwhile, regarded them as practicing lukewarm Judaism. Now they seized the chance to be the vanguard fulfilling the old secular Zionist value of settlement. At the same, they believed, they were proving their superior religious commitment, since they were keeping what Filber described as the "commandment that is as important as all the others combined, the commandment of settling the Land."

Had the conquests been temporary, a sobering up would likely have followed the postwar intoxication. When the government held on to the occupied territories, began settling them, yet left their ultimate political fate uncertain, it created the perfect conditions for an ideological storm.

The greatest practical difficulty that Labor governments faced in building settlements was a lack of willing manpower. Their Likud successors faced the same problem recruiting people to settle deep in occupied territory. Young secular Israelis generally treated settlement as a value to be honored, not acted on. Partnership with religious Zionists of the Kook school provided the foot soldiers. In turn, religious settlers became the role model for the Orthodox Zionist community. After the emergence of Gush Emunim in 1974, the National Religious Party metamorphosed into the faction representing settlers and ultranationalist faith.

The government's alliance with religious settlers was fraught with ignored dangers. Religious settlers were subcontractors in a project with strategic implications, but saw government decisions restricting where they would settle as illegitimate. The government was outsourcing a project that combined defense and foreign policy to an ideological camp that read pragmatic restraint as a lack of faith.

Of course, the settlement project meant more than a philosophical move for religious Zionism. Settlers migrated physically, from inside the Green Line to occupied territory. And among settlers, the religiously motivated ones were most likely to move to the small settlements farther from sovereign Israel, between Palestinian towns and villages in the mountains of the West Bank. The state made that migration easier: Israelis moving to settlements deep into the West Bank received the largest financial incentives.

Most religious settlers also moved from cities to a new kind of exurb. Ofrah created the model. Until its founding, the settlement ideal meant building a kibbutz or moshav, a socialist community whose members worked in agriculture or jointly owned industry. Nearly all the settlements established by Labor governments stuck to that pattern, with the exception of a few towns. But socialism had gone out of fashion. After much discussion, Ofrah defined itself as a "community settlement." That meant a small residential community, managed by an association responsible for "preserving the character of the settlement," as Gush Emunim reports explained. New residents would have to be accepted as members, so that all would share an "ideological-social background." They would enjoy "single-family homes, quiet streets, fresh air," a dream beyond the reach of middle-class apartment-dwelling Israelis. The community would grow no larger than a few hundred families, attracting educated professionals to an "island" of a "selected population," deliberately "closed" and "homogenous." The shade of one's religious commitment, even the precise degree of modesty in women's dress, could be a criterion for membership. When the Likud came to power, it adopted this model and built many more settlements on the same lines.

Young Orthodox Jews who had grown up in urban Israel, contending with a cacophony of political and cultural argument, moved to small communities of people like themselves, comfortable colonies with Palestinian towns and villages as scenery. Many commuted to cities inside Israel to work. But in their new homes, they did not need to face the secular Israelis who had mocked them on their way home from Bnei Akiva meetings. They became a sect, apart from the Israel they sought to lead.

Yet from the start, Orthodox settlements saw educating Jews from within the Green Line as both an ideological goal and a solution to the problem of livelihood. The economic chapter of an early Gush Emunim master plan called for establishing yeshivot and boarding schools in settlements to create jobs. Another option was commuting to teach in state-funded religious schools inside Israel. The state has backed both options. Extra funding for education has been one pillar of the structure of financial incentives supporting settlement. Free education begins two years earlier in settlements than inside Israel; the Education Ministry pays for longer school days than in most of Israel; the Interior Ministry provides extra cash to the municipal governments of settlements to pay for education. Teachers living in settlements get benefits that can boost their salaries by up to 20 percent, whether they work in the settlement or inside Israel.

The combined effect is a striking disparity: in the Israeli population as a whole, 12.7 percent of employees work in education, according to the Central Bureau of Statistics. In West Bank settlements, the parallel figure is 21.9 percent, nearly twice as much. These official figures don't distinguish between large suburban settlements and the small communities deeper in the West Bank. But the proportion of teachers is almost certainly higher in the latter, where the desire to pass on intensely held beliefs makes teaching a much more valued profession.

One day in 2003, I visited the spacious home of Moti and Lea Sklar in Ofrah. At the time, Lea Sklar was an administrator in the Jerusalem city schools, supervising education for "Judaism, equality, and democracy." On the range of religious and political views among settlers, Sklar put herself at the moderate, even iconoclastic, end. She proudly described her two youngest daughters, of elementary school age, as "real feminists." To satisfy the interpretation of Orthodox law requiring a married woman to cover her hair, she wore a small knitted cap, with her chest-length curls hanging out— a statement of both accepting and defying rules.

The second Palestinian uprising was still raging.

Discussing her reasons for staying in Ofrah despite the increased dangers of terror attacks, Sklar said it was a warm community and the only home her five children knew. But she also stressed that Ofrah was "part of the State of Israel," and that settling there was a direct continuation of early Zionist pioneers' creation of the first kibbutzim. "I don't believe in a distinction between [the land we held] before 1967 and after," she said. "It's all part of a process." In the political arrangement that would complete that process, she suggested, the West Bank's Palestinians would have "human rights to life, security, health" and a measure of autonomy— for instance, to run their own school system—under Israeli rule. They would not be citizens. "They can't vote for my government, because then it would be an Arab government," said the woman then in charge of education for democracy in the schools my children attended.

For children who have grown up and been educated in the closed, warm communities of the settlements, those views represent the liberal end of the spectrum. Inside Israel, settler educators have had a particularly strong presence in state religious schools and other institutions serving the Orthodox Zionist community.

In their partnership with Orthodox settlers, secular politicians underwrote the indoctrination of a new generation in radical religious culture. The dangerous results have become clear only as that generation has come of age.

IV.

CHILDREN OF THE HILLS

The handbill hung on the study-hall notice board. Only one of the thirty students was in the hall at midday. He had the wispy beard of a young man who has never shaved, and thick blond sidelocks that hung over his shoulders. The name of the institution, "Sing Unto the Lord Yeshivah," and the slogan, "The Lord Is King," were painted rather sloppily on the outside of the prefab building. A donkey and large yellow tractor for construction work stood in the dusty parking lot at Havat Gilad, Gilad's Farm, an illegal outpost southwest of Nablus. It was late October, the height of the olive harvest.

Driving in, I'd seen Palestinian families working in the groves, picking the fruit that provides the deep green oil that is the West Bank's premier product.

The writing on one side of the handbill was printed over a soft photo of an olive grove. On the other side, the background showed a Palestinian woman wearing a white headscarf and standing next to a mutilated olive tree. The Hebrew text was written in the diction of Jewish religious law, *halakhah*, and cited classical religious works from the Bible onward.

The ripening of the olives, said the leaflet, provided the opportunity to fulfill Moses' command to the twelve spies he sent into Canaan, "Be strong and take from the fruit of the land." The way to show who really had title to the Land of Israel was to "bring its good fruit from its temporary occupants"—meaning Palestinians—"to its true owners"—meaning Jews. All the soil of the Land of Israel and all the trees belonged to the Jewish people, it said, so that by taking the fruit, Jews are "returning what has been stolen to our own hands and not stealing from others."

In places where harvesting olives from Palestinian groves was impractical, the handbill's unsigned author continued, the proper alternative was to follow Ecclesiastes' words, "A time to plant and a time to uproot," and cut down the trees. A war was in progress, and "one of the important means . . . to victory over our enemies is driving him out of our land by harming his property." The text ends with the prayer for a speedy end to the infamy of "strangers consuming our inheritance" and the shame of them being able to do so "with the help of the establishment and various security bodies that have forgotten their Jewish identity."

The handbill tacked to the notice board demonstrated an old principle: with enough determination, an interpreter of sacred texts can turn them inside out, making a sin into an obligation. On the simplest level, the writer had to explain away the explicit commandment in Deuteronomy 20:19 against chopping down fruit trees as a means of waging war. He rationalized an obvious act of theft as reclaiming one's own property. He also ignored an ancient and well-known rabbinic gloss on the disagreement between the shepherds of Abraham and his nephew Lot in the book of Genesis: Lot's men, the tradition says, grazed his herds in fields owned by Canaanites, rationalizing that God had promised the land to Abraham's descendants. But Abraham rejected that excuse. The story teaches that a divine promise for the undefined future cannot justify theft from the land's here-and-now inhabitants. This is a tradition that schoolchildren learn.

Historically, religious groups that believe God's kingdom on earth is near are particularly vulnerable to this kind of photo-negative morality. There's no better way to demonstrate that a new age has dawned than to say that new rules have replaced the old. In Judaism, the classic example is the seventeenth-century false messiah, Shabtai Tzvi, whose followers turned adultery into a ritual. In our time, theologies that absorb extreme political doctrines suffer similar vulnerability to sanctifying sins—as shown by Islamic radicals who have turned the forbidden act of suicide into heroism.

The religious settlement movement is doubly vulnerable: it springs from the faith expressed by Tzvi Yehudah Kook that "we are already in the middle of redemption," and from recasting nationalism, at its most tribal, as religious doctrine.

The combination is expressed by a quotation that appears on the website of Shvut Ami, another illegal outpost in the Nablus area. On the cusp of the messianic era, it says, "the most important point is the land of Israel. From it everything flows, and except for holding tightly to it, there is no way to bring holiness into the world." The words are those of Rabbi Ya'akov Moshe Harlap, a disciple of the elder Kook, who died in 1951. Whatever Harlap's original intent, his words open the door to a "moral" system in which seizing territory outweighs obligations to human beings.

The leaflet represents the attitude of a significant wing of the settler movement. The West Bank olive harvest has become an annual low-level battle, with settlers stealing from and ravaging Palestinian groves, and with outpost settlers as prime suspects. Israeli human rights groups documented over thirty attacks on Palestinian property in the first six weeks of the 2010 harvest alone. Near the settlement of Talmon, unidentified Israelis set a grove on fire while Palestinians were picking the olives. A hundred trees were poisoned and another forty uprooted at Turmusayya, a Palestinian village close to the Adei Ad outpost. Attacks were rampant in the Nablus region; Gilad's Farm is just one of the extremist settlements and outposts that ring the Palestinian city. Near Shvut Ami, fifty trees were broken or cut down, and the fruit of two hundred others was stolen. Gilad's Farm itself is wedged between the Palestinian villages of Fur'ata and Tell. Hundreds of trees in a 120-acre area belonging to the two villages were set aflame. The olives from another of Fur'ata's groves were harvested and stolen. One cannot presume that the offenders necessarily came from the closest settlement, especially when the campaign is so widespread. But one can be certain that each destroyed tree represented part of someone's labor and livelihood; each incident is part of the effort to drive "the enemy . . . out of our land by harming his property."

The handbill's concluding prayer expresses the furious antipathy of many outpost settlers toward "the establishment." That term is a catchall: it includes the Israeli government; the Civil Administration; the police, Shin Bet security service, and IDF; and often the first-generation leadership of the settlement movement, Orthodox politicians, and insufficiently radical rabbis—all of whom are judged to lack Jewish consciousness. The irony is that the outposts are actually a joint project of the young settlers and much of that establishment. The outpost settlers are a far-right twist on the college student who despises her parents' bourgeois hypocrisy, demands independence, and awaits the next cash infusion from home. Politicians, government agencies, and middle-age settlement leaders play the role of parents who oscillate between encouraging their child's idealism, lecturing her about restraint, and arguing with each other and themselves.

Gilad's Farm is one of the many variations on this theme. The outpost was established by Itai Zar in memory of his older brother Gilad, who was murdered by Palestinian gunmen in a drive-by shooting on a nearby road in 2001, early in the bloodletting of the Second Intifada. Their father, Moshe Zar, is a prominent figure among the first generation of settlers, a well-known land dealer, and a convicted member of the Jewish terror underground of the early 1980s. According to Itai Zar, the outpost stands on land that his father bought, but for which he had not legally registered ownership. Prime Minister Ariel Sharon gave verbal approval for settling at the spot and sent the family to Amana chief Ze'ev Hever to make the arrangements, Itai Zar told me.

Not all the details of Zar's account can be independently confirmed, but it fits the pattern of the outposts. The details that he leaves out also fit the standard story line: the new settlement lacked approval from the cabinet, the defense minister, and the planning bodies of Israel's Civil Administration in the West Bank, meaning that it was illegal several times over. One slightly unusual event in the history of Gilad's Farm is that in October 2002, Sharon's defense minister, Binyamin Ben-Eliezer, decided to remove the outpost, apparently as symbolic proof of his willingness to enforce the law. A thousand young settlers showed up to block the evacuation bodily. Over ninety police, soldiers, and settlers were wounded in the struggle as the flimsy structures were razed.

The evening after the melee, Itai Zar and his companions returned to reestablish the outpost, with the backing of the Council of Settlements in Judea, Samaria, and Gaza, the main settler leadership body. By 2009, twenty-five families lived at Gilad's Farm, and thirty young men were studying at the yeshivah. Zar speaks with deep disdain of established settlements as mere "neighborhoods with TV sets"—in contrast to the "hilltops," the outposts, which are home to young idealists. He uses a dismissive pejorative for classic religious Zionists who support Israeli institutions, calls secular law "drivel," and aspires to see Israel governed only by religious law. Like the anonymous leaflet writer, in short, he has very little use for the political, religious, and settlement establishments that have helped put him on the map.

Gilad's Farm and the outpost enterprise as a whole deserve attention not as aberrations, but as symptoms of a larger syndrome. Since the Oslo Accord of 1993, the split in Israel's personality has widened into a gulf.

On one hand, Israel recognized the Palestine Liberation Organization and the reality of Palestinian peoplehood. It has intermittently engaged in a diplomatic process whose only logical outcome is creation of a Palestinian state in the West Bank and Gaza Strip. In parallel, the government stopped approving new settlements in occupied territory. It even removed the small number of settlers from the Gaza Strip. Could these changes only be taken by themselves, they would mean that Israel had made the long-delayed, necessary choice to give up the occupied territories for peace and for the sake of its own future as a democracy and a Jewish state.

Yet in the same years, the machinery of the state has aided and abetted a dramatic expansion of West Bank settlement. Cabinet ministers, officials, and settlers have joined in pervasive disregard for the law and for responsibility to democratic decisions. Reversing one of the signal achievements of Israel's early years, the government ignores court decisions upholding human rights as a matter of course. A new generation of settlers has come of age, as radical or more in its theologized politics, alienated from the institutions of the state that have so assiduously fostered its growth.

The meaning of these changes is a democracy in greater danger, a state that is weaker and less capable of ending the occupation. To understand the outposts, it's necessary to look at the wider changes that spawned them.

Yitzhak Rabin was able to sign the Oslo Accord because the heat of the Palestinian uprising, the Intifada, transmuted his understanding of the conflict. As defense minister when the uprising erupted in December 1987, Rabin promised to suppress it with "force, might and beatings." Yet in the cabinet, Rabin eventually became the strongest voice insisting that the Intifada was "a popular, national uprising" that could not be stopped by military means, according to former Shin Bet chief Yaakov Perry. Put differently, he realized that Israel would have to reach a modus vivendi with the Palestinian national movement.

I mention Rabin not to endorse the great-man reading of history, but from a literary perspective: as in Shakespeare, the tragedies of aristocrats represent the inner battles of the common man. In Israeli society of the 1980s, to speak of two states for two peoples was to place oneself on the radical left. At first glance, it was the Oslo Accord that made such ideas legitimate. In fact, the agreement was possible only because the uprising burned away many Israelis' indifference to the occupation.

Yet Rabin was not ready to go directly to a peace agreement including borders and evacuation of settlements. The Oslo Accord created an interim stage leading to an unknown outcome. The Great Decision actually contained another refusal to decide. In that way as well, Rabin represented the common man.

Postponing a final-status agreement proved disastrous.

Under Oslo and its follow-up agreements, a Palestinian Authority was created to exercise limited autonomy in parts of the West Bank and Gaza. Since no settlements were evacuated, the PA received fragmented enclaves. The map of autonomy was dictated by the map of settlement that Ariel Sharon had drawn. Meanwhile, both Israelis and Palestinians had every motivation to "create facts" to predetermine the permanent-status agreement. But Israel had more power to do so: setting up Palestinian institutions in East Jerusalem could not have the same impact as building new Israeli neighborhoods there.

Since settlements remained in place, the Rabin government embarked on a West Bank road-building program so that Israelis could drive around Palestinian-controlled cities. The bypass roads made the commute from settlements to Israeli cities safer, and had the unintended effect of shortening the drive considerably—thereby making it easier for Israelis to move to settlements deep in the West Bank. The new roads were a particular boon for rightists who had been dithering between convenience and their desire to join a settlement to help block a future withdrawal. Rabin quite literally paved the way for his opponents. "The greatest of the settlement builders was Yitzhak Rabin. What caused Ofrah to develop? The road came to us," says Pinchas Wallerstein, the longtime head of the Mateh Binyamin Regional Council, the local government for settlements north of Jerusalem. The praise is backhanded; neither Wallerstein nor other settlers who express the same idea think that Rabin had any intention of helping them.

At the time the Oslo Accord was announced, settlers had

no praise, even ironic, for the prime minister. Protests began even before the signing of the accord on September 13, 1993. At mass rallies, secular right-wing politicians such as Knesset members Ariel Sharon and Benjamin Netanyahu spoke—but the protesters were almost all Orthodox settlers and supporters. For the settlers, the accord was much more than a political defeat. Though the agreement did not immediately require evacuation of settlements, it pointed in that direction—threatening their homes, their understanding of their place in society, their life's work, and the theology that gave it meaning. After years of believing they were Israel's vanguard, settlers now felt like a betrayed minority. The sacred state was relinquishing sacred land, introducing a contradiction into the heart of their beliefs.

Rabbis of the religious right described the threat in incendiary language. Rabbi Nachum Rabinovitch, head of the state-supported Birkat Moshe yeshivah in the settlement of Ma'aleh Adumim, compared anyone who carried out orders to evacuate a settlement to Jewish collaborators with the Nazis. In an article published by the Committee of Rabbis in Judea, Samaria, and Gaza, Rabinovitch described "any activity reducing our hold on the Land or banishing Jews from regions of our soil" as violating an underlying "purpose of the Torah" and referred readers to a medieval text prescribing capital punishment for blasphemy.

"Visionaries have seen their vision torn asunder before their eyes," wrote ideologue Dan Be'eri in the settler journal *Nekuda*, half a year after the accord. Be'eri was describing the spiritual crisis among believers in "redemptive Zionism." More specifically, he was explaining what brought Kiryat

Arba settler Baruch Goldstein to murder twenty-nine Muslim worshippers in the Hebron holy place known to Jews as the Tomb of the Patriarchs and to Muslims as the Ibrahimi Mosque on February 25, 1994. Beforehand, Goldstein told friends he had a plan for ending the Oslo process. He stopped shooting only when Palestinians managed to kill him.

Yitzhak Rabin was not alone in describing Goldstein as "mentally ill," a description that erased the context of the settler movement rebelling against the state that had nurtured it. Meanwhile, the extreme edge of the religious right eulogized Goldstein as a hero and martyr. Among his posthumous admirers was Bar-Ilan University law student Yigal Amir. On November 4, 1995, Amir carried out his own plan to prevent dividing the Land of Israel. He assassinated Yitzhak Rabin.

It is impossible to measure Amir's share of responsibility in the breakdown of the Oslo process. History cannot be rewound and run again, with Rabin alive, for comparison. But Rabin's successor, Shimon Peres, a much weaker candidate, lost the 1996 election to Netanyahu by a mere 1 percent. Netanyahu spent three years as prime minister trying to avoid diplomatic progress.

As for the trauma of Rabin's murder, much of the public reaction focused on the fact that a Jew had killed another Jew, as if violating ethnic solidarity were Amir's primary offense. Defending his university, for instance, Bar-Ilan president Shlomo Eckstein said, "We try to educate our students to love all Jews." The operative corollary was to seek "national unity," meaning Jewish unity: reconciliation between secular and Orthodox, or between Jews on the left and right.

When Labor's Ehud Barak defeated Netanyahu in 1999 on a platform of renewing peace efforts, he showed fealty to the unity story by bringing the pro-settlement National Religious Party into his coalition and making its leader, Yitzhak Levy, the housing minister. Levy accelerated building of new homes in settlements to an unprecedented level; Barak acquiesced as the concrete mixers worked overtime.

The unity narrative evades the significance of Amir's act: beyond the normal horror of murder, it was a poor man's version of a coup, an attack on the elected leader in order to change a democratically chosen policy. Amir acted as the self-appointed messenger of a political camp that saw the state as legitimate only insofar as it fulfilled its purportedly God-given mission—holding the Whole Land for the Jews. Afterward, avoiding conflict between Jew and Jew served politicians as another justification to support settlement, thereby making a future confrontation over democratic decisions all the more likely.

Between 1993 and the unsuccessful Camp David summit in 2000, the number of Israeli settlers in the West Bank and Gaza Strip grew 70 percent, from 116,000 to 198,000. Throughout the Oslo years, Palestinians could watch the red-roofed houses of the settlements spreading on the hills, making it harder to believe that Israel really intended to allow Palestinian independence. The reason for the failure of the Israeli-Palestinian talks in 2000 remains the subject of intense debate, but the growth of the settlements surely figures as one factor. More important for the present discussion, by talking peace while building houses in Ofrah, Ma'aleh

Adumim, and a host of other settlements, successive governments showed strategic schizophrenia and undermined their own credibility.

By mid-2010, despite Israel's pullout from Gaza, the number of settlers had grown to 300,000. That is, during seventeen years in which Israel was officially committed to reaching a permanent agreement with the Palestinians, the settler population increased by over two and a half times. These are official Israeli figures, which do not include another 185,000 Israelis living in the annexed areas of East Jerusalem.

This increase is not a natural population explosion. Rather, it is driven by a deluge of government financing for the settlement project, which continues with no accurate accounting. A 2003 report on the Housing Ministry by Israel's state comptroller complained, "The ministry's budget does not make it possible to identify what portion . . . is allocated to Judea, Samaria and the Gaza District." That is true of other ministries as well. The same year, a Finance Ministry spokesperson said, "We don't have any way of making an estimation" of government outlays on settlement. It was an answer I'd learned to expect. In 1986, the first time I set out to investigate settlement costs, Yaacov Tsur, the absorption minister, told me he had asked the Finance Ministry, Central Bureau of Statistics, and Bank of Israel how much the government was spending on settlement, and "no one had any figures." Even as a cabinet member, he found that the total outlay was "a bigger secret than the [Mordechai] Vanunu affair," referring to the closed-door trial that year of an Israeli convicted of leaking information on Israel's nuclear program.

The difference between the nuclear secrets and the settlement budget was that the latter could not be leaked; it had never been added up, and remains uncalculated to this day. Settlement outlays are scattered throughout the state budget. Many of the incentives were originally intended to help "national priority areas" inside Israel—mainly poor Jewish towns far from the country's urban center. Later, settlements were quietly added to the list of priority areas. The perks for educators, for instance, were intended to attract qualified teachers to towns where they were in short supply. Settlements do not have that problem, but got the money anyway. Grants to investors building factories in settlement industrial parks are part of the same budget as subsidies designed to bring jobs to economically depressed areas inside Israel.

Municipal governments in settlements impose lower local taxes than towns inside Israel, and receive much more funding via the Interior Ministry—meaning that residents pay less and get better services. In most settlements, the Housing Ministry cuts the costs of homes by giving discounts on the already artificially low price of land, at the same time offering subsidized mortgages. Cheap land makes it possible to build a type of home unavailable inside the Green Line: a single-family house as small as 750 square feet, with the option to expand later. This means a young couple can buy a home in a settlement for the cost of renting in the city and feel secure in beginning a family. Later, when their income grows, the house grows too, making it easier to fulfill religious expectations to have a large family. The goal of settlement subsidies may not have been to boost fertility, but they have done that, too. Even "natural growth" in settlements enjoyed an unnatural cash stimulant.

If the ongoing occupation and settlement expansion have had a silver lining, it's that they've helped spur other Israelis to create human rights and pro-democracy groups. Such organizations have regularly turned to the judicial system, especially to the High Court of Justice. Meanwhile, the court itself has taken a more activist role. Since the 1980s, it has gradually opened its doors to petitioners—including human rights groups—not directly harmed by the government actions they are challenging. The Supreme Court gained additional power through its interpretation of two "basic laws"—pieces of Israel's still incomplete constitution—passed in 1992. One guaranteed "human dignity and freedom," the other protected the right to pursue the livelihood of one's choice. In a 1995 ruling that was the Israeli equivalent of *Marbury v. Madison*, the Supreme Court asserted its authority to declare normal legislation unconstitutional if it contradicted a basic law.

In 2006, the High Court of Justice ruled on a petition by three organizations defending the rights of Israeli Arab citizens. The petitioners argued that the list of national-priority areas for education discriminated against Arab communities inside Israel, violating the principle of equality. The court not only accepted the petition regarding education, it recommended that the government review all other benefits under the national-priority system. As of July 2010, the government was still allocating funds as if the country's highest court had never spoken, and settlers were still receiving the largest benefits. That outcome, too, reveals Israel's split personality in the post-Oslo years: On one hand, citizen activism and the Supreme Court's 1995 constitutional revolution have taken the country further toward fulfilling the principles of liberal democracy. On the other, the government's disregard for this and other court decisions undermines judicial review, a retreat from the precedent set by David Ben-Gurion's response to the *Kol Ha'am* decision.

Citizen activists have also tried to determine how much money the government is devoting to settlement. In 2002, the Peace Now movement hired Dror Tzaban, formerly a top Finance Ministry official, to analyze the previous year's state budget. Tzaban identified $430 million in extra outlays for settlers, beyond what the state would have spent on the same citizens if they had lived inside Israel. That came to $2,000 per person, in a country where the GDP per capita was about $17,000.

Tzaban stressed that this was only a piece of a much larger, unknown total. Many parts of the state budget contain no geographic breakdown, and spending on the settlements is included in the national total, as if they were inside Israel. Moreover, Tzaban explained, "The defense budget is a black box"; the breakdown is classified. In a 2008 study by Shlomo Swirski, director of the Adva Center, a social research institute, he described the settlements as "probably Israel's single most costly civil—or rather, civil-military—project in the post-1967 era." The word *probably* hints at a price not measurable in monetary terms. Financial transparency is essential to democratic debate. Yet the extent of the state's spending on settlement is unknown to the Israeli public and its elected representatives.

One prayer at the Al-Asqa Mosque in Jerusalem is worth five hundred elsewhere, a leader of the Islamic Movement among

Palestinian citizens of Israel told me in 1999. He was quoting, or slightly misquoting, a hadith, a tradition attributed to the prophet Muhammad. Events the next year suggest that a death at Al-Aqsa—also known as the Temple Mount—certainly has the impact of hundreds in another place. On September 28, 2000, Ariel Sharon, then leader of the right-wing opposition in the Knesset, made a highly publicized visit to the contested holy site. On the morrow, Friday prayers at the mosque erupted into violent demonstrations. Israeli police shot four Palestinians dead. The Second Intifada had been ignited.

However spontaneous its eruption, the underlying reasons for the Second Intifada appeared clear. After the failure at Camp David, many Palestinians despaired of achieving independence through diplomacy, and hoped to end the occupation through violence. Israel's overwhelming military response had the effect of spraying lighter fluid from fire hoses. A decade later, over 1,000 Israelis had been killed—most of them civilians—and over 6,000 Palestinians. Yet filling the graveyards did not bring Palestinian independence.

Prima facie, Israel did make two significant concessions after Sharon succeeded Barak as prime minister in 2001. With suicide bombers shredding themselves and other human beings in Israeli cafés and buses inside the Green Line, Sharon acceded to public pressure to build a fence to keep terrorists from entering Israel from the West Bank. Like previous prime ministers, Sharon had heretofore resisted marking a de facto border between Israel and occupied territory. Had the fence been built on the most obvious route, the Green Line, it would have been a psychological breakthrough, the surfacing of repressed national memory. The project would also have avoided local and international legal challenges, and could have been built more cheaply and quickly than Sharon's brainchild.

Sharon, however, adapted the fence to fit his strategy of fragmenting Palestinian territory with "fingers" of Israeli settlement. Working closely with an IDF strategic planner, Colonel Dany Tirza, Sharon designed a tortuous route that looped through the West Bank to put as many settlers as possible on the "Israeli" side of the fence. In the process, it trapped thousands of Palestinians in enclaves between the fence and the Green Line, caught tens of thousands in areas completely surrounded by the barrier, and left others separated from their farmlands.

In 2003, Tirza described the route as a "reference line" for an Israeli-Palestinian border. At a legal conference in 2005 Tzipi Livni—then justice minister in Sharon's government—said the fence was "the future border of the state of Israel." In fact, the fence route was no more workable as a border proposal than an M. C. Escher drawing would be as a blueprint. Meandering tentacles stretched deep into the West Bank, reaching almost to Nablus in one spot and most of the way from Jerusalem to Jericho in another. Along most of its route, the barrier was designed as a swath of barbed wire and sensors, with military patrol roads on each side—a confession written by bulldozers that the IDF would remain deployed on both sides of the fence.

One small example of the route's effect on Palestinian lives is the village of Azzun Atma, on the western edge of the West Bank. The barrier twists through the foothills to separate the Palestinian community from settlements on either side of it. Azzun Atma is completely enclosed, with one road out to the rest of the West Bank. In January 2008, the secretary of the village council, Abdulkarim Ayoub Ahmed, confirmed reports that women often left the village near the end of pregnancy to avoid the risk of going into labor at night, when the IDF gate on that road was unmanned and shut. A few weeks before, one woman had given birth in her car at the closed gate.

Rather than redividing Israel from occupied territory, the fence entangled Israel more deeply in the West Bank. Like the checkpoints that proliferated during the uprising, like prohibitions on Palestinians using the same roads as Israelis, the fence was presented publicly as protecting Israel from terror, but was designed in large part to secure the settlements.

Sharon's announcement in February 2004 that he would withdraw the IDF from the Gaza Strip and evacuate Israeli settlements there appeared to be a much larger concession, and more out of character. Sharon, though, regarded "disengagement" as a tactical move, a shortening of the lines to protect his forces. The idea was born after the Bush administration issued its 2003 Roadmap to a Permanent Two-State Solution. One of Sharon's closest advisers, Dov Weisglas, described disengagement as "providing the proper quantity of formaldehyde" to embalm the American proposal "so that there won't be a diplomatic process with the Palestinians." Israel would maintain external control of access to the Gaza Strip. By removing 9,000 Gaza settlers, along with 600 residents of four tiny, isolated communities in the northern West

Bank, Sharon intended to protect the settlement project as a whole. The evacuation was set for August 2005.

The Israeli religious right took Sharon's decision as a betrayal worse than Rabin's. Sharon had been the Orthodox settlement movement's closest secular ally for thirty years. Worse, the disengagement plan hinted at the failure of what believers had convinced themselves were divine promises. The answer was denial. The country's former chief rabbi, Mordechai Eliahu, announced that the edict would be canceled by the eve of Passover in April 2005, vanishing like the last crumbs of leavened bread that religious Jews burn before the holiday. The holiday passed; Sharon failed to repent. In June, speaking before thousands of opponents of "uprooting and expulsion" who gathered at the Gaza settlement of Neveh Dekalim, Eliahu again played prophet, proclaiming, "It will not be." Many Gaza settlers were farmers who wanted to show their faith by planting crops weeks before the pullout date. Since banks would not give them the usual loans that farmers need, activists organized the Believe and Plant Fund, which collected money from thousands of supporters—as loans, to be repaid when the crops were harvested.

Along with demonstrations of faith came political protest. Since the council of Gaza settlements had an orange flag, its supporters distributed orange ribbons. At one stage, the "orange camp" tried to convince Israelis to wear orange six-pointed stars, modeled on the yellow stars that Jews were forced to wear during the Holocaust. The tactic equated leaving Gaza to being shipped to the east in boxcars, and the Israeli government to Nazis.

In late July 2005, 40,000 demonstrators gathered at Kfar

Maimon, an Orthodox moshav near the Gaza Strip, planning to march to the Gaza settlements to prevent the evacuation. Thousands of police and soldiers stood in their way. On the third day of the standoff, the column of protesters tried to march out of the moshav, with Wallerstein, Hanan Porat, and other graying settlement leaders at the front of the line and angry teens behind them. When the police commander refused to let them through, the middle-aged leaders decided against a hand-to-hand fight and ended the march.

For that moment, loyalty to the state that they regarded as sacred won out over sacred soil. The leaders deserve credit for avoiding bloodshed. Nonetheless, the choice they made was, in religious terms, between one form of idolatry and another. They treated the state, "at most something of instrumental political value," as being "something of ultimate value," to borrow terms from philosopher Avishai Margalit. Their younger opponents treated a piece of the Land of Israel—also something of instrumental value for achieving political and religious goals—as possessing ultimate value.

Afterward—after fire did not descend from heaven to prevent withdrawal; after hundreds of young infiltrators managed to enter the Gaza Strip, barricade themselves in the synagogue of the Kfar Darom settlement, and fight police with stakes and steel rods before being dragged away; after the last disbelieving settlers were evacuated—after all this, the name "Kfar Maimon" became a code word. Among some veteran settlement leaders, it stood for doubt, self-castigation, failure. Among the young, the most radical rabbis, the unbending ideologues, it meant "sell-out."

The withdrawal itself showed that secular Jews and the

state had abdicated their roles in redemption. Radical settlers sometimes distinguished between Jews and Israelis. Jews were settlers, or Orthodox supporters of settlement. Israelis were secular and lived on the coast, the land of the Philistines in biblical times. In the outpost of Amonah, on a mountaintop overlooking Ofrah, a young settler explained to me that the biblical Abraham's departure from the city of Ur taught that Jews should not live in cities. The subtext was that Ur stood for the West and for Western-facing urban Israel, all of which was opposed to true Jewishness. The name Kfar Maimon signified one more stage of alienation: the settler leadership, extreme as it might appear to "Israelis," was altogether too moderate and law-abiding for "Jews."

As formaldehyde, the disengagement failed. With Israel still occupying the West Bank and controlling access to Gaza, international pressure for peace talks resumed quickly. At the same time, the pullout left many members of the religious settler movement, especially young ones, doubting the legitimacy of the state and bitterly determined to mount a stronger, more violent opposition the next time around.

Yet none of this interrupted the momentum of state support for settlement, or for institutions that barbarized Judaism. One example: the Od Yosef Hai yeshivah is located in the settlement of Yitzhar near Nablus. The yeshivah's violent history goes back at least as far as a 1989 rampage in the Palestinian village of Kifl Harith, during which sixteen-year-old Ibthisam Bozaya was shot dead. Four yeshivah students received brief sentences for that incident after a plea bargain. The head of the yeshivah, Rabbi Yitzhak Ginsburg, responded to their arrest by declaring, "Any trial based on the assumption that Jews and goyim are equal is a total travesty of justice." Ginsburg went on to write a eulogy for the mass murderer of Hebron, Baruch Goldstein.

In late 2009, two other rabbis from the yeshivah, Yitzhak Shapira and Yosef Elitzur, published a book called *The Law of the King*, which purports to elucidate Jewish religious law on when it is forbidden or permitted for a Jew to kill a gentile. The book's repeated themes are that a Jew's life is worth more than a gentile's, and that for a Jew to kill a gentile is a lesser sin than killing another Jew. In a war between Jews and non-Jews, Shapira and Elitzur assert, Jews are permitted to kill anyone from the opposing side who poses a threat, even in the most indirect way. Enemy civilians who show emotional support for their troops are therefore legitimate targets, they say. There is no moral problem, the authors state, with the death of civilians who live near an army base or weapons plant, even if they are children, because they stand in the way of a legitimate target. Indeed, they claim, there is even a basis in religious law to argue that children may be intentionally targeted, "if it is clear that they will grow up to harm us."

Without mentioning the Israel Defense Forces, the book is a broadside against the army's rules on avoiding harm to enemy civilians. Such restrictions, in the authors' views, are un-Jewish. Rather than a leaflet rationalizing theft, this is a full volume justifying war crimes, desecrating the faith in whose name it is supposedly written.

In the years 2006 to 2010, the government allocated an average of nearly $400,000 annually to Od Yosef Hai. For the years in that period for which the yeshivah's full balance sheet is available, nearly half of its budget came from the state. The funding continued in 2010, after *The Law of the King* appeared and caused national controversy. The allocations, I should stress, do not mean that the officials who signed off on the allocations endorsed the ideas of Ginsburg, Shapira, and Elitzur. But even after *The Law of the King* made headlines, it seems no one in the Education or Welfare ministries considered whether the government should be funding an institution that taught racism.

Finally, sometime during 2010, both ministries suspended their funding, apparently in response to legal letters from the Israel Religious Action Center, the civil rights arm of Reform Judaism in Israel. The letters argued that for a government body to fund an institution engaged in racist incitement violated the "fundamental values of the State of Israel" and was "unreasonable in the extreme." The letters, implicitly but unmistakably, were first drafts for a legal challenge before the High Court of Justice. The ministries were concerned enough to stop issuing checks. But apparently fearing either political backlash or a countersuit, they avoided admitting that they would halt funding a yeshivah over such a questionable offense. Instead, the spokespeople of both ministries insisted that the delay was due to reviews of Od Yosef Hai's accounting and possible overreporting of the number of its students. By implication, once the bookkeeping problem was resolved, the flow of money could resume.

On a hilltop eight miles to the northeast of Yitzhar as the crow flies is the outpost known as Skali's Farm: a handful of sheds, mobile homes, and tiny wooden houses, with a watch-tower and stone synagogue. The founders, Yitzhak and Cheftziba Skali, live in one of the wooden houses with their four small children.

Cheftziba Skali belongs to the generation that knows not life inside Israel. She grew up in Kiryat Arba, next to Hebron. Her childhood friends, she says, are today "at the front line," scattered among outposts and other relatively new settlements. She moved to the hilltop in 1999, when she was twenty, after marrying Yitzhak. She is a thin woman with a narrow face, her hair covered almost entirely by a knit cap, her sleeves reaching her wrists in strict religious modesty. The second generation of settlers is more liberated than the first, she tells me—less concerned with "the pressure of the law," more prepared to live in open country, beyond the fences of established settlements. Just six other families live at the outpost.

She speaks of the veteran settlement leadership as if it has passed its expiration date. The Council of Settlements "doesn't run things here," she says. The outpost does not belong to Amana, though the organization did provide a generator. She does not mention that the Housing Ministry has invested nearly $200,000 in improving the site, even though two-thirds of the land is privately owned by Palestinians and the settlement has never been approved by the government. The settlers at the outpost have no contact with local Arabs, Skali says: "We're not murderers and thieves."

As it happens, a married couple from Skali's Farm were suspects in the 2004 armed robbery of two donkeys from elderly shepherd Aziz Hneini of Beit Dajan, a Palestinian village just to the south. According to the Israeli human rights group Yesh Din, which monitors law enforcement in the West Bank, Hneini testified that the man was also one of several settlers who later beat him so seriously that he was hospitalized for five days. After cursory investigations, the police closed both files on the grounds of "unknown perpetrator," Yesh Din reported. Yesh Din cited the incidents as examples of "the continuous failure" of the Israeli police to enforce the law against settlers suspected of attacking Palestinians.

In themselves, the unsolved crimes are merely an epilogue to the 1982 Karp Report. They are evidence not of change, but of business as usual. So is settling on land owned by Palestinians; so is building without going through the planning process that Israel itself legally requires.

For years, says Ronny Goldschmidt, an architect formerly in charge of town planning for the Mateh Binyamin Regional Council, the de facto process for establishing a settlement had nothing to do with the de jure planning procedure. Rather, it began with a "trigger"—a Palestinian terror attack or a diplomatic initiative "that threatened the settlement enterprise." In response, "settlement leaders" identified land—state land, in Goldschmidt's account—where it was possible to build, then got together mobile homes and people willing to be the founders, and moved them into the site. The term "settlement leaders" in this account apparently includes the top officials of the regional councils, along with other activists. After the first settlers moved in, the pressure started on government officials to approve the plans and permits that should have been completed ahead of time. Long before the plans were signed, the state had built what the community needed, from sewage lines to classrooms. The principle was always to seize political openings, move in, get generous state help, and legalize the settlements later—if ever.

And yet the outposts do represent two important shifts. The government's role in building the outposts shows a new level of audacity, of politicians proclaiming one policy while doing the opposite, of state agencies violating the law. Among settlers, the outposts are the flagship project of the militant second generation.

Attorney Talia Sasson's government-commissioned report, submitted in 2005, provides the most detailed description of state involvement in the outposts. Sasson, a highly respected lawyer, had only recently left the State Attorney's Office, where she headed the Department for Special Assignments. Sharon's decision to have her investigate the outposts was one of the most surprising acts of his career. The prime minister was apparently under pressure from the United States to explain why the outposts were proliferating, and to identify which ones had been established after he took office in March 2001. Under the 2003 Roadmap, Israel was required to remove those outposts.

Sasson is the first to stress that her report is incomplete. Many of the gaps can be filled in from other investigations and from the testimony of outpost settlers themselves. The picture that emerges is that between the mid-1990s and 2005, about one hundred outposts were established in the occupied territories. Though the government's declared policy was not to allow new settlements, state agencies provided funds and other forms of support, using an arsenal of subterfuges. The Housing Ministry funneled money through the settlers' regional councils. The councils then hired contractors to build infrastructure and public buildings at outposts, hiding the ministry's role. The Housing and Interior ministries and the state-funded Settlement Division of the World Zionist Organization fictitiously designated outposts as expansions of older, existing settlements so that they could allocate money without government approval of new settlements. The chain of collusion reaches at least as high as ministry directors-general, the top level of the civil service. Avigdor Lieberman, director-general of the Prime Minister's Office under Prime Minister Netanyahu in 1997, issued instructions to the Settlement Division to assist new settlements as if they were neighborhoods of older ones. Another top-level official, Ron Shechner, who served as defense minister Shaul Mofaz's assistant for settlement affairs beginning in 2003, instructed the Settlement Division to budget outposts as if they were approved settlements, and permitted settlers to move mobile homes to illegal outposts.

But responsibility for the rogue operation reaches beyond civil servants. Sasson names at least one cabinet minister who was apparently directly involved. Numerous reports point to Ariel Sharon's role in the outpost effort, as a cabinet member and as prime minister.

For all practical purposes, Israeli governments have not approved any new settlements since before the Oslo Accord. When Rabin was elected prime minister in 1992, he froze settlement planning, though some building continued in existing settlements. In July 1996, after Netanyahu took power, his government lifted the planning freeze. The same cabinet decision, though, stated that no new settlement could be established unless the full cabinet voted to make an exception. That hasn't happened. The 1996 decision also imposed strict rules on new projects in existing settlements. At five points in the planning process, the defense minister—the second most prominent elected official in the country—personally had to sign off on a project. Any construction without those signatures would be illegal *by Israel's own standards*, leaving international law aside.

In an era of peace talks, the government understood that it was "internationally impossible" to approve new settlements. Yet the "ideology of expanding the state" through settlement continued to guide government officials, says Sasson.

Setting a precise date for the birth of the outposts is impossible, as there is often conflicting testimony on when half a dozen people started living in mobile homes pulled onto a hilltop. Though outposts were set up during Rabin's term to protest government restrictions on building, the real wave began under Netanyahu. The idea was to establish a presence, usually on high ground, to mark more land as being under Jewish control, to make it more difficult for Israel to give up land in peace negotiations.

In October 1998, in an effort to keep the Oslo process from collapsing, U.S. president Bill Clinton corralled Netanyahu and Palestinian Authority president Yasser Arafat into a summit meeting at the Wye River Plantation in Maryland. As foreign minister, Ariel Sharon also took part. The summit ended with an agreement that included Israel promising to hand over another 13 percent of the West Bank's land to Palestinian Authority rule. Returning home, Sharon used an appearance on Israel Radio to urge settlers to take action.

"Everyone there should move, should run, should grab more hills, expand the territory," he said. "Everything that's grabbed, will be in our hands. Everything we don't grab will be in their hands."

Sharon's words summed up the inner contradiction of the Oslo process: it promised to turn the relations between Israel and the Palestinians into an interaction between two states. But because it postponed marking the border, it encouraged Israeli leaders to act as if they had returned to the 1940s and could determine how the land would be partitioned by establishing settlements. It exacerbated their tendency to think and act like members of a national movement locked in conflict with another ethnic group over the entire land between the Jordan and the Mediterranean, and to treat laws as minor obstacles to be dodged for the cause.

Amonah was one of the early outposts, established no later than 1997 on privately owned Palestinian land, without cabinet approval or building permits. The first settlers were young men who had grown up at Ofrah. By February 2003, twenty-five young families were living in mobile homes spread in a line along the mountaintop. The Mateh Binyamin Regional Council had built the road from Ofrah up the mountain, one resident said. She wasn't sure who had paid for the high-power floodlights placed around the outpost's perimeter for security. For more security, IDF soldiers were stationed at Amonah. At the south end of the ridge, a flat shelf had been cut in the rock to create lots for a row of houses. In 2005, Sasson reported that the Housing Ministry had spent about half a million dollars on infrastructure at Amonah. By then, the concrete frames of nine houses stood at the end of the ridge.

In 2001—the year that Sharon became prime minister and that immigrant political leader Natan Sharansky became housing minister—the Housing Ministry "created a special budgetary clause, named 'general development misc.,' and used it for financing unauthorized outposts," Sasson wrote. Responding to her questions, the ministry admitted to spending $16 million between 2000 and 2004 on outposts— but "it seems the actual sum considerably exceeds" that amount, she wrote. The ministry also bought hundreds of mobile homes for the regional councils of settlements in the West Bank, deliberately evading regulations on government purchases. Many of the dwellings were placed in outposts, including five at Amonah. The decision, the ministry told Sasson, was made by housing minister Effie Eitam, Sharansky's successor and leader of the National Religious Party.

The lawbreaking extended further. The IDF failed to prevent the violation of property rights. The Civil Administration illegally approved hooking up outposts to the Israeli national electric grid. The Settlement Division illegally allocated state land to outposts. This is a very partial list from the 343-page report that Sasson marked as "interim" because she had exceeded the time she'd been given and was far from completing the picture of the state's attack on its own laws.

As a cabinet minister identified by name in Sasson's report, Eitam is unusual. Working with limited time, within a limited mandate, against bureaucrats' stonewalling, Sasson was rarely able to follow the paper trail all the way to cabinet members—though a top Housing Ministry official asserted that one housing minister after another "assisted in setting up unauthorized outposts." If defense ministers including Barak and Mofaz were unaware of state involvement in building outposts in occupied territory, they worked hard at ignorance.

Sasson did not find evidence directly implicating Ariel Sharon. Neither did she declare his innocence. The prime minister's support for the outposts was a matter of record since his exhortation after the Wye summit. In 2003, the daily *Ha'aretz* reported that Sharon was meeting weekly with Amana chief Ze'ev Hever to pore over maps. Adi Mintz, a former director-general of the Council of Settlements, has described continual discussions between settlers and Sharon when he was prime minister on where to build outposts.

The locations of the outposts fit Sharon's approach perfectly—seizing high points and filling in tendrils of settlements that separated Palestinian communities. For instance, a string of outposts links the extremist settlement of Itamar, near Nablus, with settlements to the east, on the slopes overlooking the Jordan River. The post-Oslo innovation was that a tiny number of people could stake a claim to large areas. By 2009, the outposts were home to only about 4,000 people.

Even that small number has its social divisions. At Amonah, as a settler told me in 2003, the community consisted of two camps, half-seriously called the Grays and the Greens. The Grays hoped that the outpost would grow up to look like Ofrah, with suburban houses along quiet streets. She identified with the Grays, whom she described as accepting Western culture; she herself was a university graduate. The Greens were upset that paving the road to Amonah had scarred the mountain, hoped for houses that would fade into the folds of the hills, and wanted nothing to do with Western culture.

Schematically, she was describing two faces of the outpost population as a whole. Those whom Amonah calls the Greens are the better-known side. From the start, some outposts attracted teenage boys who could not cope with the long hours of religious study expected in yeshivah high schools. The outposts gave the "hilltop youth" a chance to rebel by claiming to be better settlers than their parents. To proclaim their piety and to show they had no interest in being part of mainstream Israeli society, many adopted the ultra-Orthodox custom of growing long sidelocks. They took Ginsburg and similar rabbis as their religious guides. Politically, wrote one researcher, "most of the hilltop youth identified with the . . . path of [Meir] Kahane," the American-born rabbi whose doctrine included expelling all Arabs from the Land of Israel. Some of those teens grew up, married young, and began families in the outposts. The hilltop youth were the flower children of the radical right, seekers of spiritual enlightenment and of other people's land. Their lifestyle became a model for other hilltop settlers. Allegations of violence by outpost settlers against neighboring Palestinians are rife. Convictions, not surprisingly, are rare.

By fostering the outposts, government officials from Sharon down fomented the growth of a theologically driven far-right movement that saw the state and even the established settlement leadership as illegitimate.

In July 2005, the Peace Now movement petitioned the High Court of Justice, demanding that the Civil Administration raze the nine as-yet-unoccupied houses at Amonah. In a pretense of law enforcement, the Civil Administration had issued demolition orders the year before and then done nothing about them. Responding to the suit, the state promised to remove the houses once the withdrawal from Gaza was out of the way.

After repeated delays, the operation was set for February 1, 2006. The Council of Settlements called on supporters to come to Amonah to block the demolition. Several thousand Orthodox young people answered the summons, barricading themselves in and on top of the houses and forming chains around them, determined to erase the shame of Kfar Maimon and the Gaza pullout. Over 7,000 police and troops were deployed against them. In a last-minute legal gambit, the Council of Settlements asked the High Court of Justice to allow it to move the houses to state-owned land. When the court rejected the request, the police advanced. Cursed as "Nazis," bombarded with stones, lightbulbs, and concrete blocks, they pushed their way to the houses with baton blows, some rendered from horseback. Over 200 police and demonstrators were injured by the time the houses were razed.

The following week, the council held a protest in downtown Jerusalem. The crowd, again, was very young, and was not enamored with the organizers. The middle-aged leaders' latest offense was offering the court a compromise before the demolition. The council is known in Hebrew as "Yesha"—an acronym for Judea, Samaria, and Gaza that just happens to mean "salvation." Teenage girls held up hand-scrawled signs saying, "Get rid of the Pesha Council," using the Hebrew word for "crime." The same pun appeared as a headline on flyers that boys handed out to passersby. Teens wore T-shirts that read, "Disengage from the State—Connect to Torah."

After Amonah, a stalemate set in. The Sasson Report, two scathing reports by the state comptroller, a warning from attorney general Meni Mazuz that anyone "allocating government funds for illegal purposes" could be prosecuted, and a wave of legal actions by human rights groups all combined to cool officialdom's ardor for outposts. Since 2005, establishment of new outposts has virtually stopped, and development of existing ones has slowed. At Gilad's Farm, Itai Zar says he has been unable to get approval for a power line "because of Ariel Sharon, because of the Sasson Report." Cheftziba Skali testifies that development "is choked now." At Migron, the largest of the outposts, with over 300 residents, the community's security coordinator says that development stopped in 2005. Sporadically, the Israeli police and army have razed new buildings at outposts.

Yet the Sasson Report did not push the government to remove existing outposts. Nor has it fulfilled its obligation under the Roadmap to evacuate the outposts established after March 2001. Four years after she submitted her report, Sasson spoke with frustration about her recommendation for a criminal investigation of implicated officials. "An investigation was opened, but what came of it? We've never heard," she said.

In response to petitions to the High Court of Justice by human rights and peace activists against illegal building in outposts and older settlements, the government has manufactured reasons not to act. Migron is the classic case. Itay Harel established the outpost in 1999, on high ground overlooking the bypass highway from Jerusalem to the settlements north of Ramallah. The settlers could be called Grays—young professionals and university students, not hippies of the right. Harel, who grew up in Ofrah, is a social worker. Still the moving spirit at Migron, he is the son of Yisrael Harel, founder of the Council of Settlements. The land is owned by Palestinians, though settlers claim that a company owned by the Mateh Binyamin Regional Council bought part of it in 2004. The claim rests on a document that the man purportedly signed and had notarized in California over forty years after he died.

In 2006 the Palestinian landowners, assisted by Peace Now, asked the High Court of Justice to order the IDF to remove Migron. The state's reply confirmed that the outpost was on stolen land. The defense minister hoped to reach an agreement with the settlers so that they would leave peacefully, the state's lawyer wrote. Over two years later, in February 2009, the Defense Ministry reported to the court that it had reached an agreement with the Council of Settlements for Migron's residents to leave voluntarily once a neighborhood was built for them in the nearby settlement of Adam. One flaw with that plan: the settlers had no intention of carrying out the agreement reached by the council, and were not shy in saying so. Even among the Grays, the old channels of collaboration between the government and the settlers have no hold. Nonetheless, the Defense Minister continued to report to the court on the sham agreement, and Migron stayed in place.

The Supreme Court justices, however, are painfully aware that the proceedings in settlement cases have become a mockery. In September 2009, the court held a hearing on a petition by Yesh Din to implement demolition orders against five apartment buildings on stolen Palestinian land next to the Beit El settlement. The state's representative in court gave what had become the standard answer: the government has to set priorities in enforcing demolition orders in the West Bank, and the court should not interfere. Chief Justice Dorit Beinisch answered angrily. "We have heard many cases like this, and out of all the declarations about law-enforcement priorities, in not one case have we seen the orders implemented," she said. "There are no priorities, because nothing is ever done."

Beinisch's remark was a verdict on a country with a split personality, a government divided against itself. Civil society was flourishing. The justice system was ready to review executive action. The government condemned violations of the law in the West Bank. Yet it had often collaborated in those offenses, and it would not end its collusion with the settlers. So Supreme Court hearings became theater, disconnected from the real world. With the executive branch uninterested in enforcing the law or carrying out court decisions, the judicial branch was powerless to protect human rights.

Yet more is at work here than politicians' pro-settlement policy or concern that the ruling coalition will come undone if they evacuate settlers. There's another fear. "They'll only say it softly, as a secret: it might break the back of the army," says Talia Sasson. "A large portion of the combat troops today are settlement supporters. They're the backbone of the army." The fear has a basis. The army has changed, and that change is another part of the story of a country taking itself apart.

V.

DISORDERLY CONDUCT

Captain Moshe Botavia said no. It was August 18, 2005. Botavia was a company commander in the IDF combat engineering corps, deployed in the northern West Bank—in official Hebrew, Samaria. That day, police and troops were evicting settlers who had refused to leave Neveh Dekalim and Kfar Darom, two of the largest Israeli communities in the Katif Bloc of settlements in the Gaza Strip. A deluge of news from Gaza poured from Israeli television and radio.

Botavia, a career officer, had grown up in Kiryat Arba. His unit was assigned to help remove two of the four small

West Bank settlements included in the disengagement plan, along with a nearby army base. The settlements, Ganim and Kadim, on the outskirts of the Palestinian city of Jenin, were already ghost towns. Many residents who'd come in search of a quiet, comfortable community rather than out of ideological zeal had left for safety during the fury of the Second Intifada. The rest accepted the government's instructions and moved out by August 2005. Whatever the engineering unit had to remove or raze was inanimate. Nonetheless, Botavia could not bear taking part. He was expecting a last-minute miracle to save him from the task. When no miracle came, he told his commander that he could not lead his soldiers in the field.

Botavia was arrested, held for three weeks, then released from prison and from active duty pending trial. Under questioning, he said he'd refused orders under "family pressure." In prison, he wrote a letter expressing remorse. Just before his trial, though, when the settler newspaper *Besheva* interviewed him and other soldiers and police who'd refused to take part in the withdrawal, he proudly recounted that he had told his commanding officer, "I can't get up in the morning . . . say prayers about the wholeness of the Land and its sanctity, and in the afternoon do something that's the complete opposite." Sacrificing his military career wasn't easy, he said, "but everyone has limits, values that he has grown up on."

The court-martial sentenced Botavia to time served and let him keep his rank for reserve duty. The judges, explaining their leniency, cited his "extreme and tragic dilemma . . . between his devotion to his ideology . . . and his zealotry for the IDF." On appeal by the prosecution, a higher military court demoted him to second lieutenant, thereby allowing him to remain an officer. The appeals court's ruling is a tangle of conflicting allegiances. Citing a 2002 Supreme Court ruling on left-wing reservists who refused to serve in the occupied territories, it describes insubordination on political grounds as being "particularly severe." A few sentences later, under "arguments for leniency," it portrays Botavia as coming from an exemplary family whose "love and devotion for the homeland" had led them to settle in Kiryat Arba. Refusing orders for ultranationalist reasons was good and bad at the same time.

In the last legal round, Supreme Court chief justice Dorit Beinisch refused to hear a further appeal by the prosecution to cashier Botavia. Beinisch's brief ruling says the military appeals court erred in treating Botavia's ideology as cause for lighter punishment. But appeals by the prosecution, even if allowed under Israeli law, should be kept to a minimum, she said. Beinisch concluded with the hope that there would be no need for the Supreme Court to lay down clearer guidelines on commanders refusing orders for political reasons—in other words, that such insubordination would not recur.

Beinisch's hope is a fragile one. Over the last two decades, the Israeli military has drawn ever more of its combat soldiers and commanders from two overlapping groups—the religious right and the settlers. Many come to the army directly from religious institutions whose rabbis teach that both military service and the Whole Land of Israel are pillars of Judaism. The army welcomes them as replacements for the sons of the secular elite who once reliably filled frontline roles. Yet in doing so, it is acquiescing in the influence of a politicized clergy over troops and the dominance of the religious right in key units. The authority of the elected government over the military is steadily being eroded.

Formally, Israel has had a universal draft from its birth. Culturally, as historian Motti Golani argues, the combination of the Holocaust and the victory of 1948 reversed traditional Jewish reticence toward the use of force. The Holocaust justified military power as morally necessary; the 1948 war showed that Jewish arms were effective. Henceforth, one's Israeliness "was measured by one's ability to fight," Golani says.

In reality, the army was never the great equalizer of Israeli myth. Only small groups of Israeli Arabs, minorities within the minority, were subject to conscription. The deferral for a few hundred yeshivah students developed into a near-blanket exemption for the ultra-Orthodox. Orthodox women could opt out of serving. Returning to the army annually for reserve duty was a ritual that lasted into one's fifties—for Jewish men. Civilian class differences carried over into the military. Secular Jews of European ancestry—especially from kibbutz and moshav—were more likely to serve in the most respected combat units and the officer corps, with Middle Eastern Jews assigned support jobs. Combat roles, until recently, were entirely closed to women. If service and sacrifice equaled citizenship, some Israelis were more authentic citizens than others. They also had an avenue of advancement closed to others. In Israel's early years, the economy was largely controlled by politicians, and the founding politicians resolutely held on to power. An army career was a way for a man from the right background to climb toward leadership and prominence.

By the 1980s, a shift began to emerge. Israel's 1982 invasion of Lebanon ignited unprecedented public debate about the government's use of the military. A purportedly limited operation turned into a march to Beirut aimed at remaking the Lebanese regime—a war of choice, not of self-defense. The crisis of confidence was greatest among the Israelis who had identified most strongly with the military—secular Jews from kibbutzim and the urban middle class. For the first time, reservists rejected call-up orders, on grounds that could be described either as political opposition to the war or as conscientious objection to immoral use of force. According to the pro-refusal movement Yesh Gvul ("There's a Limit"), 168 "refuseniks" were jailed for refusing to serve in Lebanon, with the army quietly refraining from prosecuting many others. An unknown number chose "gray refusal," using pretexts such as illness to avoid duty in Lebanon. The eruption of the First Intifada at the end of 1987 sparked a new wave of refusal to serve in the West Bank and Gaza Strip, as did the Second Intifada in 2000. Some of those who chose jail over serving in occupied territory were combat officers, poster boys for the old ethic of self-sacrifice.

In the meantime, the Israel economy was expanding, privatizing, and becoming more technological. There were new paths to success. None of this meant that secular teenage boys stopped aspiring to be pilots or commandos. But as a source of combat soldiers and officers, the old elite was no longer as reliable—either in the numbers it could supply or in unquestioning identification with the mission.

Among the Orthodox, the shift took the opposite direction. From independence on, religious Zionists valued military service while fearing the army's corrosive influence on young souls. Religious soldiers, especially in combat units, faced intense social pressure—not to pray thrice daily, not to keep the Sabbath, not to stand out by being Orthodox. A desk job or a place in the army rabbinate allowed one to slide more easily through the military.

In the 1960s, the IDF agreed to a new program for Orthodox men—the *hesder* ("arrangement") yeshivah. It was modeled on the Nahal Brigade, whose soldiers alternated between active duty and paramilitary farming outposts. Instead of farming, *hesder* soldiers studied Talmud. During active duty, they served in separate companies, or later in separate platoons. While in yeshivah, they were available for immediate call-up. *Hesder* soldiers had to commit themselves to extra time in the combined program, but spent fewer months than other conscripts in active service.

Only one *hesder* yeshivah existed before the Six-Day War. Afterward, amid the messianic fervor that merged nationalism and religious revival, more Orthodox men wanted to combine combat service and religious study. The government had a practical reason to lend support: like a Nahal outpost, a *hesder* yeshivah was a way to create a presence in newly conquered territory. One was established next to Kfar Etzion, another in Kiryat Arba. When the Likud took power, more were set up in the new religious settlements. They attracted rabbis who saw the Whole Land of Israel as a signpost to redemption. The army got a new source of combat soldiers with high morale. The yeshivot produced young teachers for

Orthodox schools who were imbued with the theology of nationalism, and new recruits for ideological settlements. The "arrangement" was one more way in which the state, in a fit of absence of mind, promoted religious radicalism.

Yet the *hesder* program had limited appeal. A young man signing up for it after finishing an Orthodox high school had to commit himself to several more years of studying Talmud. The most prestigious units would not take *hesder* soldiers, who would serve too little time to justify the investment of long training. Socially, *hesder* soldiers faced criticism that by spending less time on active duty, they were shirking their fair share of the military burden.

A new kind of religious institution, the premilitary academy, offered an alternative. The first academy, Bnei David, opened in 1987, in the settlement of Eli on the road from Ramallah to Nablus. One of the founding rabbis, Eli Sadan, was a disciple of Tzvi Yehudah Kook; the other was an ex-colonel, Yigal Levinstein, who found right-wing religion after leaving the uniform. They aimed at preparing Orthodox recruits to serve in the same units as secular soldiers and resist pressure to give up religion. They also sought to inspire their graduates to volunteer for elite units and rise through the ranks. To enroll, students received a one-year draft deferment. The academy put less stress than a yeshivah would on Talmud study. Instead, it served up large portions of "faith studies," inspirational lessons intended to fortify students' belief and imbue in them the sacred significance of being a Jewish soldier. The program included physical conditioning to help graduates qualify for top combat units.

According to Levinstein, a conversation with General

Amram Mitzna, then the head of the Central Command, prodded him to start the academy. Secular, born on a kibbutz, Mitzna was the classic Israeli general. (Years later, he would make a failed run for prime minister as Labor's dovish alternative to Ariel Sharon.) The general said Israeli society was in a "crisis of values" that could infect the army. The Orthodox community had "deep values" and "should make a higher-quality contribution to the army." In Levinstein's depiction, Mitzna was passing the torch of military service from secular society to the Orthodox.

Bnei David flourished and invited emulation. More academies were established. They eventually included nonreligious ones, each with its own formula for preparing motivated soldiers. By 2000, there were fifteen pre-army academies; by 2010, there were thirty-six. The Orthodox ones attracted more students, especially in proportion to the community on which they drew, since only 14 percent of male conscripts each year were graduates of religious schools. In parallel, more *hesder* yeshivot sprang up.

In inventing the premilitary academy, the religious community could for once lay claim to setting a trend. In making military service into a supreme ideal, though, it was coming late, just as it had in embracing the ideal of settlement after 1967—seizing a value just as it became passé in the wider society.

Predictably, the secular value was reborn as a religious one—or rediscovered as having being religious all along. A eulogy for Sergeant Yossi Weinstock, a *hesder* soldier who fell in South Lebanon in 1995, illustrates ideas that permeated the religious Zionist community. It was true, said a friend of

Weinstock's father, that Orthodox Jews had long been under-represented in defending the Jewish people, though that was changing. But, he said, what had actually motivated the secular founders of kibbutzim, along with secular "paratroopers, infantrymen . . . and pilots," was the Jewish religious passion that they inherited from their forefathers. "That passion is weakening as each generation grows more distant from the [religious] wellsprings." That was why secularists were willing to give up parts of the Land of Israel for "momentary convenience," the eulogist said. In contrast, there were men such as Sergeant Weinstock. They showed they "loved the Lord with all their soul" by "giving up their lives for the [Jewish] people and the Land." These were common themes. Earnest students in religious high schools learned to describe fallen soldiers as "martyrs" worthy of emulation.

In these descriptions, I should stress, a soldier was not precisely defending the country. He was defending the Jewish people and the Land of Israel—the ethnic group and its territory—whose welfare was described as being virtually identical.

The effect of the academies can be seen statistically. Nearly all IDF officers begin service as privates. Those who excel are offered the chance to volunteer for officers' training, which means signing up for longer service. In 1990, according to an internal IDF study, just 2.5 percent of the men finishing the infantry officers' course were graduates of Orthodox high schools. In 2007, close to a third of new infantry officers were Orthodox. Penetrating higher ranks took longer. But by 2010, six of the eight top commanders in the Golani Brigade, one of the IDF's main infantry units, were

Orthodox, with ranks of colonel or lieutenant colonel. At least five of the six were alumni of yeshivot known for messianic nationalism or of the Bnei David academy.

The exact overlap between Orthodox officers and settler officers is unknown. But the proportion of the latter has also climbed. The army magazine *Bamahaneh* reported in 2010 that 12.5 percent of all company commanders in the ground forces were residents of settlements, though settlers made up just 5 percent of Israel's Jewish population.

Similar changes have taken place at lower ranks. Alumni of the pre-army academies are represented in high numbers in combat units, especially selective ones such as commandos. The proportion of religious Zionists among infantrymen killed during the Second Intifada has been estimated as twice their proportion among Israeli Jewish men.

The IDF has not simply become a place where more soldiers are Orthodox. In the frontline forces and officer class, the role of men whose identity has been shaped in the crucibles of theological nationalism keeps growing. When the change began, the IDF could believe it had found a solution to a problem. It was getting soldiers who had no questions about service in occupied territory. They would not refuse orders on political grounds.

That was before the army got orders that put military service and sanctifying the land at odds with each other.

Here I must pause. The classic Israeli ideal of military service deserves to be judged with care, with respectful ambivalence. So does selective refusal of military orders.

The importance of subordinating one's life to a collective

need is rooted deeply in Israeli history. In American English, the word *pioneer* conjures up a lone frontiersman. The equivalent Hebrew word calls up an early kibbutznik, the very shirt on his back belonging to the commune. A friend of mine, born on a kibbutz in the 1940s, was given her name not by her parents but by a vote of the kibbutz general meeting. This symbolized an era: selflessness, living for the cause, could give an individual a great deal of meaning, but not a large amount of room to be an individual.

After independence, the army became the last great communal effort in which everyone could, supposedly, take part. At the peak of conscription, Israel drafted over 90 percent of eligible men, more than any other country in the twentieth century—so Reuven Gal, formerly the army's chief psychologist, told me in the mid-1990s. This figure was misleading: Arabs were not eligible. The egalitarianism of universal service was a facade for an ethnic definition of being Israeli.

By the 1990s, in any case, universal service was also fading among Jews. The army still needed as many smart, fit combat soldiers as it could get, but a rising population provided too many conscripts for other jobs. With politicians afraid to question the universal draft, the IDF was left to improvise. It exempted more eighteen-year-olds on physical or psychological grounds, and quickly discharged soldiers who didn't fit in. For the right, especially the religious right, the drop in military service is one more proof that Israel is losing touch with its core values. In fact, the right's insistence that settlement and military service must remain Israel's core values is anachronistic.

Politically, universal conscription and extended reserve

duty have had contradictory effects. They can encourage citizens to think as soldiers, to identify with generals and expect military answers to every threat. Yet reservists have repeatedly brought the message to civilian society that something has gone wrong in the separate universe of the army. Reserve soldiers revealed in 1972 that the IDF had expelled thousands of Beduin from their homes in the occupied Sinai on General Ariel Sharon's orders. Reservists protesting the failure to prepare for war in 1973 drove prime minister Golda Meir and defense minister Moshe Dayan from office. Protests against the 1982 invasion of Lebanon grew as reservists returned from the front. For worse and better, a citizen's army cannot be completely separated from politics.

The strongest statement that a citizen-soldier can make is selective refusal to serve. Israeli law requires a soldier to disobey an order that "bears a black flag of illegality." This principle was established after a 1956 massacre in which troops followed orders to shoot anyone returning to an Arab village after curfew. The problem—so a tall, gaunt reservist named Itai Haviv told me in 2002—is when no single order is patently immoral but the sum total is. Haviv, a captain in the artillery corps, had refused to continue serving in occupied territory. "You're told to demolish a house, because it commands a road and [Palestinian gunmen] have been shooting from it. Militarily, it's the absolutely right thing to do . . . but when it goes on for thirty-five years [since 1967], it turns into a black flag."

Most of the Israeli left has rejected that stance as bringing politics inside the military and violating the rules of democracy. In the Supreme Court's 2002 ruling against reservists who refused to serve in the occupied territories, Chief Justice Aharon Barak wrote, "The line dividing opposition to one policy or another and conscientious objection to carrying out that policy is thin, sometimes thinner than thin." Were selective objection allowed, the army could break into a collection of separate units, each unwilling to carry out certain tasks, he said. "Today, the objection is to serving in Judea and Samaria. Tomorrow the objection will be to removing outposts," Barak wrote.

Barak was right—particularly about how difficult it is to distinguish between political and conscientious objection. In an imperfect world, countries need to defend themselves, and an army needs discipline. Decisions on using the military must be made by the elected government, not by each soldier.

Yet unless we are to surrender utterly to relativism, there are moments when a person must obey a moral principle rather than a democratically enacted law or policy. When my son was small, I read him a children's book about a devout Christian family in antebellum America that helped slaves on the Underground Railroad to freedom. The father in the book explained to his son that he believed in obeying the law, but he could not obey the law requiring him to return fugitive slaves.

And if we are not to surrender utterly to relativism, it matters which principle a soldier cites as obligating him to refuse the order of an elected government. Barak was right that selective conscientious objection corrodes both discipline and democracy. Nonetheless, there is a distinction between someone rejecting an order because he believes it would require him to violate the sanctity of human life and dignity, and someone refusing an order because it means giving up land that he regards as the sacred territory of his nation, as "ours." It seems to me that the difference between the two is not a thin line; it is the gulf between ethical concern and national egotism.

In the run-up to the withdrawal from the Gaza Strip, the threat of religious soldiers selectively refusing orders became a national issue. In October 2004, former chief rabbi Avraham Shapira, then the religious right's leading authority on Jewish law, spoke out. He declared that religious soldiers must tell their commanders that they would no more follow an order to evacuate settlers than they would obey an order to eat pork. "Heaven doesn't want this," Shapira asserted, supremely confident that he knew the divine will, in an interview published in the settler newspaper *Besheva*. The following day, sixty rabbis—including several prominent heads of *hesder* yeshivot—issued a proclamation stating, "It is forbidden for any Jew to participate or assist in dismantling settlements."

When the evacuation ended, IDF chief of staff Dan Halutz announced that sixty-three soldiers had been tried for refusing orders, among them twenty-four *hesder* soldiers. The numbers were small enough that it seemed that military discipline and religious Zionists' loyalty to the shared "people's army" had more or less held up. Sanguine analyses noted that many well-known rabbis had publicly disagreed with the calls for insubordination. Besides, it was argued, Orthodox soldiers' requests for direction from their rabbis more often dealt with how to maintain a religious lifestyle in the army, or with combat ethics, than with the disengagement.

In fact, the official number of soldiers disciplined is a poor indication of what happened in the summer of 2005. It would be a mistake to use those figures to dismiss the risk of future insubordination or mutiny. What took place before and during the disengagement is better understood as a portent of a growing danger.

It's true that the religious Zionist community is anything but monolithic. Not all Orthodox soldiers are on the right, and not all those on the right phrase their politics in theological terms. It's also true that some religious Zionist rabbis joined in calling on Orthodox soldiers to "recognize the authority of government and Knesset decisions" and obey orders. They provided a reminder—sadly necessary at that moment—that Orthodox Judaism and democracy are compatible. Some of the best known among them, however, were already tainted in the eyes of the religious right as being far too moderate—men like Rabbi Yehudah Amital, dean of the Har Etzion *hesder* yeshivah, who had accepted the idea of relinquishing land for peace since the 1980s.

Some rabbis from what became known as the *mamlakhti*, or statist, side of the theological right also called on soldiers to obey orders—lest the sacred state be endangered and the chance of overcoming its secular character be lost. Rabbi Avihai Ronski, head of the *hesder* yeshivah in Itamar, articulated that view. Ronski, a colonel in the reserves, worried that political insubordination would weaken the army. But besides that, he argued, "Our sons and students have been enlisting . . . in the best units and slowly climbing the ladder of ranks and responsibilities." ("Our" in that sentence referred to Orthodox settlers and their ideological supporters.) Deciding which orders to follow, he said, would "mortally injure" progress toward the change they sought—having "the leaders of the country and commanders of the army rooted in the tent of Torah." The investment in creating an entirely different Israel would be squandered.

A more influential dissent came from Shlomo Aviner, rabbi of the settlement of Beit El and, like Shapira, a highly regarded authority on religious law among settlers and their supporters. Aviner sought to adhere unbendingly to the sanctity of both the state and the Land. A soldier could not contribute to the destruction of the army by explicitly rejecting an order, he wrote. But the army's job was to guard the Land, not give it up. So it was unthinkable that a soldier would be capable of carrying out such orders. As the disengagement approached, Aviner wrote an article stating that anyone "expelling" Jews—alluding to the expulsion of Jews from various lands during their history—would be violating nine of the Ten Commandments. Aviner admitted that he had not yet found a way in which evicting settlers constituted adultery.

With his contradictory counsel, Aviner was actually recommending "gray refusal," finding a quiet way to avoid evacuation duty. He was not alone.

The association of pre-army academies, religious and secular, also issued a statement against refusing orders. It made sense that the deans of the Orthodox academies assented. They had an ideological investment in the military and the advancement of religious soldiers, which would be undermined by mass insubordination. The head of the association was Rabbi Moshe Hagar, dean of the Beit Yatir academy and a colonel in the reserves. Hagar later described to me a conversation with his students before the disengagement. He instructed them not to refuse orders. He also told them, "I wouldn't be able to carry out this mission." Rabbi Yitzhak Nissim, head of the Elisha academy, gave a similar message: "I told my students, 'It's impossible to call for refusal, because that's a mutiny. But no one should carry out such orders.'" The result was that "of my students who were there, none refused, and none carried out orders." In short, whatever the statement for the public said, they agreed with Aviner.

By the nature of gray refusal, there are no exact numbers on its extent. *Besheva* challenged the army statistics on how many soldiers were disciplined, reporting that it had found over a hundred soldiers who were court-martialed. There were many more cases, the settler paper asserted, in which commanders "preferred . . . to end the affair quietly" when soldiers refused orders or avoided carrying them out. *Besheva* clearly sought to magnify the problem. But the army had an institutional interest in showing that all was well in the "people's army," and did not acknowledge the full extent of resistance in the ranks.

Moreover, the government and the army's top command carefully chose who would carry out the disengagement in order to avoid more dissent. Ten thousand police were assigned to the operation—over a third of the total police force in Israel. The police could be expected to see the job professionally, not politically. The IDF contingent numbered 15,000. Units such as Golani and Givati brigades, with large numbers of Orthodox soldiers, were not assigned to evict civilians. To help the police remove the settlers, the army created temporary units consisting of career officers from support units and command posts and of cadets training to be pilots or naval commanders. Like the police, they were committed to a career in uniform and could be counted on to identify with their orders, as Israeli political sociologist Yagil Levy wrote afterward. The IDF also deployed a large number of women soldiers—who were less likely to belong to the religious right, since many Orthodox women opt out of army service.

All these measures were needed to remove 9,000 settlers, almost all from the Gaza Strip, to which the army could control access with relative ease. The national police force stretched its resources to the maximum, and had to be backed up by troops drawn from select, limited sources. Despite the IDF's effort to avoid using units in which refusal was likely, political resistance in the ranks did take place—some visible, more beneath the surface.

A pullback from the West Bank would be a challenge on a different scale. At the unrealistic minimum often discussed in Israel—a peace agreement based on withdrawing to the security fence—over 65,000 settlers would have to return to sovereign Israel. Any more realistic map of Israel's borders with a Palestinian state would mean a larger evacuation. The ideological settlement movement would face not a setback but the final shattering of its vision of redemption through the Whole Land of Israel. Its core communities—Kiryat Arba, Ofrah, Elon Moreh, Yitzhar, and many others—would face evacuation. The army would have to confront a young generation of settlers determined not to repeat the "shame" of Gaza. It would have to operate in a larger area, where its opponents could move much more easily.

Yet since 2005, the army's dependence on soldiers coming out of the Orthodox academies, *hesder*, and other yeshivot aligned with the theological right has increased. Graduates of those institutions have taken a larger place in the officer corps, advanced to higher ranks, and gained command of larger units. By playing down what happened in 2005, the state and the army have allowed the threat to democratic control of the military to grow.

Following the disengagement, Chief of Staff Halutz did take one step aimed at convincing pro-settlement soldiers to obey orders. In 2006 he appointed Rabbi Avihai Ronski of Itamar to be the IDF's new chief rabbi. Ronski had been a battlefield commander. He was a founder of Itamar, one of the extremist settlements ringing Nablus. He'd studied at Ateret Kohanim, Rabbi Aviner's yeshivah, provocatively located in the Muslim Quarter of Jerusalem's Old City. Probably unknown to Halutz, he had also been a founder of the far-right Od Yosef Hai yeshivah. As listed in the Sasson Report, Ronski's yeshivah was located in an illegal outpost outside Itamar, a detail Halutz either didn't know or didn't see as significant. Yet Ronski had supported obeying orders to evacuate settlements. He believed in doing what your commander said because he was a Spartan in the original sense: he was a militarist. Halutz's aim was transparent. Soldiers from the extreme right could see Ronski as a spiritual authority—and hopefully be swayed by his views on army discipline.

Ronski, however, had views on other matters. In the past, he'd written to an army medic that keeping the Sabbath took priority over saving a gentile's life. The medic could treat a wounded Arab captive on the seventh day only because it was necessary to avoid causing hatred toward Jews, and to interrogate the captive, he wrote. Challenged by a leading figure in the moderate Orthodox camp, Ronski added that in any clash between religious law and the army's ethical code, religious law took precedence. In context, the implication was that religious law required less concern with non-Jews' lives—a view I can only describe as defiling Judaism.

In office, Ronski quickly showed that he was not satisfied with catering to soldiers' religious needs. He wanted the rabbinate to take over the task of educating the army, stiffening its will by teaching his militant version of Judaism. During Operation Cast Lead, the IDF invasion of Gaza in January 2009, the rabbinate issued a booklet for soldiers, containing selections from the teachings of Shlomo Aviner. In it, Aviner wrote that the Torah forbade "giving up a millimeter" of the Land of Israel to gentiles, even by allowing Palestinian autonomy. Jews were commanded to go to war to conquer the Land, Aviner said. He explicitly rejected the idea that saving Jewish lives might be more important than territory.

Gentile life, however, was cheaper in Aviner's view. Erasing any distinction between enemy combatants and civilians, he advised fighting from a distance, with air and artillery attacks, to avoid losses to Israeli troops, stressing, "Cruelty is a bad quality but it all depends when." Providing another reason for going to war, Aviner said that any time the Jewish nation is humiliated, "it is a desecration of God's name," which a Jew should give up his life to prevent.

The pocket-sized booklet showed how the religious right had taken the principles of the secular Zionist far right from the 1930s and '40s—militarism, national pride, the Whole Land of Israel—and dressed them in theology. Aviner's comments on cruelty directly contradicted the IDF's official ethical code, which instructs a soldier to "do everything in his power to prevent harm" to noncombatants. His explanation of "desecration of God's name" turned the classic Jewish concept on its head. In the traditional view, a Jew sanctifies God's name—that is, shows the purity of his religion and God—when he is strictly honest or avoids anger. When he is crude, dishonest, or cruel, he "desecrates the Name." In Aviner's description, God's reputation in the world rested on whether Jews looked strong or weak.

When a dovish Orthodox soldier, upset that this had become "the official voice of Judaism in the IDF," turned the booklet over to Breaking the Silence, an organization that publishes testimony from soldiers about serving in the occupied territories, Ronski claimed he hadn't seen it. Meanwhile, Ronski's rabbinate published an article in its weekly Sabbath leaflet for soldiers, describing the war in Gaza as shattering the "materialist culture and blurring of values" that afflicted Israeli society. In a lecture later that year at a *hesder* yeshivah, Ronski said that a soldier who "keeps his sword from blood" and "shows mercy toward his enemy when he should not" is "cursed." He added that in Operation Cast Lead, "one of the great innovations" was that the army had finally behaved as if it were really at war.

The IDF's behavior in Gaza, especially toward Palestinian civilians, was intensely controversial—not just abroad, but within Israel. Half a year after the war, Breaking the Silence published firsthand testimony from twenty-six soldiers who fought in Gaza. They reported that in order to prevent casualties, the army had used firepower with less restraint than in the past, ignoring the price to enemy civilians. If that description is correct, Ronski's "educational" activity was certainly not the main cause of the change. Yet he did provide legitimation, from within the military, for ideas that sharply diverged from the IDF's official position—and that some officers had already heard from their rabbis in pre-army academies and yeshivot. On the religious right, I should note, the standard criticism of the army's behavior in Gaza is that it was altogether too worried about Palestinian civilians.

Ronski served as the IDF's chief rabbi for four years—a year longer than his original appointment. His successor was the dean of a pre-army academy. Attempting to co-opt rightist rabbis to shore up discipline, the military was instead legitimizing the religious right's antihumanistic attitudes and its claim to be the voice of Judaism, and eroding the IDF's own standards of behavior. In its own way, it was proving the truth of the traditional Jewish warning, "One sin leads to another."

Next to Gilad's Farm, on a country road through the West Bank mountains, I picked up two young men hitchhiking. Both wore the long, thick sidelocks and extra-large skullcaps popular among outpost settlers. It was an autumn day in 2009. Four years had passed since the disengagement, less than a year since Operation Cast Lead. One of my passengers lived at the outpost and studied at the yeshivah in Yitzhar, the nearby far-right settlement. He was nineteen, recently married, and said he intended to avoid service in an army that "hurts Jews" and "goes against the laws of the Torah." His latter accusation reflected his view of how the IDF had fought in Gaza the previous winter. The army "doesn't want to kill Arabs because it wants to look nice in the world," he said, and had thereby endangered its own soldiers. The other hitchhiker, son of a prominent Kiryat Arba disciple of Meir Kahane, lived at Gilad's Farm. He'd ignored his first draft order, been arrested, was inducted into the army, and discharged after three months as "unsuitable," an outcome that suited him, for reasons like those of his friend.

Earlier, in the living room of his mobile home at the outpost, Itai Zar told me that "the IDF has betrayed its people," meaning the Jewish people. He was a reservist in the Givati Brigade. After the disengagement, when he got a call-up order for training, he told his commander, "I'm not coming to an army that evacuates Jews." He was court-martialed before a higher-ranking officer who "didn't want to screw me" and wrote "that I'd been sick or something" rather than disciplining him. Zar noted that the former spokesman of the Gaza settlements, Eren Sternberg, had gone to school with him. After the disengagement, Sternberg began urging Orthodox youth not to serve in the IDF. Sternberg called it "the army of destruction"—using the traditional Hebrew word for the destruction of the ancient Temple in Jerusalem by the Romans.

When Zar was called up to fight in Lebanon in 2006 and in Gaza in 2009, he decided to report for duty, because "I love my buddies" in the unit. In Gaza, though, he was "outraged" by the army's concern for Palestinian noncombatants. In the command post, "there was an officer from our army who was in touch with the Arabs in Gaza and *was concerned about their rights*," he recounted, with utter disbelief. "He'd say not to shell a neighborhood because they were evacuating the wounded. And we'd let the ambulances evacuate them—tell me, is this a war? They're crazy! . . . In the last five, ten years, the army has turned into a welfare office for Palestinians."

After the Gaza pullout, doubts about idolizing the IDF were to be expected. Indeed, draft dodging by potential soldiers who object to the IDF's ethical code and its commitment to carrying out democratic decisions is a gain for the army, not a loss.

But the hilltops around Nablus are home to a radical fringe, and outright refusal to serve hasn't been the standard answer to the "uprooting" of Gaza's settlers. The more common reaction is to believe more fervently than ever that army service is holy, and at the same time that orders to dismantle settlements are sinful—in the best case, a sin that must be accepted.

One portrait of this dissonance comes in a study of religious Zionist boys approaching draft age. The researcher, Bar-Ilan University graduate student Keren Levi, gave a series of questionnaires on religious identity and values to students at yeshivah high schools, the most respected and most ideological of the Orthodox Zionist schools. The test group was split between teens living inside Israel and settlers.

The results showed that both groups saw the army as sacred. The difference was that young settlers were even more eager than the Orthodox teens from inside the Green Line to serve in combat units and become officers. At the same time, nearly a third of settler teens would disobey orders if national policy conflicted with religious demands. More than half were unsure what they'd do.

The difference between the two groups, in short, was that the young settlers identified even more with the IDF—as long as it fulfilled what they saw as its God-given purpose. If the government chose to use the army differently, if the IDF wasn't guarding the Whole Land of Israel for the Jews, they didn't know why they should follow orders.

Nonetheless, the gap between the two groups wasn't huge. Religious Zionist teens on both sides of the Green Line had been taught to see the state as sacred because it gave Jews power, conquered the Land of Israel, and thereby advanced redemption. The idea of a state as a human institution, subject to the consent of the people it governed, meant to serve their needs within moral and legal limits, had a small place, if any, in their curriculum.

Levi's study dealt with boys who had not yet enrolled in pre-army academies or *hesder* yeshivot, as many would do. There they would meet rabbis whose debate on insubordination has only grown sharper since the Gaza pullout. Yet even among educators belonging to the religious right's *mamlakhti* camp, which stresses continued identification with the state, the message can be ambivalent.

One of the best-known *mamlakhti* rabbis is Eli Sadan, dean of Bnei David, the oldest and largest of the pre-army academies. Bnei David takes pride in the fact that over half its alumni have become officers. In the spring of 2006, Sadan published an impassioned plea to Orthodox youth not to "disengage from the state." He denounced calls to use violence to prevent any future "expulsion" from settlements, warning that civil war would destroy Israel. He affirmed the feeling that the government had betrayed settlers, but insisted that the process of redemption continued, and promised that the Gaza settlements would yet be rebuilt.

Sadan defended the honor of religious soldiers who carried out orders in the summer of 2005—on the grounds that their units had not been asked to participate directly in evacuating settlers. By speaking of the past, Sadan did not say what religious soldiers should do in the future if they received order to remove settlers. A stand on that question is strikingly absent from his "Letter to Youth."

Other teachers left no room for uncertainty. In his column on Jewish law in *Besheva*, Rabbi Eliezer Melamed repeatedly called on soldiers not to take part in evacuating settlements. Melamed headed the *hesder* yeshivah in Har Brakhah, another of the settlements ringing Nablus. In 2003 he explained that historically, rabbis had only allowed cooperation with secular Zionists in order to fulfill the commandment of settling the Land of Israel. That partnership did not extend to "actions uprooting this great commandment," such as removing outposts. In a column a year after the disengagement, Melamed affirmed that Orthodox men should serve in the IDF "to fulfill the tremendous obligation of defending the [Jewish] people and the Land"—but only if they could stand up to commanders and refuse to take part in "expulsion." Mass refusal would not cause the army to collapse, he asserted, since, "If many refuse, such an order will not be given."

Melamed's views gained attention outside the settler media after two incidents involving *hesder* soldiers in the Kfir

Brigade, a unit created to maintain order in the West Bank. In October 2009, at the Western Wall in Jerusalem, the brigade's Shimshon Battalion held its swearing-in ceremony for recruits finishing basic training. Several times in the weeks before, the brigade had removed settlers who had returned to the site of Homesh, one of the four West Bank settlements dismantled in the disengagement. During the ceremony, two soldiers held up a sign reading "Shimshon Won't Evacuate Homesh." For the unprecedented political protest at an army ceremony, the two men got twenty days in the stockade.

The following month, six soldiers in the Nahshon Battalion, also part of Kfir, unfurled a sign at their base that said, "Nahshon Also Doesn't Expel." That day, the police had demolished two buildings at an illegal outpost, with Nahshon troops deployed nearby to secure the operation. The Nahshon protesters also received brief sentences in the stockade. The two ringleaders were demoted and removed from combat duty.

In the chain of events after the protests, defense minister Ehud Barak ejected Melamed's yeshivah from the *hesder* program. According to Rabbi Haim Druckman—the head of another *hesder* yeshivah, a central figure in the Orthodox settlement movement since its start, and a former Knesset member—Melamed's writings on refusing orders contributed to the decision, along with his refusal to sign a letter against demonstrations within the army.

On the surface, Barak had finally taken a stand. Yet the sanction against Melamed obscures the government's acquiescence as clerics of the theological right continue to politicize the military. No action was taken against other *hesder* rabbis who called for insubordination. Interviewed on the Melamed affair, Druckman himself said that if a soldier was ordered to do "something forbidden—like evacuating settlements in order to turn them over to the enemy, as with the Katif Bloc—absolutely, *he shouldn't do it*."

In reality, a vicious cycle is at work. Israel continues to hold the West Bank and expand settlements. Policing occupied territory and protecting settlers are military burdens, increasing the need for combat soldiers and officers who have no qualms about the occupation. To meet that need, the army depends ever more on recruits from the religious right. Yet this increases the danger of fragmenting the military when an Israeli government finally does decide to pull out of the West Bank.

For politicians, this is one more reason to postpone difficult, necessary decisions. The longer they wait, though, the greater the risks. The problem is not one of individual conscientious objectors. There are already whole units that the IDF fears using. As men who believe in the inviolable sanctity of the Whole Land of Israel climb the ladder of command, possibilities loom that are worse than refusal: outright mutiny, even decisions by senior officers to deploy their units to prevent withdrawal.

Watching this process is like watching a film of the *Altalena* affair run in reverse: the smoke returns to the ship, the shell to the cannon. The opposition unloads its arms at the Kfar Vitkin beach. Israel evolves backward, returning to the moment of a fragile state facing an armed faction dedicated to fantasies of power and expansion.

VI.

THE LABOR OF THE RIGHTEOUS IS DONE BY OTHERS

I'm standing in the Kerem Avraham neighborhood of Jerusalem. Across the street is the stone-faced building where Israeli novelist Amos Oz grew up in a small ground-floor
apartment.

Back then, in the 1940s, Kerem Avraham was home to
"petty clerks, small retailers, bank tellers or cinema ticketsell-
ers, schoolteachers or dispensers of private lessons," as Oz

writes in his memoir, *A Tale of Love and Darkness*. They observed the last vestiges of Judaism—lighting Sabbath candles on Friday night, attending services on Yom Kippur—and avidly argued the fine points of secular Zionist ideology.

While I stand on the street, a flock of teenage girls walks by, all with the pale complexions of indoor lives. The girls are dressed in blue blouses buttoned to the neck, pleated skirts, and high socks, so that no skin besides their faces and hands shows. Small boys—the age that Amos Oz was when his secular father chose an Orthodox Zionist school for his son because religion was dying anyway—are coming home, carrying book bags heavy with religious texts. A family passes, the husband in a circular, flat-topped black hat, his wife pushing a stroller, three more children younger than age six walking with them. The mother wears a wig, the common *haredi* method for married women to hide their hair in modesty. But that custom is now a matter of strident controversy, as one of the posters glued to a wall along the street testifies. It tells married women who wear wigs rather than scarves that they will be judged before the heavenly court for their licentious practice, which makes it look as if their own naked hair is exposed. On a cross street, I pass a *kollel*—a yeshivah where married men receive small salaries to study full-time. The building of the school that Oz attended still stands, but now it is an ultra-Orthodox boys' school.

Kerem Avraham today is one neighborhood in the *haredi* belt of northern Jerusalem, a land of wall posters denouncing television, Internet, and rival religious factions; of lifelong Torah study for men and countless pregnancies for women; of schools that provide scant preparation for earning a living and no preparation at all for participating in a democratic society. The neighborhood began changing in the 1950s, after the rebellious young Oz moved to a kibbutz, which he left many years later. Socialism, not religion, is now a historical memory in Israel.

Less than a mile from Amos Oz's childhood home is an apartment development put up several years ago for better-off *haredim*. The nine-story buildings surround a courtyard with a playground that is crowded with children in late afternoon. Underneath the buildings is a three-level parking garage, with small storerooms along the sides of the half-lit concrete caverns. The storerooms, a standard feature of Israeli apartments, belong to the residents who live above. But some of the small rooms have doorbells, names on the doors, water meters, and high windows looking into the dark garage. I hear the voices of a couple inside one, and an infant crying. Outside another is a metal rack on which laundry is drying. They've been rented out as apartments to young *haredi* families who can afford nothing else.

The picture aboveground is of a thriving community. Beneath the surface one can see one part of the price being paid by the *haredim* themselves, and by Israel as a whole, for the peculiar development of ultra-Orthodoxy in Israel.

Today's *haredim* are known for marrying early and having many children, even as men spend much or all of their adult lives studying Talmud rather than working. When the state was established, *haredi* society "was entirely different," says sociologist Menachem Friedman. "It was a normal working society," similar to the rest of the Jewish population. The fertility rate was about the same. So was the average marriage age, though sometimes *haredi* men married relatively late if they wanted to extend their religious studies. To get married, a man had to leave yeshivah and find work.

Rather than being a diorama of traditional Jewish life in Eastern Europe before the Holocaust, as many Israelis and visitors believe, Israel's present-day version of ultra-Orthodoxy is a creation of the Jewish state. Policies with unexpected effects fostered this new form of Judaism, at once cloistered and militant. So did successful measures by *haredi* leaders to revive a community that was shrunk by modernity and then devastated by the Holocaust.

While a similar revival has taken place in *haredi* communities in the United States and other Western countries since World War II, their dependence on government funding is necessarily more limited. In turn, the extent to which adult men can engage in full-time religious study rather than working is also more restricted. The difference was illustrated in 2000, when the daily *Ha'aretz* published a series of pictures by photographer Alex Levac, showing ultra-Orthodox men at work in New York. For the Israeli audience, photos of gainfully employed *haredi* men—a private detective, a truck driver, a technician, a contractor, a welder—were news on the level of man bites elephant.

In economic terms, the *haredi* revival in Israel has been disastrous. Israel's ultra-Orthodox community is ever more dependent on the state and, through it, on other people's labor. Exploiting political patronage, ultra-Orthodox clerics have largely taken over the state's religious bureaucracy, imposing extreme interpretations of Jewish law on other Jews.

By exempting the ultra-Orthodox from basic general educational requirements, the democratic state fosters a burgeoning sector of society that neither understands nor values democracy. And to protect their own growing settlements, *haredi* parties are now essential partners in the pro-settlement coalitions of the right.

This is a story full of ironies. Here's the first: the critical, unnoticed catalyst of the transformation of ultra-Orthodox society in Israel was the 1949 law instituting free, compulsory education.

In the Palestine of the British Mandate, ultra-Orthodox schools were few, scattered, and short on cash. After independence, most joined a school system under the roof of the Agudat Yisrael party. In a Knesset Education Committee meeting in June 1949, a government official mentioned in passing that there used to be three party-linked school systems; now there were four, including the ultra-Orthodox one. The addition sounds like something inconsequential that happened almost accidentally. In Education Committee discussions of the compulsory education law, the fact that it would provide budgets to the ultra-Orthodox schools hardly merited mention. After all, ultra-Orthodoxy was vanishing.

Instead, the opposite happened. State funding made it possible to open new ultra-Orthodox schools and pay steady salaries. Young *haredi* women could finish teacher training at Agudat Yisrael's Beit Ya'akov seminaries by age eighteen or nineteen and get elementary school jobs. Meanwhile, some of the Jews pouring into Israel from the Islamic world chose *haredi* schools for their children, creating more teaching positions. The absolute numbers were small, but the growth was astounding: in the state's first four years, Agudat Yisrael's elementary schools went from 7,000 to 24,000 pupils.

In 1953, when the Knesset voted to eliminate party-run schools and create a national educational system, it left loopholes in the State Education Law that allowed the Agudat Yisrael schools to keep operating and receive funding from the state. As the Israeli economy modernized, high school education became the norm. The state helped fund ultra-Orthodox secondary schools along with others, but the high schools for *haredi* boys were yeshivot devoted entirely to religious studies. Most were boarding schools, where students lived in a day-and-night realm of Torah study, with rabbis substituting for parents. From there, young men—not only the few brilliant scholars, as in European Europe before the Holocaust, but the mass—proceeded to advanced yeshivot.

The leading *haredi* religious figure in Israel, Rabbi Avraham Yeshayahu Karlitz, used these changes to promote a transformation in the name of extreme conservatism: *haredi* men and women would marry young. Men would keep studying Torah in *kollel* after marriage, supported by their teacher-wives. Their working parents would help out. Funds to help give *kollel* students small salaries came from Jews in Western countries. The donors were not necessarily Orthodox. Rather, they regarded their contributions as honoring the destroyed Jewish world of Eastern Europe, seen through the distorting lens of loss and nostalgia. Young *haredim* rejected Israeli society, but accepted its demand for idealistic sacrifice. Through a lifestyle based on Torah study, they were outdoing their bourgeois parents and their secular rivals.

Ironically, the army's centrality in Israeli life promoted the change, precisely because *haredi* society wanted young men to avoid what it saw as the IDF's secular press gang. Remaining a full-time Torah student allowed a man to stay out of uniform. Gradually, the state allowed the quota of deferments for yeshivah students to rise, from 400 in 1948, to over 1,200 in 1953, to 4,700 in 1968.

The deferment helped lock young men into the *kollel* lifestyle. So did the education gap: though ultra-Orthodox men spent years engaged in study, their schooling did nothing to prepare them for jobs in a modern economy. From their teens on, their curriculum was devoid of mathematics, sciences, foreign languages, and other general studies.

Thus "the society of scholars"—as Friedman named it—took shape. Older *haredi* men, who'd come of age before the change, worked for a living. A growing number of young men stayed in *kollel* after marriage, often for a decade or more. The father was a carpenter, shopkeeper, or tailor; the son was a full-time student. In a universe of arranged marriages, Torah scholars were the most sought-after grooms. The marriage age for both men and women dropped: between 1952 and 1981, the average marriage age of ultra-Orthodox men in Israel fell from 27.5 to 21.5. At the beginning of that period, the typical *haredi* groom was slightly older than the average for Israeli Jewish society. By 1981, he was four years younger than the Israeli Jewish average. Among *haredi* women, marriage before age twenty became the standard. Ultra-Orthodox couples started having children early and continued to have them often. This, too, made leaving *haredi* society much more difficult, for women as well as men.

In the 1940s, it had seemed to ultra-Orthodox educators and parents that nothing could stop young people from giving up religion. Now the exodus stopped. The gulf between the society of scholars and the secular world grew too wide to cross. Rabbis noted with satisfaction that children were outdoing their parents at piety. "The sons are more complete than the fathers," wrote Moshe Scheinfeld, a *haredi* ideologue, in an Agudat Yisrael journal in 1954. "This is the source of the 'tragedies' taking place in many homes, where the parents feel that their sons studying in yeshivot and their daughters training in . . . seminaries are rebelling against them in their hearts and demand of them, openly or secretly, greater completeness, greater sacrifice, greater consistency in [religious] practice and belief."

Those words portray a revolution in a society that believed itself to be changeless. Young *haredi* Israelis saw the previous generation as insufficiently religious—a paradox in a community for which *religion* and *tradition* were synonyms. To show they made no compromise with modernity, young *haredim* sought to follow Jewish law in the strictest fashion. They thereby created a new interpretation of Jewish practice, a strict constructionism that was itself a product of modernity. This is the shared attribute of fundamentalist movements—they are creations of the present claiming to be old-time religion.

Karlitz—known as the Hazon Ish, after his major religious work—supplied the theology of strictness. In his view, precision in following religious law (*halakhah*) encouraged a person to overcome natural urges and purify his soul. The strain, the difficulty, was the fire that removed the dross. He also provided the specifics of strictness. An example: Jewish religious law includes various measures—the minimum amount of wine required for the blessing at the beginning of the Sabbath meal, the minimum amount of matzah to eat at the Passover Seder. The measurements are ancient and imprecise—the volume of an egg, or of an olive. These are requirements written in a book. In real life, for generations, Jewish children learned how to live their religion from parents, without using cup measures or rulers. The Hazon Ish famously interpreted the minimums in maximal terms, as if eggs and olives had been larger when the ancient rabbis set the measurements and had since degenerated, just as the wisdom of the ancients had faded through the ages. One had to make sure the wine cup was large enough to meet the new requirement masquerading as the traditional one; one had to make sure to eat a sufficient amount of matzah. "It follows," as historian Lawrence Kaplan wrote, describing the sage's impact, "that though the Hazon Ish was opposed to formal *halakhic* innovation, he was one of the great *halakhic* innovators of [his] century."

The Hazon Ish applied the same innovative rejection of innovation to belief and science. The scientific knowledge of ancient and medieval Jewish sages, he asserted, exceeded that of modern scientists, and had to be accepted without question. Ironically, some of those medieval sages had regarded learning the science of their own time as a religious value. Most prominently, the towering twelfth-century rabbi, philosopher, and physician Moses Maimonides taught that knowledge of the natural world was the path to love of God. As a twentieth-century reactionary, the Hazon Ish honored the shell of medieval Jewish scholarship while negating its core. The very practical implication was that secular studies were at best a waste of time better spent studying Torah, and at worst an intellectual siren song, luring the young to the rocks where their faith would be shipwrecked.

By accepting his rulings and doctrines, yeshivah and *kollel* students were also accepting written tradition over lived tradition. Partly that was a consequence of the Holocaust and the mass migration of Jews to Israel and the West: the lived tradition was dead, buried in the rubble of Eastern Europe. Young *haredim* tried to re-create a lost world; tragically, they could only create a caricature.

But more than the historical fracture was at work. Ultra-Orthodox men growing up in Israel spent many years in yeshivot—cloistered and hierarchical religious communities. They learned from books. They learned to value obedience to rabbis in every aspect of life, to believe that effacing one's own judgment and accepting that of the great scholars of the age was the foundation of piety. The rabbis themselves, unlike their forefathers, did not need to interpret Jewish law pragmatically, moderately, for the sake of a working laity. The working laity was shrinking. Every strict ruling could eventually become the norm, in turn calling for an even stricter interpretation, so that the process of radicalization rolled onward. Rather than seek to sanctify life in the modern world, ultra-Orthodoxy tried to build a sacred preserve, apart from modern society. All of this, paradoxically, took place thanks to the funding of a rapidly modernizing and gloriously cacophonic democracy.

I should stress: in a democracy, a religious subculture has

the right to make this choice. Their coreligionists have the right to argue—as I do—that this siege mentality misinterprets the tenets of the faith. But it is not a democracy's legitimate business to intervene and finance a religious subculture. Nor should a democracy promote a kind of education that makes its graduates into economic captives of the sectarian community.

The ultra-Orthodox economy was a pyramid scheme, though no one planned it that way. At the start, any young *haredi* woman who finished secondary education could get a job teaching in elementary school. The supply of teachers was small, and the Agudat Yisrael school system was new and growing. But girls from those *haredi* elementary schools went on to seminaries, graduated, and were too numerous for the available teaching positions. They were investors who had entered the scheme too late. To support a husband who was a yeshivah student, some needed to find other jobs in business or public service, sometimes outside the *haredi* community.

Men were in a more difficult bind. They expected to find "Torah positions" when they left *kollel*. Originally, they could teach in the expanding *haredi* yeshivot, or in religious Zionists' new high school yeshivot, which had many hours of Talmud along with general studies. Or they could get work in the state's religious bureaucracy—for instance, supervising kosher food production for factories and restaurants that wanted the Chief Rabbinate's seal of approval. This was another paradox: their livelihoods depended on the outside society from which they wanted to segregate themselves.

But Orthodox Zionist yeshivot began producing their

own teachers of religious studies. The rabbinate bureaucracy did not expand as quickly as the *haredi* population. Exiting *kollel* to a Torah job gradually became harder. In the first generation, moreover, working *haredi* parents could help buy apartments for two or three or four children who were *kollel* students or students' wives. In the next generation, the parents had five or seven or nine children, and some of the fathers were lifetime students. The pillars that supported the society of scholars were weak.

Yet it kept expanding, with the 1977 election supplying the means. For the first time, Menachem Begin's Likud won a narrow plurality in parliament. As usual in Israel, Begin needed to build an alliance with other parties to govern. And for the first time since 1953, Agudat Yisrael joined the ruling coalition.

The *haredi* party had ideological reasons for working with Begin. Unlike the Zionist left, the right did not present itself as a replacement for religion. Begin, though not Orthodox, peppered his sentences with references to God. He was comfortable in a synagogue. Like American donors to yeshivot, he felt an aching nostalgia for Eastern European Jewish life.

But the real push was practical: Begin needed coalition partners and was willing to pay them well. The ultra-Orthodox community had needs and desires it could meet only through the government. The 1977 coalition agreement was a long list of promises to Agudat Yisrael on religious and budgetary issues. The 1981 agreement, after the Likud barely defeated Labor again, promised even more. The commitments included more funding for Agudat Yisrael's schools, without touching the *haredi* system's autonomy to teach—or not teach—what it wanted, and "special consideration" for other ultra-Orthodox educational institutions.

Not all the promises could be kept, but many were. The Begin government made it harder for businesses to get permits to operate on Saturday, the legal day of rest. Amending a relatively liberal law on abortion, the Knesset eliminated "difficult family or social circumstances" as grounds for the procedure. The government dissolved the committee that interviewed women to make sure they were Orthodox before granting them draft exemptions. Instead, a draft-age woman could simply sign a declaration that she was religious. The change encouraged non-Orthodox women to make false declarations, but Agudat Yisrael believed that having any female soldiers encouraged licentiousness and violated the honor of Jewish women.

These measures were meant to shape the wider society to fit *haredi* views. Other political gains protected the *haredi* subculture. The army removed the ceiling on draft deferments for yeshivah students. As a result, the number of men with deferments climbed from 8,000 in 1977 to 16,000 in 1985, eventually passing the 40,000 mark in 2005. The chairmanship of the Knesset Finance Committee became an Agudat Yisrael prerogative, in Begin's time and after, giving the small party an outsize influence over the national budget. Funding for ultra-Orthodox schools, yeshivot, and adult religion classes rose.

The state's social welfare system provided another funding pipeline. Rather than giving tax deductions to parents, Israel pays a stipend for each child, so that families below the tax threshold also get help. In the 1980s, the government reset the stipends so that small families got little or nothing. After the third child, the amounts climbed steeply. The ultra-Orthodox community, with low incomes and a high birthrate, got a cash infusion.

These policies allowed men to stay out of the workforce and entrenched ultra-Orthodox dependence on the state. Arye Naor, who served as cabinet secretary in the Begin governments, says the changes were a product of immediate coalition needs and "mutual dependency" between the Likud and the ultra-Orthodox. No one thought about the long-term impact.

In 1984 a new ultra-Orthodox party entered parliament. Known as Shas, it was led by Jews from Middle Eastern countries educated in Israeli ultra-Orthodox yeshivot. In *haredi* society, Middle Eastern Jews were kept from leadership; Shas represented a rebellion. But Shas also extended its appeal beyond *haredim* to the larger Middle Eastern Jewish underclass in Israel, portraying the community's social problems as symptoms of loss of religious tradition. Combining faith with ethnic and economic resentment, Shas attracted former Likud and National Religious Party voters. As in Agudat Yisrael, the Knesset members followed orders from a rabbinic leadership. Adept at getting out the vote, Shas was a democratic success story on the outside and a theocracy internally. *Haredi* representation in the 120-member Knesset climbed from four seats in 1981 to eleven in 1988 to a high-water mark of twenty-two in 1999. Shas set up its own school system, generously financed and barely supervised by the state.

The longer a pyramid scheme continues, the more people are caught up in it, the more difficult maintaining it becomes, and the more catastrophic is its looming collapse. For the ultra-Orthodox themselves and for Israel as a whole, this is the economic meaning of the society of scholars.

A statistical picture of *haredi* society must be drawn in rough strokes, since defining who is ultra-Orthodox bedevils statisticians. But that rough picture is striking in its implications. In 2004, by one measure, there were 470,000 *haredim* in Israel, about 7 percent of the country's population, or 9 percent of Israeli Jews. The proportion was growing, because fertility was more than three times higher among the ultra-Orthodox than among other Israeli Jews. In 2002 the average *haredi* woman was likely to have more than seven children in her lifetime.

In 2003, during the Second Intifada, Prime Minister Sharon built a coalition without the ultra-Orthodox parties. It was a product of rare circumstances: in the election that year, a significant part of the electorate feared Sharon but had lost faith in Labor, and chose a party built on secular backlash. Sharon's finance minister, Benjamin Netanyahu, began a cutback in child stipends for large families. The blow to *haredi* family finances brought only a small drop in childbearing. Economics can change culture, but not instantly. Besides, Diaspora donations to yeshivot partly ameliorated the government cuts, explains Rabbi Bezalel Cohen, a dissident former *kollel* student who has become an advocate of *haredim* getting jobs. The 2008 recession hit those donations as well, deepening the social crisis, he notes.

Again, a culture does not change direction easily, and the direction of ultra-Orthodox cultures had been set decades before. In 1979, during the Begin administration, just over 20 percent of ultra-Orthodox men aged thirty-five to fifty-four, the prime working years, were not employed. By 2000, 63 percent of *haredi* men in that age bracket were outside the workforce, and the number rose to 65 percent in 2008. By then, at least 55,000 men in Israel were *kollel* students, meaning that full-time study was the most common occupation of adult men. Despite the ideal of women supporting their scholar-husbands, employment was also low among ultra-Orthodox women. The National Insurance Institute, a state agency, reported that one-fifth of all Israeli families lived below the poverty line that year—and about two-thirds of ultra-Orthodox families.

In recent years, there has been more discussion in *haredi* society about the need to work. But there are two barriers to leaving *kollel*. On one hand, Torah jobs are scarce, despite the population growth. Yeshivot have let classes grow larger, Cohen explains. In some institutions, the teachers are paid off the books, with no social benefits, no pension fund. So teachers "keep teaching until they're ninety," Cohen says, rather than making way for younger teachers. On the other hand, *haredi* education has not given its graduates the basic tools for academic study or for work in a postindustrial economy.

And many more children are growing toward the ranks of the unemployable. Over a fifth of the Israeli *haredi* population is aged four or less. One-quarter of all kindergarten and preschool children in Israel were in ultra-Orthodox institutions in 2009. Unless those children receive a different kind of education than the one their parents and educators plan for them, they too will be lifetime dependents of the shrinking

number of working Israelis. The pyramid scheme will bank-
rupt Israel and leave the *haredim* hungry.

This large picture is made up of many individuals whose
world has gone out of kilter. In his father's generation, a semi-
employed *haredi* man told me, it was normal to leave the *kollel* by age thirty. Today, he said, men forty or fifty years old
were still studying. He himself was approaching forty, with a
relatively small family, just five children, and he made a bit of
money teaching here and there. We sat in the living room of
his apartment, in an entirely ultra-Orthodox neighborhood
beyond the Green Line. Secretly, to himself, he was a social
critic. He spoke slowly, as if each word was negotiated between a hundred arguing thoughts. His wife had work, so
his family was getting along, but the Torah job he'd grown
up to expect never materialized. "Little by little, a situation
was created where everyone is studying in *kollel* and the
number of Torah positions is shrinking," he said.

Because of the economic situation, "people always have
butterflies in their stomach. A *kollel* student arranges his
daughter's wedding and he has to commit himself to amounts
[for the young couple] that he's never seen in his life." The
society's normal response is to stress faith. "They don't like to
speak in realistic terms. They like to speak in religious terms.
They'll say, 'Before you ask about the future, look back—
thirty years ago people already said things couldn't go on this
way, and look—miracles happen!'" A week before, a prominent rabbi had given a talk in his neighborhood on "trusting
heaven and being satisfied with little."

Haredi life, he said, was built on believing in what rabbis say: "It's far beyond honoring Torah scholars, as in previous generations—it's trusting that they know more, understand more" about practical and political matters, not just religion. To begin to reach one's own conclusions, he said, was a slow and dangerous process, because "when a person begins doubting what his rabbis told him, it's hard to draw a line." The whole structure of faith might collapse. Trust in rabbis, he said, "is the education they're drumming into my children." Yet he acknowledged that he had accepted the drift toward more restricted schooling. His father had attended a school that combined Talmudic studies and an academic curriculum, and whose alumni include professors and doctors as well as rabbis. He himself went to an Agudat Yisrael elementary school that taught history, math, and Hebrew composition, though no English—an essential subject in general Israeli education. His secondary school was a yeshivah with no secular studies. His sons attended *talmudei Torah*, schools outside the Agudat Yisrael system but still mostly state-funded, where general studies were allocated forty-five minutes a day. This is the normal progression of generations in Israeli ultra-Orthodoxy. The man across the table from me had joined a quiet rebellion by sending his eldest son to a private English class in the evenings, creating an opening for him to get an academic education later.

My host's wife stayed in a different room while we talked. Before I left, she called him for an urgent conversation. He returned and asked, uncomfortably, that I sign a written declaration that I would write nothing that could identify him. In a few years, they would need to arrange marriages for their children. They could not risk being known as critics or heretics.

The implications of the state's link to ultra-Orthodoxy begin with economics, but they go much further. For instance, one source of employment for *haredi* men has been the state rabbinate and rabbinic courts. The rabbinate has exclusive jurisdiction over marriage between Jews within Israel. The main function of the rabbinic courts is divorce, also a religious monopoly. For mixed couples, or for Jews who don't want to deal with a clerical bureaucracy, the only alternative to the rabbinate for marriage is going abroad for a civil ceremony. There is no alternative for divorce.

Formally, rabbinic court judges are appointed on professional grounds. In practice, positions in the courts and rabbinate are parceled out as patronage. The rising power of *haredi* parties since 1977 has allowed them to fill more of those posts with their appointees.

Rabbinic court treatment of women has been particularly shameful. Under Jewish law, the husband grants the divorce to his wife. Rabbinic judges have allowed recalcitrant husbands to deny their wives divorces for years, or to use their advantage to dictate financial and custody settlements. Religious scholars concerned with women's rights have proposed innovative interpretations of Jewish law to solve the problem. The rabbinic judges show no interest in sanctioning innovation.

In the name of tradition, however, the state rabbinic establishment has introduced startling changes into Judaism, especially regarding the question of who is Jewish. In the classical view of Judaism, Jews are a "large extended family" that accepted a covenant with God—to use Bar-Ilan University law professor Zvi Zohar's phrase. The child of a Jewish mother is a member of the clan; a convert is an adopted child and, like anyone born into the family, remains Jewish for life, whether or not she continues to observe the rules of the covenant. This is a self-understanding that fits poorly into the European categories of "nation" and "religion," though both Zionism and ultra-Orthodoxy have tried to squeeze Jewishness into those frames.

The state rabbinate has never recognized non-Orthodox conversions. In recent years, it has become skeptical of Orthodox conversions, except those carried out by a select group of rabbis. What's more, a radical thesis has taken hold among rabbinic court judges: for a conversion to be valid, a convert has to have sincerely committed herself to keeping Jewish law—and her sincerity at the moment of conversion can be measured by her behavior years later. If the convert eats nonkosher food, works on the Sabbath, perhaps if she fails to cover her hair after marriage, a court can annul her conversion.

The state's rabbinic court of appeals endorsed this view in 2008, when it upheld a rabbinic judge's ruling in a divorce case involving a Danish-born convert. Because she had not kept a strict Orthodox lifestyle, the appeals court affirmed, her conversion seventeen years earlier was invalid. Rather than issue a divorce, the judge annulled her marriage. The ruling meant she could not remarry a Jew without going abroad. Her children, raised as Jews, had just lost their identity, and were likewise added to a rabbinic court blacklist of people ineligible to marry Jews in Israel.

In religious terms, the ruling was a scandal. It uprooted the principle of Judaism that a convert must be treated as the equal of a Jew from birth. The greater scandals, however, are that the state empowered a particular set of rabbis to impose their views on other Jews, and that it allowed them to negate a citizen's civil right to marry.

The High Court of Justice subsequently sent the case back to another rabbinic court, which interrogated the woman three separate times about her observance of religious law and finally ruled that she had, in fact, converted properly. While that decision ended her case happily, it again rested on the presumption that conversion to Judaism is conditional and that the state's religious courts may cancel it. The need for the High Court's intervention underlined the entanglement of state and religion. The obvious remedies are to institute civil marriage in Israel and to dissolve the rabbinic courts. It's equally obvious that as long as secular parties depend on ultra-Orthodox ones to rule, the Knesset will not adopt those remedies.

In Israeli political discussion, the standard explanation for the ultra-Orthodox parties' clout is that they hold the balance of power in parliament: since they can sell their support to a coalition of the left or of the right, they can drive up the bids from both sides. This description is misleading. *Haredi* parties have consistently preferred right-wing governments. Yet even when Labor won the 1992 election and Ehud Olmert's centrist Kadimah did so in 2006, they sought alliances with the ultra-Orthodox. The real foundation of *haredi* strength lies elsewhere—in the exclusion of Arab-backed parties from power.

In 1992, when Rabin was elected, two parties drawing their votes mainly from Palestinian citizens of Israel won a total of five seats in parliament. By 2006, three Arab-supported parties held a total of ten seats. The meaning of Labor's 1992 election victory was that *together with the Arab parties* and another left-wing party, it won a majority in the Knesset. The same was true of Kadimah's victory.

But the iron rule, ever since Ben-Gurion disqualified the Communists, is that Arab-backed parties are not candidates for the coalition and cabinet. The most polite explanation is that as long as the Israeli-Arab conflict continues, Arab-backed parties cannot be trusted with sharing responsibility for national security. The less polite explanation is that much of the Jewish majority does not see a government resting partly on Arab votes as legitimate.

Coalition building is like shopping: the major party must pay its smaller partners in some political coin. If there are several potential partners, each must set a lower price for its support. Because the Arab parties are eliminated, the ultra-Orthodox can charge more.

To Rabin's credit, he pushed the limits on Arab participation more than any Israeli leader before or after. Without formally including the Arab-backed parties in his coalition, he reached agreements under which they supported his government in parliament. In turn, the government allocated funds to make up for long neglect of Arab communities. As one Communist Knesset member told me at the time, Rabin treated the Communist Party as a publicly acknowledged mistress, an improvement on the past but hardly sufficient. When Shas quit the coalition, Rabin stayed in power with the help of the Arab parties, which was one more factor in the right's fury against him. Since his assassination, no other leader has had the courage to follow his example or go further.

The link between *haredi* power and the exclusion of Arabs is not the only way in which the ailments of Israeli democracy compound each other. One of the most pressing social concerns within the *haredi* community is housing. Young couples, both husband and wife from large families of little means, are desperate for inexpensive apartments. The community expects its elected representatives to procure state help. At the end of the 1980s, the government began using that hunger for housing to draw *haredim* into the settlement enterprise.

In 1990, the first homes were completed at Beitar Illit, southwest of Jerusalem, and 350 ultra-Orthodox settlers moved in. The first apartments cost $60,000, with the government providing a $50,000 interest-free mortgage. Four years later, the first residents arrived in what would become the town of Modi'in Illit, east of Tel Aviv. The two communities grew faster than any other settlements in the West Bank. By the end of 2009, they were also the two largest settlements, with a total of 81,000 residents between them, a quarter of the total settlement population outside East Jerusalem. Besides the constant arrival of new residents, the internal growth of the communities was stunning. Nearly 30 percent of the people living in Modi'in Illit were aged four or under. Each apartment in one of these towns could end up housing ten people or more. The government designated additional developments for *haredim* within settlements elsewhere in the West Bank.

Virtually every extended *haredi* family in Israel now has members living over the Green Line, notes geographer Yosseph Shilhav, a veteran researcher of the ultra-Orthodox world. "Every household has a vested interest in the territories," Shilhav says. "Israeli governments over the years who sent *haredim* to these places pushed them rightward. . . . After [the *haredim*] saw what happened to the Katif Bloc, they're even more afraid . . . and that pushes them further and further to the extreme."

So the combination of self-chosen poverty and dependence on the state has made the ultra-Orthodox constituency an integral part of the pro-settlement, pro-occupation alliance. The *haredi* community, moreover, mobilizes completely at elections. The value put on trust in the leading rabbis of the generation, and the social pressure against public dissent, ensures voting as a bloc. These factors increase the community's representation and its bargaining power. Yet participation in the democratic system is entirely instrumental—and seen from the inside, defensive. The mood within the community is a strange mix of feeling persecuted by secular society and celebrating victory over it.

At noon, a third-grade class at the Nitei Meir elementary school in Beitar Illit is studying the details of religious law on ritual handwashing before meals. The two dozen boys read the text in chorus, in Yiddish-accented Hebrew. There are no girls; they study in separate schools. The kindergarten teachers at Nitei Meir are women. Their classrooms are in the basement, so that they can enter through a separate door and not be seen by the male teachers. The walls of the kindergarten rooms are decorated with pictures of great rabbinic sages.

To see the boys study arithmetic or Hebrew grammar, I would have to come later in the day. At Nitei Meir, first-through sixth-graders have religious study from 8:30 to 2:30, and then two hours of general studies. In seventh and eighth grades, religious studies last till 4:00. The general curriculum also includes "a little history," explains Rabbi Yosef Rozovsky, the educational director, and "nature," a soft version of natural science. Studying English is out of the question. In the late nineteenth century, Rabbi Yehoshua Leib Diskin, a leader of Jerusalem's Orthodox community, put a ban on studying foreign languages to keep Jewish children from enrolling in European schools that were opening in the city, Rozovsky explains. Nitei Meir's principal, Rabbi Eran Ben-Porat, adds, "The moment a boy studies English, he's more exposed to the wider world, and he naturally leaves religion and he can even engage in intermarriage, like in America."

Nor does the curriculum include geography or physical education. "And civics?" I ask. No, says Rozovsky. Instead, the boys learn *Mesilat Yesharim*, an eighteenth-century work on perfecting oneself ethically. (I refrain from saying that while *Mesilat Yesharim* may indeed help moral improvement, it says nothing about the rationale for elections or free speech.) The point of school is to shape the child's personality, Rozovsky argues. Secular education has failed at this, while *haredi* education succeeds. He does not mention the ultra-Orthodox community's inability to cope with the *shebab*—an Arabic word for youth, which originally entered Hebrew as the term for the stone-throwing Palestinian teens of the first

Intifada. *Shebab* is now used to describe *haredi* young people who no longer believe in the ultra-Orthodox lifestyle but are locked in the community by their lack of job skills and knowledge of mainstream Israel. In Beitar Illit, a resident told me, the *shebab* hang out restlessly on the sidewalks on Friday night, or have the Sabbath meal with their families and then walk out to the main road and hitchhike to Jerusalem to hit the bars.

"Every society is selective. People who don't fit in, leave," says Shlomo Tikochinski, a resident of Beitar Illit and a rarity, a *haredi* Israeli who recently completed a doctorate in history. Ultra-Orthodox society, he argues, has "no drainage. The *haredim* have sealed it hermetically." There are still dropouts, but they can't get out.

Actually, it's impossible to seal a society completely. Despite rabbinic condemnations of the Internet, one can find young *haredi* men in the Internet cafés of the Christian Quarter in Jerusalem's Old City, or in the National Library on Hebrew University's Givat Ram campus, using the catalog computers to surf the net. They assume they won't be seen by other *haredim*. Among the online temptations are *haredi* discussion sites where they can anonymously discuss ideas they fear to acknowledge having in public.

And despite rabbis' pleas to trust heaven, economic desperation is pushing men to consider going to work. Vocational and academic programs have sprung up to help *haredim* do that. The change requires turning one's self-image inside out. Ex-*kollel* student Bezalel Cohen, who now directs a job program for the ultra-Orthodox, notes that "in all their thoughts and plans for the future," many *haredi* men have never realistically considered getting a mainstream job. A *kollel* student who wants to learn a profession must also overcome practical barriers. To get a college education, he must acquire the missing pieces of a primary and secondary education. The financial crunch is most likely to hit a man over forty with a large family, Cohen explains. Yet enrolling in an academic or even vocational program means giving up his meager *kollel* salary.

Those challenges for adults only highlight the absurdity of bringing up another, larger generation trained only for "the economy of the next world," to use Menachem Friedman's phrase. Twice in the last decade, the High Court of Justice has ruled that to uphold the State Education Law and the principle of equality, the government must set a core curriculum for high schools and cease funding *haredi* yeshivot that refuse to teach it. The second ruling was needed because the state ignored the first one. The latter ruling, however, came a few days too late. While the justices were preparing to deliver it in July 2008, the Knesset passed a preemptive law, allowing the Education Ministry to fund secondary schools serving "unique cultural groups"—explicitly including *haredi* schools that only teach religious subjects.

The script of this legal drama was an Israeli cliché: the Supreme Court asserted that democracy requires honoring basic rights. The ultra-Orthodox viewed the decision as an attack on Judaism, and used their power in the Knesset to overrule it. The small variation on the genre was using the liberal-sounding language of multiculturalism to protect funding of illiberal education.

Democracy, however, is not a synonym for unbound multiculturalism. An earlier democracy than Israel's was founded on the philosophical and theological axiom "that all men are created equal, that they are endowed by their Creator with certain unalienable Rights." This is not a culturally neutral statement. It is a proclamation of a moral truth that sometimes takes precedence over cultural heritage.

In a democratic society, it is reasonable to protect parents' rights to pass their values and their faith to their children. But that right must be balanced against the rights of the children themselves, who are people, not chattel, and against the rights of other citizens. If parents' religious values include forcing teenage daughters into polygamous marriage, for instance, the state is obligated to intervene. Freedom of religion does not protect child abuse.

For an education system to deprive young people of the knowledge they will need to support themselves as adults, in order to deny them the choice of whether to leave or stay within a sectarian community, is a form of child abuse. For the state to tolerate this abuse is abdication of duty. For it to fund such education is unconscionable. By forcing those children to become wards of the public as adults, the government also violates the rights of the remaining citizens who will have to support them.

The problem with *haredi* schooling, however, is not just economic, and will not be solved only by adding job skills to the curriculum. In its current constrained form, almost devoid of the humanities as well as science, ultra-Orthodox education denies young people the chance to articulate and question opinions, to see issues from many sides, to look at the world through other people's eyes, to understand human complexity. It evades exploring the mechanics and the moral basis of democracy. It fails to give young people the basic knowledge of science needed to understand what a doctor tells them or a debate over global warming. This, too, is abuse. Not only do children have to learn to think openly, they have a responsibility to do so, because the free consideration of ideas is essential to the functioning of a democracy. Other Israelis have the right to fellow citizens who can debate issues without fear and who can vote as individuals.

Being "exposed to the wider world" does not "naturally" lead to abandoning religion. A religious education and a liberal education can and should complement each other. The Talmud, the pinnacle of classic Jewish education, is essentially the transcript of centuries of debate. It can be taught, as American Jewish educator Joshua Gutoff asserts, to develop "moral imagination," the ability to see the moral complexity of everyday life.

The state of Israel can respect the right of Orthodox parents to give their children a religious education. But by allowing religious schools to deny children a general education, it fails those children and puts its own future as a democracy at risk.

The armored personnel carrier stops in the dry riverbed. Soldiers leap to the rocky earth, spread into a line, and run uphill, weighted with guns, helmets, and battle vests. They drop, prone, to the hillside. A second line of men advances, overtakes the first, and then drops to provide cover as the first line leapfrogs past. Scattered on the slope are cardboard figures of helmeted men facing them with guns, figures ripped by the fire from the advancing soldiers. Officers without helmets walk upright behind the troops, surrealistically calm, observing their performance. In a few minutes, the men of Netzah Yehudah, the IDF's *haredi* battalion, have conquered two desert hilltops. The company commander, a clean-shaven officer who grew up in a religious Zionist settlement in the Golan Heights, is quietly pleased. The exercise "flowed," he says. He never had to interfere.

Netzah Yehudah is an unusual unit. Soldiers are required to wear skullcaps, pray thrice daily, keep the Sabbath, and attend daily Torah study with the unit's rabbis. At the battalion's isolated base, the roles normally filled by women—the education officer, the social work NCO—are staffed by men. Women do not enter the gate.

Netzah Yehudah inducted its first recruits in 1999. It was a joint project of the IDF's Manpower Branch and an association of *haredi* rabbis concerned about young men unsuited for yeshivah study. In order to gain legal employment, the men needed to acknowledge leaving yeshivah, which in turn meant they would have to serve in the army. The rabbis agreed to cooperate with the military if the unit enforced a *haredi* lifestyle. Soldiers who enlist get a bonus: they spend their final year of service either studying to complete a high school education or training for a vocation.

Netzah Yehudah started with thirty recruits. When it celebrated its tenth anniversary, it had seven hundred men on active duty, in four companies, and was expanding. The IDF sees the unit as a success. In the ultra-Orthodox world, wall posters signed by major rabbis denounce Netzah Yehudah, lest real yeshivah students sign up.

The soldiers are not all from the same mold. About a third are religious Zionist troops, who want a stricter Orthodox atmosphere than elsewhere in the army. Their presence has boosted demands from *hesder* soldiers to have separate brigades of their own. Some of the soldiers are skin-deep *haredim*. A military rabbi, interviewed about the unit, described "a young man who came to me, with beard and sidelocks, bitter and angry that they forbade him to talk on the phone on the Sabbath. . . . He did not understand why the army . . . forced him to keep religious commandments."

The unit is run in tight coordination with the rabbinical association. "The commanders don't do anything without consulting the rabbis," says Ze'ev Drori, an academic expert on the military and a colonel in the reserves who researched Netzah Yehudah. The battalion commander at the time I visited, a religious Zionist officer, said it would take time for an ultra-Orthodox soldier to rise to command of the unit, but the day would come. To develop morale, he said, "We stress [defending] the Jewish people," rather than defending the state. Most of the soldiers do not identify with the secular state and its citizenry.

The battalion's military rabbi, Lieutenant Ariel Eliahu, is the grandson of former chief rabbi Mordechai Eliahu and son of the controversial far-right rabbi of the Galilee city of Safed. Lieutenant Eliahu often conducts the daily class for soldiers, on subjects ranging from Talmud to "the justice of our cause," which includes "the truth that . . . the Land of Israel belongs to us by historical and divine decree." Drori notes that when a rabbi has an hour to teach soldiers, and "mixes in love of the land and Jewishness compared to

Arabness," he is transmitting his "personal ideological and political credo." Religious study becomes political indoctrination.

Netzah Yehudah is part of the Kfir Brigade, whose main task is policing the West Bank. The battalion carries out raids to arrest Palestinians suspected of terrorism and mans the checkpoints through which Palestinians must constantly cross. Netzah Yehudah was not assigned to participate in the withdrawal from Gaza. There was no point in placing the soldiers in that bind.

The *haredi* unit demonstrates one more way in which the strains on Israeli democracy reinforce each other. The battalion is meant to overcome *haredi* self-segregation, to help men leave the yeshivot and enter the workforce. Yet it is built on segregation within the army. It is a unit tied to a particular political community, with two hierarchies of command, military and ideological, a unit where esprit de corps is built on defending Jews and their homeland, not on defending Israel. It is the kind of unit that Ben-Gurion knew he should not have in his army.

Through Netzah Yehudah and the *haredi* settlements, a problem in Israeli society is being exported to occupied territory. There is a greater danger, however: the longer the occupation lasts, the more its ills enter Israel proper. They cannot be sealed off behind the missing border. They metastasize.

VII.

IMPORTING THE REVOLUTION

"Clearly, there's a war here, sometimes even worse than the one in Samaria," the student said. "It's not a war with guns. It's a war of light against darkness." That's why, he said, he set clear lines for himself, why he didn't let himself form any connection with Arabs, even if they lived across the hall from him.

We were sitting in a side room of the *hesder* yeshivah in Akko—or Akka, as members of the Arab minority in the

Israeli coastal city call it, or Acre, as it's sometimes marked on maps in English. The student had grown up in a settlement in Samaria, the northern West Bank. In Samaria, he said, there were clear lines dividing Jews and Arabs, which was how he liked things. He was in his early twenties, recently married, back in the yeshivah after finishing his active duty in the army. Years before, he explained, the Arabs had "started spreading" from the Old City on the southwest of Akko. The dividing line was now the railroad tracks—mostly Arabs on the west side, Jews on the east. But now Arabs were "trying to get in" on the east side as well. The battle in Akko, he said, was "psychological and overt—who will be here, who will rule here."

The yeshivah is on the west side, in the Wolfson neighborhood, in a synagogue surrounded by the Soviet-style apartment blocks built in Israel's early years: long stucco rectangles, four stories high, with multiple entrances leading to small walk-up flats. Most of the names on the mailboxes are Arab; a few are Jewish. On the main street, an Arab-owned restaurant stands next to an empty storefront, formerly a dental clinic, with a sign in Hebrew and Russian, a reminder of the 1990s wave of Soviet Jewish immigration. Near the yeshivah, a corner kiosk has been converted into a shirt-pocket police station—a more subtle reminder of the 2006 melee between yeshivah students and their neighbors, which presaged the ethnic riots of 2008.

Akko was the last capital of the Crusaders in the Holy Land. Relative to the length of the city's history, this is the recent past. Much more recently, Akka was one of the main cities of Arab Palestine—and the harbor from which many refugees fled north by sea to Beirut in 1948. Yet when Haganah troops conquered the city on the fourth day of Israeli independence, some of the Palestinian Arab residents stayed, along with Arabs from surrounding villages who'd found refuge there. Their numbers were small enough that Israel could order Arabs living in the modern, British-era section to move into the walled Old City, with room left inside the walls for Jewish immigrants to join them. Akko was now one of Israel's "mixed cities," mostly Jewish, partly Arab.

To the victors went the street names. Along the beach runs Haganah Street. The Comprehensive Arab High School, just outside the Old City walls, is on the Street of the Two Eliahus, named for Eliahu Hakim and Eliahu Bet Zouri, members of the Lehi terror group who in 1944 assassinated Lord Moyne, the British Minister Resident in Egypt. They died by hanging and became martyrs of the Israeli right. Those who named the street for them surely did not think of the potential lessons that their choice might have for Arab high schoolers. The blaze of ethnic conflict blinds people to how their actions might be seen in the other side's eyes.

In the 1960s, Jews moved out of the Old City to the modern apartments of Wolfson. Later, as Arabs also found homes in the neighborhood, Jews moved on, to newer parts of town or to the nearby all-Jewish town of Nahariyah. In Akko, Muslims went to the Old City for public prayer; the government refused permission to reopen pre-1948 mosques outside the walls. Meanwhile, the big synagogue in Wolfson slowly emptied. Palestinian citizens of Israel moved into Akko from nearby Galilee villages, where growing populations collided with government policies that made both land and building permits into scarce commodities. In the 1990s, Russian-speaking Jewish immigrants arrived. Overall, Jews remained a large majority in the town.

Here enter two more hard-line nationalist Eliahus: former chief rabbi Mordechai Eliahu and his son, Rabbi Shmuel Eliahu. In the late 1990s they established a project to place groups of their followers in Israeli towns to work with the poor and bring Jews to their version of "redemptive" Judaism. While the agenda of the urban "settlement groups" was supposed to be religious education and social projects, the first city that Mordechai Eliahu targeted was Akko, which he saw as being abandoned by Jews. His son picked Nachshon Cohen, a rabbi who had studied at the yeshivah in Hebron, to be the group's spiritual leader. Cohen later recounted that he recruited three of the group's original families from the Jewish settlers in Hebron. The project's administrator, Yishai Rubin, was a native of Elon Moreh.

They were moving back into Israel. But they were not leaving behind the sectarian nationalism distilled in the West Bank hills. They were bringing that way of seeing the world back home, reimporting the message of ethnic struggle for each acre of land. And in doing so, they embodied the long-term effect of the settlement effort on society within Israel.

By 2009, more than eighty families belonged to the religious settlement group in Akko. Members of the group and their supporters often describe the city as if it were a battlefield, on which two armies thrust and parry via the real estate market. Akko's Arabs have been "taking control of neighborhoods in the north and east," the settler newspaper *Besheva* reported just after the 2008 riots. But by moving into one of the eastern neighborhoods, the settlement group "stopped the Arab encroachment." There is "an Arab nationalist push for young families living in the Galilee to invade into Akko," says Sara Paparin, development director of the *hesder* yeshivah. The interpretation of Arab migration to the city as an organized campaign is one I heard repeatedly in Akko. Its basis appears to be psychological: a projection of what Jewish nationalists are doing onto the actions of the perceived enemy. The enemy should know its place. "We certainly won't expel them," Nachshon Cohen says of the city's Arab residents, but "the question is whether . . . they accept not only that we are here, but that Akko is a Jewish city."

Akko's *hesder* yeshivah opened its doors in 2003. The idea came from the settlement group. The yeshivah website explains the importance of bringing Jews to the city: "Akko of our days is the front line. . . . The risk [here] of losing the Jewish majority and the Zionist identity of the city is the highest in the country." At one time the site also declared that the students "project power, determination and confidence in everything having to do with the Jewish future of the city," though the language has since been toned down. One way of projecting power, intentional or not, particularly disturbed the yeshivah's Arab neighbors: When students on leave from the army visited the yeshivah, they carried their military assault rifles. Even if students were from within Israel, the combination of skullcaps and guns fit the evening-news image of West Bank settlers.

In 2006, during the Muslim holy month of Ramadan,

someone in Wolfson tried to make up for the lack of mosque and minaret by putting a loudspeaker on an apartment house roof to sound the chant announcing the daily end of the fast. The yeshivah students saw that as violating the religious status quo. That year, the Jewish holiday of Simhat Torah—traditionally marked by dancing with Torah scrolls—fell during Ramadan. The procession of dancing yeshivah students left the study hall for the streets and "private Arab areas," according to a Knesset report. The report avoids stating whether the students or Arab bystanders started the brawl that followed. This ambiguity is wise, given how a brawl smolders from shouts to pushes to blows. The shots fired in the air, however, clearly came from a student's army-issue rifle. The police arrested the student and broke up the melee. Afterward, the street-corner police station was established to keep the peace in Wolfson.

The response was not sufficient. The city burst into flame two years later, again on a religious holiday. In Jewish areas of Israel, the streets are empty of cars on Yom Kippur, the holiest day in the Jewish calendar. The custom is that no one drives. Near midnight on Yom Kippur, 2008, an Arab resident of Wolfson drove to the east side of town to pick up his daughter at a relative's apartment. Young men hanging out on the street—the kind of bored toughs who do not spend the holy day fasting and praying but are quick to defend Jewish honor—began hurling stones at the car. The driver and his two passengers took refuge in his relative's apartment, which was surrounded by an angry crowd. A rumor spread in the Old City that Jews had killed someone. Young Arabs tried to reach the apartment, clashed with Jews, and smashed car and shop windows on their way home. Arabs living on the east and north sides of town fled their homes, several of which were torched; Jewish rioters threw stones at Arabs and police and chanted "Death to Arabs." The violence lasted four days.

This time neither the yeshivah nor the settlement group was at the center of the storm, though someone in Wolfson did express his view of the yeshivah by tossing a Molotov cocktail through the office window, causing a small fire. Arab activists cited the presence of the yeshivah and settlement group among the ignored portents of the explosion. "That's the trend of recent years—a trickle of the extreme right into Akko. They've turned everything upside down," an Arab resident of Wolfson told a reporter.

Afterward, the settlement group "took the lead in making the statement that this is a Jewish city and it's ours," administrator Yishai Rubin told the settler magazine *Nekuda*. On Simhat Torah, a week and a half after Yom Kippur, the group hosted 600 young Orthodox Jews from out of town who "flooded the streets of Akko and raised morale," Rubin said. Once again, the ritual was religious, but the statement was nationalist. The riots were over. The "psychological war" was not.

Akko is only one of the mixed Jewish-Arab cities in Israel that religious nationalists have set out to "save" by importing the settlement model. Two families from the West Bank settlement of Beit El established the original toehold in Lod, southeast of Tel Aviv, in 1995. By 2009, the Lod group had expanded to 250 families, and was building a housing development on the "seamline" between mainly Jewish and mainly Arab neighborhoods. That was the defensive tactic, meant to create a wall blocking Arab migration. For offense, the settlement group established a premilitary academy in a majority-Arab neighborhood. "We're absolutely starting a process that declares that we are not abandoning the area and that we're going to Judaize it," the group's director told *Nekuda*.

One of the Lod settlers, Ariel Ben-David, helped establish a parallel group in the neighboring town of Ramleh. "I grew up as a settler," he told the settler magazine. "It was hard for me to leave the settlements, and it was important for me to live in a place where there was also a national struggle," meaning a struggle between Jews and Palestinians. Many of the Ramleh settlers came from the hypernationalist communities of Beit El, Elon Moreh, and Yitzhar.

Another settlement group has moved into Jaffa. Until 1948, Jaffa was the commercial center of Arab Palestine. Since then, it has been the southern end of Tel Aviv, the one part of the metropolis with a mix of Arabs and Jews. A *hesder* yeshivah followed the settlement group. The dean of the yeshivah, Rabbi Eliyahu Mali, moved to Jaffa from Beit El. Mali, an extremely wary interviewee, told me that "Arabs don't interest us." His goal, he said, was to connect to local Jews. The yeshivah, however, is in Ajami, the Arab-majority part of Jaffa.

A few blocks away from it is a state-owned lot for which the Bemuna company has acquired development rights. The company's name means "In Faith"; it builds for "the religious Zionist public" and announced it would sell the apartments exclusively to Orthodox Jews. Among the company's other projects is one in the West Bank settlement of Pnei Hever and another in Arab a-Sawahra, a Palestinian neighborhood of East Jerusalem. The head of the company told an Orthodox news site that one attraction of the Jaffa project is that it provides "ideological value added" for religious couples. The news site's sympathetic report forthrightly describes buyers as "settling in Jaffa."

"Akko is not alone," Knesset member Uri Ariel of the far-right National Union party wrote after the 2008 riots. Arabs were engaging in deliberate block-busting in Israeli cities, he said. After Jews were pushed out, neighborhoods became "hothouses of crime, drugs and prostitution," wrote Ariel. "In Israeli cities, a creeping Arab conquest is taking place." Religious settlement groups, in his description, were a first line of defense, "stabilizing the situation in many cities and preventing Jewish flight." But on the national level, the solution was "to encourage voluntary emigration of the Arabs." Ariel, a veteran leader of the West Bank settlement movement, did not specify how Arabs were to be so "encouraged." His article does make clear that in the view from the settlements, the Green Line had truly been erased. Israeli cities and West Bank hills were fronts in the same war.

In *God of Vengeance*, Sholem Asch's classic Yiddish play, a character in an unnamed Eastern European town a century ago runs a brothel in his basement while trying to bring up his daughter as a chaste Jewish girl on the floor above. To protect her purity, he places a Torah scroll in his home. He has a matchmaker find a pious groom for her. His plan fails. A wooden floor cannot keep the two realms of his life apart.

Reverence for a sacred scroll cannot ward off corruption when people ignore the words written in it.

Let us read Asch's drama as an allegory for what happens when a fragile democracy tries to maintain an undemocratic regime next door in occupied territory. A border, especially one not even shown on maps, cannot seal off the rot. Nor can politicians' declarations of reverence for liberal values.

In recent years the corrosive effects of the occupation on Israel have been glaring, especially the vocal, shameless efforts of the political right to treat Israeli Arabs as enemies of the state rather than as fellow citizens. "Settling" in Israeli cities is just one symptom of this illness. Unchecked, the offensive against democracy has grown wider. The political right uses charges of treason to attack critics of policy in the occupied territories, and seeks legislation to curb dissent and the rights of Arab citizens and to bypass the Supreme Court.

Obviously, the occupation is just one factor in the inequality of Israel's Palestinian citizens, which dates to the beginning of the state. The abolition of the military government over Israeli Arabs in 1966 did not instantly end discrimination or the ideas on which it was based.

An example: the unnatural survival of the Jewish Agency and Jewish National Fund was a statement that Israel had not yet learned to see itself as a state rather than as a national movement. Both bodies were established to serve Jews in their struggle for self-determination. Independence made them obsolete, but they were not dismantled. Instead, their relation with the government was defined by law, and they provided services in its place. The agency built the infrastructure for rural Jewish communities; Arab communities remained less developed. The JNF owned land designated for the use of Jews alone. Much of it was "absentee property"—land that Arab refugees left behind, which the government seized and sold to the JNF.

The JNF's role, which lasts to today, is just one expression of planning and land-use policies that reflexively serve Jews rather than citizens in general. A recent wave of eviction notices against Jaffa's Palestinians illustrates the problem. After 1948, Arabs who remained in Jaffa were forced to move into a small section of the city. Many moved into buildings that other Arabs had left behind, becoming the state's tenants in what was officially "absentee property." Jaffa as a whole was annexed to the municipality of Tel Aviv. When the city enacted a new town plan for Jaffa in the 1990s, it set rules that virtually forced gentrification. By finding Arab residents in breach of contract and evicting them, the state can sell the property at the new, high market value to developers who will sell to well-off Jews.

Land use, moreover, is part of a larger picture. In 2008, Palestinian citizens were 17 percent of the Israeli population, but only 6 percent of the civil service. The class size in Arab elementary schools was nearly one-fifth larger than in Jewish schools. The proportion of young Jews enrolled in Israeli universities was almost three times larger than the proportion of young Arabs. This is but a sampling of the effects of years of institutional and informal discrimination.

It's also true that abolishing the military government was a milestone in a slow process of emancipation of Arab citizens. Accessible higher education paved the way for the rise of a new generation of Israeli-born Arab intellectuals, some of whom led a political transformation. The old client-patron relation with Jewish-dominated parties faded; the number of parties representing Israeli Palestinians grew, as did their total representation in the Knesset. Over time, as part of the growth of civil society, organizations defending Arab rights began using the courts to challenge discrimination.

The effect of the occupation on this picture is complicated. In some ways it actually seemed to enhance Israeli Arabs' emancipation. Ultimately, though, it is sabotaging the process.

After June 1967, Arabs inside the Green Line could reconnect to Palestinians in the West Bank and Gaza Strip, and to their own identity as Palestinians. Yet something else happened, which fit into political rhetoric less well: they noticed that they were different from those living across the invisible border. The Hebrew words in their Arabic marked them as Israelis. They were second-class citizens—but unlike Palestinians living in occupied territory, they were citizens. The new reality made them more Palestinian and more Israeli at the same time.

The first stage of planning of Israel's security fence, in 2002, highlighted the difference in status and confidence between Israeli and West Bank Palestinians. Much of the route meandered through the West Bank. In one spot, though, it cut through Israeli territory—on the outskirts of the Israeli Arab town of Umm al-Fahm, putting nearly 250 acres of local farmers' fields on the West Bank side. The army's planners preferred the topography of that route. Whether they would have drawn the same line on hillsides farmed by Jews is a separate question. A committee including the mayor and a local human rights lawyer, Tawfiq Jabareen, met with Defense Ministry officials and warned that townspeople would physically block the work. A Knesset member from the town, Hashem Mahameed, contacted Prime Minister Sharon and asked to change the route.

"They saw that Umm-al Fahm, like the settlers, is very strong . . . and politically mature," attorney Jabareen told me afterward. The Defense Ministry sent officials to negotiate, and within a month the state agreed to a route that took only twelve acres of town land. Otherwise, the barrier ran just inside the West Bank, on land taken from West Bank Palestinian villages. In principle, Jabareen said, he opposed any fence, "but we must be realistic. We cannot defend all of the Palestinian people." The campaign was pragmatic, forceful, and waged by people who felt that they were more than halfway inside the system. West Bank villagers who lost land to the barrier could only dream of such negotiations, or of their success.

But the barrier's barbed wire has been no more successful than the erased Green Line in keeping occupation psychology from infiltrating sovereign Israel. That mind-set sees the entire territory from the Jordan River to the Mediterranean as the arena in which Jews and Arabs fight for hegemony. It is a pre-state attitude, but guides the actions of the state. In that mind-set, Israeli Palestinians are not second-class citizens; they are at best denizens of the first circle of occupation, at worst a fifth column.

Such thinking shaped government policy. The Likud government that took power in 1977 used the "community settlement" model, as developed at Ofrah, to draw settlers to the West Bank. But the government also began creating the same kind of exclusive community inside Israel, especially to "Judaize the Galilee"—to draw Jews to northern Israel, which has a large Arab population.

As in the West Bank, hilltop neighborhoods of private homes were planted between Arab communities. To move in, prospective residents had to first meet the approval of the community's admissions committee. The method, I should note, also made it possible to exclude Jews of Middle Eastern ancestry, single parents, or people of the wrong religious stripe, according to the whim of the committee. The more consistent impact, however, was to exclude Arabs.

Yet inside Israel, the attitudes of occupation confronted the attitudes and the institutions of democracy. In 1995 Aadel and Iman Ka'adan, a couple from the Israeli Arab town of Baqa al-Gharbiyah, tried to buy a lot in the nearby community settlement of Katzir. As young, educated professionals eager to live in a place with good schools so their daughters could get into the right universities, they fit the Katzir profile. As Arabs, they were told that there was no point even in applying for membership. The state had allocated the land to the Jewish Agency to create a rural community, and the Jewish Agency establishes communities for Jews only. As citizens of a democracy, the Ka'adans turned to the Association for Civil Rights in Israel, which filed suit before the High Court of Justice.

In its judgment five years later, citing sources ranging from Genesis to *Brown v. Board of Education*, the court ruled that "equality is one of the foundational principles of the

State of Israel," and that the state must not discriminate against Arab citizens in allocating land. Nor could it use the Jewish Agency as its middleman in order to discriminate, for "what the State cannot do directly, it cannot do indirectly." After many delays, Katzir's admissions committee weighed the Ka'adans' application. It concluded that they were "unsuited" to "fit in socially" and denied their application.

Again, the couple's lawyers petitioned the High Court. Among the exhibits they presented was the Jewish Agency's internal policy document written in response to the court's ruling in 2000. It recommended "not making noise . . . and continuing doing what we are doing"—in other words, continuing to discriminate. Finally, after a hearing in which the justices' furious comments made clear that the state would lose, the Ka'adans were allowed to buy a lot in Katzir. In 2007, they were able to start building their home. Shortly afterward, a coalition of Israeli human rights organizations—representing Arabs, gays, and Jews of Middle Eastern ancestry—asked the Supreme Court to ban the entire admissions-committee procedure. As of this writing, that case is still pending.

To this point in the story, it illustrates the defining contradiction of Israel's history, the inner clash between chauvinism and liberalism, between ethnocracy and democracy. More than that, it shows the progress upward, painfully slow but real, of a country weighted by its past but climbing toward its ideals.

In politics, however, most actions produce reactions, often unequal. In recent years, the national figure who has most embodied political reaction is Avigdor Lieberman. Lieberman's themes are a bellicose foreign policy, the need for a regime based on a powerful, unfettered leader, and—most of all—the danger of domestic enemies.

The enemies list begins with Arab citizens. "Every place in the world where there are two peoples—two religions, two languages—there is friction and conflict," Lieberman once told me, in an interview in his Knesset office. The solution, he asserted, was total political division, meaning that Israel had to rid itself of its Arab minority.

He also spoke of his admiration for Winston Churchill and for Peter the Great, the early-eighteenth-century autocrat who dragged Russia into modern Europe. He saw both as models of sticking to one's vision in the face of opposition and mockery. Lieberman said his favorite book, the one that he had read "at least three hundred times," was the historical novel *Peter the First*. Written during Stalin's reign by Alexey Tolstoy, a distant cousin of the author of *War and Peace*, it sympathetically portrays Peter the Great and, implicitly, Stalin as well. "To drag the people out of the age-old swamp, open their eyes, prod them in the ribs. Beat them, lick them into shape, teach them"—so the czar describes his life's mission. When he faces a counterrevolution, "The prisons were filled and thousands of new corpses swayed . . . on the walls of Moscow." Peter himself participates in the torture of the conspirators. Lieberman said that whenever he needed something to calm himself, he opened the book and began to read.

Lieberman was born in Soviet Moldova in 1958, and came to Israel at age twenty. After graduating from Hebrew University, he became a Likud functionary and moved to the small West Bank settlement of Nokdim, in the hills southeast of Bethlehem. When Benjamin Netanyahu was elected prime minister in 1996, Lieberman took the position of director-general of the Prime Minister's Office, the equivalent of a U.S. president's chief of staff. Lieberman gained a reputation as Netanyahu's enforcer within the Likud—and the following year was forced to resign in order to repair the prime minister's shattered relations with his party colleagues.

In the 1999 elections Lieberman ran on his own ticket, flaunting his immigrant identity along with a hard-line rightist platform. Nearly a million immigrants had poured into the country from the former Soviet Union during the previous decade. The number of engineers in Israel quadrupled; the number of physicians doubled. Disappointed professionals became semiskilled laborers, sometimes competing with Israel's Arab underclass. The name that Lieberman gave his party, Israel Is Our Home, was the loud declaration of those actually not quite at home. Read with the stress on *Our*, it also implied that there were other people in the country who should be considered aliens.

Explaining the psychology of the anti-Semite, Jean-Paul Sartre wrote, "By treating the Jew as an inferior and pernicious being, I affirm at the same time that I belong to the elite. This elite . . . is an aristocracy of birth." What shall the person who seeks membership in an aristocracy do if viewing Jews as pernicious is not possible for him? "If the Jew did not exist, the anti-Semite would invent him," Sartre wrote. Lieberman's message appointed Israel's Arabs to fill in as hated outsiders who made it possible for others to be insiders.

Israel Is Our Home won four seats in its first election. By

the 2009 election, it won fifteen seats, and Lieberman led the third largest party in the Knesset. Over that time, Lieberman's views on the Palestinian issue underwent an evolution. Initially, he aligned his party with the far-right National Union, which called for the "voluntary transfer" of Palestinians out of the West Bank and Gaza Strip in order to keep the Whole Land of Israel. In 2004, he suddenly declared that he favored partitioning the land between Jews and Palestinians. This fit a trend: at that moment, a whole slice of the right seemed to accept the left's argument that Israel could not remain a Jewish and democratic country if it kept all of the occupied territories. Deputy prime minister Ehud Olmert, a lifelong advocate of the Whole Land of Israel, had come out for withdrawing from most of the West Bank. Prime Minister Sharon had announced his plan to "disengage" from Gaza.

But Lieberman had his own twist: he proposed that Israel keep its largest West Bank settlements—and cede some of its own territory near the West Bank boundary, areas populated by Arabs who are Israeli citizens and voters. From the Knesset podium, he advocated expelling Arab citizens from elsewhere in Israel to the new Palestinian state.

Before the 2006 election, possibly to avoid having his party disqualified as racist, he stopped speaking of forced population transfer. Instead, his platform called for making citizenship conditional on taking a loyalty oath to the state, the flag, and the national anthem. Any Israeli adult who declined the oath would remain a resident but could not vote. Israel's flag, with its Jewish star, and its anthem describing the "Jewish soul stirring" have long spurred opposition from Arab citizens, who feel that the symbols exclude them. Lieberman's plans exploited that position to label them as disloyal and to disenfranchise them. "Such a law is customary in advanced Western countries, chief among them the United States of America," the party platform claimed. In fact, the proposal appears modeled on the law used by post-Soviet Estonia to deny citizenship to non-Estonians.

The meaning of Lieberman's political shift was that he changed targets: rather than focus primarily on Palestinians in the occupied territories, he portrayed Israel's own Palestinian citizens as the primary enemy.

Lieberman's success in the 2009 election showed that his rhetoric of resentment resonated beyond the immigrant community. But that success was just one facet of the rise of the radical right. The Likud's moderate wing had bolted three years earlier to form the new, centrist Kadimah party, which largely replaced the Labor Party in representing the centrist Israeli middle class. Afterward, the Likud was pulled further rightward by a group called Jewish Leadership, based among ideologically extreme settlers. The group's website proclaimed that if it gained power, it would immediately take Israel out of the United Nations, destroy the IDF's nonlethal crowd-control weapons, and establish an exclusively Jewish upper house in the Knesset.

Jewish Leadership's supporters signed up as Likud members. When the Likud central committee chose its Knesset candidates for 2009, the group's representatives voted as a bloc, helping hard-liners fill the party ticket. After a near tie in the national election between the Likud and Kadimah, Likud leader Benjamin Netanyahu refused to share power with Kadimah, in part because the leader of the centrist party, Tzipi Livni, demanded that the new government pursue peace with the Palestinians based on a two-state solution. Instead he formed a coalition with Lieberman, the religious parties, and the directionless remains of the Labor Party. Lieberman was appointed foreign minister. A legislator from his party, West Bank settler David Rotem, became chair of the Knesset's influential Law Committee, and the new justice minister, Yaakov Neeman, was Lieberman's choice.

What followed was an intense effort to use parliamentary power against basic democratic principles. That offensive, I must stress, faced resistance within the Knesset and in the general public. Nonetheless, the tidal wave of legislation aimed against the Arab minority, human rights activists, and critics of the occupation was unprecedented.

Following his party's platform, Rotem introduced a bill to condition citizenship on a declaration of allegiance to Israel as a "Jewish and Zionist state" and "to the state's flag, and to the national anthem." Lacking sufficient support for that sweeping measure, Israel Is Our Home and its right-wing allies submitted more limited measures. One bill from Lieberman's party proposed that civil servants be required to declare allegiance to "the Jewish and democratic state of Israel." The clear purpose was to push Arabs out of the civil service. Another bill, cosponsored by the far-right National Union, sought to rein in the country's cinema industry. Recent Israeli films had won international acclaim for their artistic quality and their searing examination of Israeli society, but the cinema renaissance depended on government subsidies. Under the bill, for a production to receive funding, everyone working on it would have to declare fealty to "the State of Israel, its symbols, and its Jewish and democratic values."

One of Lieberman's bills received Netanyahu's forceful backing. In October 2010, the cabinet voted to back an amendment to Israel's citizenship law. Rather than simply declaring allegiance to Israel to be naturalized, an immigrant would have to affirm loyalty to Israel as "a Jewish and democratic state." The proposed amendment did not apply to immigrants coming to Israel under the Law of Return. That is, only people with no ethnic connection to being Jewish would have to declare allegiance to Israel as a "Jewish state." At the cabinet meeting, Lieberman made clear that he saw the bill as a stepping-stone toward fulfilling his wider program to require a loyalty oath of everyone in the country. The utterly unhidden message was that Palestinian citizens were disloyal and must be excised from the polity.

The right's second front, in parliament and outside, was against domestic dissent. An organization called Im Tirtzu launched an offensive in early 2010 with a study alleging that Israeli human rights groups were part of a conspiracy to besmirch the army and "deter IDF soldiers and commanders from the very willingness to fight." The tentacles of the purported conspiracy included the Association for Civil Rights in Israel, Yesh Din, Breaking the Silence, and B'Tselem, which monitors human rights violations in occupied territory. At the center of the plot allegedly stood the New Israel Fund (NIF), a philanthropy that raises funds abroad to support a wide variety of Israeli groups working for civil rights, economic equality, and other liberal causes. By manipulating statistics, Im Tirtzu alleged that NIF-backed organizations had supplied the bulk of negative material from Israel for the United Nations' highly critical Goldstone Report on the IDF invasion of Gaza in 2009.

Im Tirtzu followed with a personal campaign against NIF president Naomi Chazan, a former Knesset member. Demonstrators outside her house held signs depicting Chazan with a horn sprouting from her forehead—playing on the fact that the Hebrew word for "fund" also means "horn," but echoing anti-Semitic myths about Jews having horns. Speaking to me, Im Tirtzu chair Ronen Shoval asserted that the various human rights groups were "really the different hands" of the NIF, "which instigates and directs them to incite against IDF soldiers and Israel." As if deliberately trying to conjure up the ghost of Joseph McCarthy, he also accused NIF-supported groups of using rhetoric that "serves Communist interests."

Afterward, the campaign moved to parliament, where right-wing Knesset members threatened legislation and investigations to expose the sources of funding to human rights organizations. Early in 2011, for instance, the Knesset plenum approved sending two resolutions to committee. One, submitted by an Israel Is Our Home legislator, called for a parliamentary commission to investigate "foreign foundations and governments" supposedly funding Israeli organizations to take part in "the campaign of delegitimization against IDF soldiers." The second, submitted by Likud member Danny Danon, demanded a Knesset inquiry into the role of "foreign bodies and governments in funding anti-state activities and organized attempts to purchase its land."

When the vote sparked intense public criticism, Lieberman responded by charging, "We're talking about groups that are nothing more than collaborators with terror, whose only purpose is weakening the IDF."

Israeli law already required nonprofit organizations to submit detailed financial reports to the state's Registrar of NPOs, which makes those reports available to the public. So the parliamentary efforts to "reveal" their funding sources were pure theater. The goal was to attack civil society, the most vibrant part of Israeli democracy, and to portray challenges to government policy in Gaza and the West Bank as subversive.

Danon's allegations that terror groups could be buying Israeli land alluded to the right's third front—preventing Arab citizens from buying or renting homes where they wished in the country. Outside the realm of parliament, the most vocal figure in that effort was Shmuel Eliahu, the chief rabbi of the Galilee city of Safed. The local college attracted many students from surrounding Arab communities, who often sought housing in town during their studies. In late 2010, Eliahu published a manifesto saying that Jewish religious law prohibited selling or renting homes or land to non-Jews anywhere in the Land of Israel.

"Their way of life is different from ours, they despise us and they harass us to the point of endangering lives," Eliahu wrote. Anyone who sold to a non-Jew, he said, caused financial damage to his neighbors by lowering property values. To prevent this, he said, people should publicly admonish the offender, "keep away from him, avoid doing business with him . . . until he reverses the great damage he has done to the public." Initially, the manifesto was cosigned mainly by other rabbis from Safed; when Eliahu came under public criticism, he gathered the signatures of the state-salaried rabbis of dozens of other towns and settlements for his racist interpretation of Judaism.

Within the parliamentary realm, meanwhile, the Knesset passed a bill that aimed at preserving the restrictive admissions-committee system in community settlements, even before the High Court of Justice ruled on it. Sponsored by members of four parties—including the centrist Kadimah—the law protected the committees' authority to reject candidates who "do not match the social-cultural fabric" of a community. As the Ka'adan case showed, that was enough to enshrine housing segregation in community settlements. Indeed, the legislation's purpose was to write a new ending to the Ka'adan story, an ending in which chauvinism defeated liberalism, in which the country's past won out over its ideals.

The article appeared in *Olam Katan* (Small World), a free weekly given out in synagogues on the Sabbath, in the summer of 2010. It announced that Israel's single national police force had a new recruitment program, aimed at men who'd studied in Orthodox pre-army academies and gone on to serve as army officers. It offered them a three-and-a-half-year course, at the end of which each would receive a BA and a police rank equivalent to being an officer in the military. Part of that time they would spend engaged in religious study—at the Elisha academy in the West Bank. That is, they would prepare for a law-enforcement career at an outpost established in defiance of the law.

Yehonatan Chetboun, chair of the Raananim movement, which was working with the police on the project, explained to *Olam Katan* how he would show young religious Zionists the importance of serving in the police: "I'll invite them for a nighttime patrol with me and the station commander in Lod or Ramleh, so they understand that the central issues facing the Israel Police are the most meaningful national issues." Lod and Ramleh, of course, are Israeli cities where Palestinian citizens of Israel make up a large part of the population. The way to attract army veterans, in Chetboun's explanation, was to show them that police work inside Israel will be a seamless continuation of the ethnic conflict in occupied territory. For the police force, the payoff would be enlisting "people at a very high level," a top police officer said.

The program was beginning small, with thirty-five recruits. It was another barely noticeable change, launched by a state agency to meet immediate practical needs, with little thought about consequences. In one more way, the occupation was coming home.

None of this has happened without resistance. Rather it is part of the cycle of action, reaction, and counterreaction. The attack on civil society is evidence that Israelis, voluntarily organizing, have determinedly tracked and opposed the abuses of power in the occupied territories and within Israel. The attempt to disenfranchise Palestinian citizens testifies to their concerted effort to assert their equality and their identity. In turn, the bids to conduct parliamentary witch hunts have provoked criticism not just from the left, but from some of Likud's veteran politicians.

Yet it has proven impossible to maintain a regime in occupied territories in which Palestinians and Jews live under separate laws, or under no laws at all, without undermining law and democracy within Israel. By acting like a movement rather than a democratic state beyond the Green Line, Israel has become less of a state in its own territory.

Only months after Israel conquered the West Bank, philosopher and dissident Yeshayahu Leibowitz warned that continuing the occupation would "undermine the social structure we have created and cause the corruption of individuals, both Jew and Arab." Leibowitz's warning has proved all too prophetic. One reason for reaching a two-state solution is to bring peace. Another, at least as important, is to begin the work of repairing Israel itself.

VIII.

THE REESTABLISHMENT
OF ISRAEL

I write from an Israel with a divided soul. It is not only defined by its contradictions; it is at risk of being torn apart by them. It is a country with uncertain borders and a government that ignores its own laws. Its democratic ideals, much as they have helped shape its history, are on the verge of being remembered among the false political promises of twentieth-century ideologies.

What will Israel be in five years, or twenty? Will it be the

Second Israeli Republic, a thriving democracy within smaller borders? Or a pariah state where one ethnic group rules over another? Or a territory marked on the map, between the river and the sea, where the state has been replaced by two warring communities? Will it be the hub of the Jewish world, or a place that most Jews abroad prefer not to think about? The answers depend on what Israel does now.

For Israel to establish itself again as a liberal democracy, it must make three changes. First, it must end the settlement enterprise, end the occupation, and find a peaceful way to partition the land between the Jordan and the Mediterranean. Second, it must divorce state and synagogue—freeing the state from clericalism, and religion from the state. Third and most basically, it must graduate from being an ethnic movement to being a democratic state in which all citizens enjoy equality.

Proposing these changes provokes several reflexive objections, inside Israel and beyond. First, many Israeli Jews translate any call for full equality of all citizens as a demand that Israel cease to be a Jewish state. The supposed choice is a false one. Israel can be a liberal democracy and still fulfill the justifiable desire of Jews, as an ethnic national group, for self-determination.

The liberal meaning of self-determination begins with the rights of *individuals*. As Israeli political thinker Chaim Gans argues, it expresses the justifiable desire of members of an ethnic group to maintain a basic aspect of their humanity and personal identity: their culture. To live in their culture and preserve it, they need a place where that culture shapes the public sphere. The natural and most justifiable place for that to happen is their homeland, or part of it.

But in the real world, in contrast to utopias, individual rights clash. The classic metaphor for this is the man crying fire in a crowded theater: dogmatically preserving his right of expression robs others of their right to stay alive. Nation-states can be liberal democracies, but each faces the constant challenge of balancing the right of self-determination and other rights.

Israel does not have to give up being a Jewish state. It does need to establish a very different balance of rights. In a country with a significant Jewish majority, it is reasonable for the usual language of the public sphere to be Hebrew. It is reasonable for offices to close on Jewish holidays, because most people would not show up for work on those days anyway. It is also reasonable for the kitchens in government institutions—such as the army—to be kosher, since this preserves the right of Jews who observe religious dietary laws to participate fully in society. It is not acceptable for the government to favor Jews in the allocation of jobs, land, or school buildings, or for it to prevent Muslim citizens from maintaining a mosque in a mixed Jewish-Arab neighborhood. Nor is it acceptable for the government to condition the rights of non-Jewish citizens on their swearing fealty to this particular balance of rights.

A second objection is that creating and sustaining two states between the river and the sea is no longer possible. Settlements are too large, Israel and the occupied territories too entangled; the tipping point has been passed. All that is possible now is a one-state solution. Especially outside Israel, this practical argument often hides a psychological tendency: even progressives sometimes fight the last battle, especially if it was a heroic fight for which they were born too late. One person, one vote was the answer in South Africa, they say; therefore it is the solution for Israel.

In fact, a one-state arrangement would solve little and make many things worse. Imagine that tomorrow Israel, the West Bank, and the Gaza Strip are reconstituted as the Eastern Mediterranean Republic, and elections are held. With the current population, the parliament will be split almost evenly between Jews and Palestinians. One of the first issues that the parliament and judiciary will face is the settlements that Israel built on privately owned Palestinian property, whether it was requisitioned, stolen, or declared state land over Palestinian objections. Palestinian claimants will demand return of their property. The problem of evacuating settlers won't vanish. Rather, it will divide the new state on communal lines.

Likewise for refugees. Palestinian legislators will demand that Israel's Law of Return be extended to cover Palestinians returning to their homeland. Jewish politicians will oppose the move, which would reduce their community to a threatened minority. Palestinians will demand the return of property lost in 1948 and perhaps the rebuilding of destroyed villages. Except for the drawing of borders, virtually every question that bedevils Israeli-Palestinian peace negotiations will become a domestic problem setting the new political entity aflame.

Issues not at the center of today's diplomacy will also set the two communities at odds. Israel has a postindustrial Western economy; the West Bank and Gaza are underdeveloped. Financing development in majority-Palestinian areas and bringing Palestinians into Israel's social welfare network would require Jews to pay higher taxes or receive fewer services. But the engine of the Israeli economy is high-tech, an entirely portable industry. Both individuals and companies will leave, crippling the new shared economy. Meanwhile, two nationalities who have desperately sought a political frame for cultural and social independence would wrestle over control of language, art, street names, and schools. Psychologically, it would be a country with two resentful minorities and no majority.

Even in the best case, the outcome would be the continued existence of separate Jewish and Palestinian political parties. And even the more liberal-leaning parties of each community would be hard-pressed to bridge the divide to form stable coalitions. Israel would become a second Belgium, perpetually incapable of forming a stable government. In the more likely case, the political tensions would ignite as violence. The transition to a single state would mark a new stage in the conflict. For a harsh example of the potential fluctuation between political stalemate and civil war, Palestinians and Jews need only look northward to Lebanon.

A single state would not be a solution—or even a workable arrangement, which is what politics normally offers in place of solutions. It would be a nightmare: another of the places marked on the globe as a country in which two or more communities do battle while the most educated or well-connected members of each look for refuge elsewhere.

A third objection to a two-state solution, from the Israeli right and its overseas supporters, is that it requires Israel to sacrifice too much for peace. This reflects an old habit of thought in which territory is the coin that Israel reluctantly pays for a peace agreement.

It's true that peace is an essential end in itself. But Israel must also give up land to reestablish itself as a state and a democracy. It needs to put a border back on the map. Within that border, the government needs to rule by the consent of the governed. It needs to restore the rule of law and end the ethnic conflict.

Peace with the Palestinians is a *means* for achieving these goals. It provides the way for Israel to end its grip from outside on the Gaza Strip and leave the West Bank safely. "Hold too much, and you will hold nothing," the Talmud says. If the state of Israel tries to continue holding the West Bank, there will be no state.

Politically, ending the occupation is also the precondition for disestablishing religion and creating equality for the Arab minority. Since 1967, Israeli politics has been clenched around the issue of territory. Once, during Israel's First Republic, "left" and "right" had the same meaning as in Europe. The left was socialist, the right capitalist. After 1967, the meanings shifted. To be on the left meant willingness to give up land; to be on the right meant compulsively keeping it. Building a coalition around other issues has become almost impossible. The conflict with the Palestinians provides legitimacy for excluding Arab-backed parties from coalitions. The right cannot rule without the ultra-Orthodox parties, but neither can the left form coalitions without including the ultra-Orthodox. So a government that would establish civil equality or separate religion and state is unachievable.

The coalition arithmetic merely reflects national habits of thought: as long as Jews and Palestinians are wrestling for control of the same homeland, both Jewish and Arab Israelis have a harder time envisioning a shared civic identity. Meanwhile settlers, and especially religious settlers, assert that they are the most dedicated Zionists, and their claim resonates with much of the Jewish public. In reality, the methods of their Zionism are taken from the pre-state era. The authentic Zionist task of the moment is dismantling the settlement enterprise so that Israel can deal with all the issues it has postponed.

This task is the key to Israel's future. I do not pretend to predict the precise circumstances under which it will take place—whether as a result of international pressure and recognition of a Palestinian state, or in a freely embraced agreement by an Israeli government less blinkered than the one in power as I write, or through some combination of those factors.

But the domestic upheaval will be more easily managed, the risk of violent opposition more easily reduced, if Israel's elected leaders do embrace the goal of bringing settlers home. By doing so, they can present it to the public, correctly, as the next national project that Israel must undertake. They can speak to the settlers themselves—at least the more moderate ones who may be able to hear this message—acknowledge that those who settled in the West Bank believed they were serving their country, and ask them to serve it now by returning to Israel peacefully.

Against the idea of evacuating settlements, two counterproposals are often raised. The first is to allow Jewish settlers to stay put as citizens of a Palestinian state. In principle, this makes sense. For Palestinians to achieve self-determination, their country need not be homogeneously Palestinian, just as Israel need not be homogeneously Jewish. Rather than Israel sending its police and army to evict people, or its Finance Ministry's representatives to negotiate payment for them to move, the government could announce that on a given date, Israel will turn control of land over to Palestine. The settlers can decide whether to stay or return to Israel, as settlers have decided when other empires retreated.

This is theory. In reality, residents of the large settlements closer to the Green Line would have no inclination to live in a Palestinian state. They moved to their subsidized suburbs expecting to remain members of the Jewish majority of Israel and to improve their standard of living. By staying, they would become a minority in a country with one-tenth of the per capita wealth. The sole value of the government declaring that they could remain in their current homes would be to reduce their ability to extort exorbitant compensation for moving.

This may be a worthwhile bargaining tactic—but it cannot be offered to the residents of the small ideological settlements, who might accept it for the worst reasons. Their hope would be to carry out a Rhodesian option—to impose minority rule over the Palestinian majority by force—or at least to destabilize the new state. A treaty that left them in place would be an agreement for chaos, not peace.

The second approach to reducing the number of evacuees is for Israel to annex West Bank areas in which the most heavily populated "settlement blocs" are located, and to compensate the Palestinian state with land within the Green Line. To reduce the extent of the land swap, diplomatic experts have suggested maps for Israeli-Palestinian borders that look like caricatures of gerrymandered American congressional districts. A moderate version appears in the 2003 Geneva Accord, which was negotiated by pro-peace Israelis and Palestinians to provide a blueprint for an official accord. The accord's border map shows narrow tendrils of Israeli territory stretching into the West Bank so that large settlements such as Ma'aleh Adumim can stay in Israeli hands.

Initially, such borders might reduce the cost of moving settlers. Yet Israel would still have to evacuate the settlers most bitterly opposed to leaving—those in the settlements far from the Green Line. After the peace agreement, the suburbs that Israel kept would be isolated, constricted, unable to grow. In any sensible policy, they would no longer receive subsidies. They would wither at the end of their territorial vines. In five years or twenty, their residents would demand government help to move to the old Israel. The state will pay for them twice—first in land, then in compensation to the settlers. The land-swap alternative is really only practical for settlements that actually hug the Green Line and in annexed East Jerusalem, where nearly 200,000 Israelis live in compact neighborhoods close to the old border.

So for Israel to move forward, most settlers must move home. The sane policy is not simply to stop building settlements, but to begin the process of evacuating them immediately, without waiting for a signature on a peace agreement. When an agreement is signed, it should include a transition of several years to permit gradual evacuation of settlers.

The logical first step in evacuation is for the government to conduct the accounting it has avoided for decades—to comb the state budget for incentives for living in settlements, to publish the cumulative cost from 1967 until today so that the public understands what it has paid for is a doomed enterprise, and to end the subsidies. In their place, the government should offer help to settlers ready to move—assistance buying reasonable housing inside Israel, retraining settlers who have made their livelihood in the inflated settlement bureaucracy and education system, counseling to ease adjustment. The explicit policy must be that the financial assistance offered at the outset is the upper limit for what will be offered later: Waiting will be costly, not profitable.

Even in a settlement of believers, there is likely to be one couple that has doubts about the future and would like to leave, though neither husband nor wife would dare say so aloud to their neighbors. Right now, practicalities such as the low market value of their home help keep them where they are. If that family is able to leave, three more may begin to discuss the heretical possibility. This is precisely why settler leaders and allies have opposed past proposals to begin paying compensation to settlers willing to leave.

One incentive, though, should not be on the table: moving a community or part of it en masse to a new location inside Israel. Nor should settlers be encouraged to "Judaize the Galilee" or the Negev, or to move as groups to Israeli cities. Such arrangements might appear to ease the transition by keeping communities together and avoiding the loss of purpose that settlers are likely to feel. But here, too, the costs later will be too high. The point of evacuating settlements is to end the ethnic conflict, not to import it. The settlement ethos does not need to be artificially revived, yet again, inside Israel. It makes as little sense in twenty-first-century Israel as covered wagon trains would make in twenty-first-century America.

In re-created settlements, evacuees are likely to stoke each other's anger and refusal to accept the new reality. It is harder to look forward when everyone around you is looking back with fury. Beyond bureaucratic bungling, this helps explain why evacuees from Gaza have had such a painful readjustment.

The government's goal should be reintegrating settlers into Israeli society. As an added religious benefit, some are likely to leave the "process of redemption" behind them psychologically. Misreading current events for the footsteps of the messiah is much easier when everyone around shares that misreading. Within mainstream Israeli society, it may be easier to accept that the state is merely a state, a political means of achieving practical results, and not a sacred institution whose existence signals history's end. The hallucinatory expectations that have warped Orthodox Zionism may begin to fade.

Peace is a necessary means for fully ending the occupation. Unlike the French in Algeria, Israel cannot simply leave the West Bank to its fate. Unlike Palestinians, Algerian nationalists did not claim France as part of their birthright. A sea separated France from whatever happened in its former colony. For Israel safely to end its military control of the West Bank, it needs a peace accord with a stable—and hopefully, a democratic—Palestinian republic.

And what if the divide between the rival Palestinian political factions, or the instability of the Palestinian government, or the wider volatility of Arab politics, or a simple inability of Israeli and Palestinian negotiators to reach agreement, even with the strongest intentions to do so, prevents peace?

Even in that case, Israel's vital interest is to remove the settlements, reestablish the border, and reduce the occupation to its bare bones, its minimal military skeleton.

Diplomatically, the idea that the settlements are a bargaining chip is an illusion. The settlements do not improve Israel's bargaining position; rather, they destroy Israeli credibility and chain Israel to the occupied territories. If they are not removed, they will grow, and the chains will grow heavier. Meanwhile, the effort to maintain them corrodes the state and brings the one-state nightmare closer to reality. Removing them is a public statement that Israel is eager to give up military control the moment it can.

In the meantime, a military presence in the West Bank is enough of a bargaining chip. Its purpose should be only to prevent attacks on Israel itself, maintain public order, and— if need be—allow international actors to help build or rebuild Palestinian governing institutions.

Even under the best conditions, the last act of the settlement drama is likely to involve Israelis in uniform forcibly evacuating settlers who do not want to go. The numbers may be small, or reach the tens of thousands. At least 65,000 Israelis live in exclusively Orthodox Zionist settlements, where opposition to leaving will be greatest.

Nor can anyone predict the level of resistance. But there is a potential for violence beyond what happened during the Gaza withdrawal. Settlers will be defending the vision—or the illusion—on which they have built their lives for two generations. Were there a withdrawal, outpost settler Cheftziba Skali told me, "Maybe I'll lay down my life, maybe not. I don't know." Yisrael Ariel, a settler at Yitzhar near Nablus and a founder of the Od Yosef Hai yeshivah, told me settlers would not engage in "bloodshed" but would use "any other level" of resistance. This estimation may make him a moderate. Before Yitzhak Rabin's assassination, *hesder* yeshivah dean Nachum Rabinovitch argued that settlers should "plant explosive charges around the whole area" of their settlements to prevent soldiers from evacuating them. Justifying that approach, he said that Israeli troops who carried out orders to evacuate settlers would be "really evil." He added, "We remember that the German soldiers also acted under orders."

Facing this potential for physical opposition, the government must be able to depend on the army to carry out its policy. For that to happen, it must put an end to the existence of units that have ideological profiles, to the creeping development of an officer corps that could obey a radical clergy instead of the government, to the web of ties between the military and the religious right.

As one step in that process, the IDF should immediately begin phasing out the *hesder* yeshivot. It should start by ejecting institutions whose deans have taught soldiers to refuse orders on political grounds. This is not a question of freedom of expression or religion. Those rabbis have the right to oppose ceding land or evacuating settlements. But the *hesder* yeshivot operate as adjuncts of the military, on state funds. The time that soldiers spend in the study hall partially substitutes for time in uniform. It is absurd for army-affiliated institutions to instruct soldiers to place the political agenda of the Whole Land of Israel above orders. The fact that the political agenda is shot through with religious beliefs does not justify the absurdity.

In the longer term, as part of the separation of religion and state, the *hesder* program should be dismantled entirely. Similarly, state funding should end for pre-army academies that are exclusively Orthodox and centered on religious studies. Netzah Yehudah, the *haredi* battalion, should be dissolved. The principle of equality indeed demands that *haredim* serve—but it is trumped by the principle of not permitting the existence of ideological combat units that are beholden to clergy. The army rabbinate should be reconstituted as a chaplaincy corps, whose responsibility is limited to seeing to the religious needs of soldiers. On one hand, the new corps should include clergy for the minority of soldiers who are not Jewish. On the other, uniformed rabbis should not engage in "educating" soldiers about the sacred value of land or of Jewish power—that is, teaching a barely masked political message in the guise of Judaism.

As soon as a policy decision is made to dismantle settlements, career officers and soldiers should be required to move back into Israel. If they prefer to engage in political activism against evacuation, they should be allowed to do so—as civilians. Officers, in particular, must hear a simple message: If you are not willing to lead your troops in the evacuation, you should resign your commission and leave the army honorably, rather than end your career with a court-martial, a loss of rank, and possible imprisonment.

It is true that the army may lose some talented commanders. That cost, however, pales next to the risk of the armed forces dividing along ideological lines. Before a second *Altalena* affair takes place, the lessons of the first must be remembered and reapplied: the country has one army, responsible to the elected government. Again, the history of Lebanon provides a gory warning of the dangers of permitting armed groups linked to political factions. Depoliticizing the army is essential not only in order to carry out the specific mission of removing settlements, but also in order to restore Israeli democracy and ensure the stability of the state.

Once a border is again drawn on the map, Israel can finally complete its long-delayed transition from national liberation movement to liberal nation-state. The competition between Jews and Palestinians for control of the entire land, from river to sea, can be put in the past, where it belongs. Within its smaller and clearly defined territory, Israel will be a country with a four-fifths Jewish majority and a Palestinian minority that must enjoy equal citizenship.

Naturally, there will be no agreement among Jews about what it means to be Jewish or to live in a country where the public sphere is overwhelmingly Jewish. This, perhaps, is the best definition of a Jewish state: the place where Jews can argue with the least inhibition, in the most public way, about what it means to be Jews.

To this argument, I offer a simple definition of what will

make the country Jewish in its values, and not just in its ethnic makeup. The most basic Jewish memory is that "we were strangers," we were the minority and were badly done by. In secular terms, this memory derives from long historical experience. Religiously, it is recorded in Judaism's founding text. The most basic Jewish aspiration should be to do better as a majority when we have the opportunity. If Israel did not have a non-Jewish minority, it would almost be necessary to import one in order to fulfill this aspiration.

Since, fortunately, the minority is already here, all forms of discrimination against it should be ended. In some realms, affirmative action is needed to make up for past injustices. The nation as a whole desperately needs massive investment in education, but a disproportionate amount must go to Arab-language schools to compensate for years of neglect. Universities should actively seek to recruit Arab students; the civil service must enlist Arab staff and actively seek to advance them in the hierarchy.

Israel's system of state ownership of land is eminently sensible if used to prevent concentration of property in a few private hands. But state land must be equally available to all citizens. Admissions committees and other techniques of housing discrimination against Arabs should be assigned to history books. The land still owned by the Jewish National Fund must really be nationalized—that is, turned over to government ownership. JNF representatives should not sit on the boards of the government bodies controlling land.

This is just part of the necessary divorce between the state and the anachronistic "national institutions"—the JNF, the Jewish Agency, and the World Zionist Organization. If Diaspora Jews want to support Israel philanthropically through a single, United Way–type organization, it should be entirely independent of the government.

Civil equality does not mean that cultural differences and ethnic identity will vanish. The government needs to encourage a shared civic identity while respecting the differences. Parents must have a choice of schools in which the main language of instruction is Hebrew or Arabic. In both sets of schools, the other language should be taught from the lowest grades, with the aim of fluency by the end of high school.

The fear sometimes expressed today on the religious right that familiarity with Arab culture will produce "assimilation" is one of many signs that the right has yet to free itself of Diaspora anxieties and accept that Jews have their own country. Assimilation is a legitimate concern of minorities, not of a majority. Besides, religious Jews will gain something of particular value to them from learning Arabic. Much of Judaism's classical literature was produced by Jewish scholars living in the Islamic world and was written originally in Arabic or in Hebrew shaped by Arabic. The language is a key to fully unlocking the treasures of that era of Jewish-Islamic coexistence.

At the same time, the state must avoid locking citizens into ethnic categories. It's likely that some Arab politicians will demand autonomous institutions for their community as part of the system of government. That demand serves those politicians better than their constituents, and should be resisted. It makes ethnic identity a legal and political fact rather than something a person can freely define for himself or herself—a freedom that is particularly vital for members of a minority. While Arab citizens should be free to create representative organizations, those bodies should be voluntary.

One realm in which neither Jewish nor Arab citizens will want instant integration is the military. The pain and fear produced by a conflict do not vanish the day after signing a treaty. Nor, given the Middle East's instability, will the risk disappear of conflict erupting again with an Arab state. Israel's Palestinian citizens overwhelmingly regard the IDF as a Jewish army that fights Arabs and would feel deeply uncomfortable serving in it. And as Chaim Gans writes, a basic justification for Jews to have an independent state is to provide themselves a safe refuge—not just for their culture, but also for their physical existence. Given "that the Jews are a minority in the region," Gans writes, they "must rely on their strength." They justifiably see the IDF not just as protecting the state, but also as protecting Jews from destruction.

For the foreseeable future, therefore, it is reasonable for Arabs to be exempt from the draft, and for the army to remain under Jewish hegemony. Equal service may eventually be a result of building a shared identity as Israelis. It cannot be a precondition for equality. Whether young Arabs should be required to perform a civilian form of national service depends on whether Jews are required to do the same if they are not drafted. What does need to change—and almost certainly will if peace breaks out—is the attitude of equating military service with being a real Israeli, or being a real Jew in Israel.

Removing the settlements and reestablishing Israel's borders will put to rest the question that until now has left little space for a normal political agenda. Parties will have to take clear stands on the free-market policies that have put much of the country's wealth in the hands of a few families, on funding for schools and health care, on gender issues, and more—or become irrelevant.

The realignment is likely to make new alliances possible, weakening the clerical parties and allowing for long-delayed reforms. A full bill of rights can finally be enacted, and the Supreme Court's power of judicial review can be anchored in a basic law, meaning that it will have constitutional status. The divorce of state and synagogue can finally begin.

The purpose of this divorce is not only to protect the rights of secular Israelis. It is also to free religious Israelis from a clerical bureaucracy. Nothing does more to alienate Jews from Judaism in Israel than the various reminders of state "support" for religion—the experience of marriage and divorce through the rabbinate, the jingoistic pronouncements of some deans of state-funded yeshivot, the ever-rising cost of underwriting *haredi* society. "There is no greater degradation of religion than maintenance of its institutions by secular state," Yeshayahu Leibowitz wrote in 1959, and again his words proved prophetic.

A comparison with America is necessary here. Constitutionally, the United States is the most secular country in the West. Yet as a society, America is strikingly religious. Nearly two-thirds of Americans report that religion is important in their lives, compared to a median of 38 percent in developed countries. This is not a contradiction. As sociologist of American religion Brenda Brasher argues, the United States is the most religious country in the West precisely because of its sharp separation of church and state: since religious institutions must survive by attracting people to come through their doors, the United States has become a hothouse of religious innovation and variety. In Israel, once the state ceases to fund and sanction specific varieties of religion, Judaism is likely to flourish, invite wider interest, and take new forms.

As Leibowitz wrote half a century ago, religious communities should fund their own needs, starting with paying their clergy. Having taxpayers pay rabbis creates justifiable resentment among the nonreligious. It also creates a bloated class of clergy with little connection to the communities they supposedly serve. The residents of my Jerusalem neighborhood, for instance, range from secular to modern Orthodox; the salaried rabbi of the neighborhood is ultra-Orthodox. If all I knew of Judaism were his sermons, I'd give up faith.

This does not mean Israel can or should follow the American model exactly. In the United States, clergy are empowered by the government to perform marriages. Israel, with its history of the state deciding who qualifies as a rabbi, is better off making a clean break: marriage for legal purposes should be purely a civil procedure. Couples wanting a religious ceremony can turn to the person of their choice to perform the ceremony. If they need a religious divorce, they can take their choice of rabbis offering that service.

In education, on the other hand, the separation should be less sharp. Israel's ethnic and religious divisions, along with the centrality of religious study in the practice of Judaism, make the American model of a single state-supported school system unworkable. It will be a difficult enough social revolution for the state to require a shared core curriculum in all schools. The government should fund that curriculum, and only that curriculum, in every school. It should allow parents to establish schools with additional hours of religious studies, for which they will pay. This balances respect for cultural diversity, the need to get government out of the religion business, and the need to teach a shared foundation for identity.

The core curriculum must include the subjects that children will one day need to earn their livings in a postindustrial economy—and the history, civics, literature, and arts that will help them understand other members of their society and become thinking participants in democratic debate.

Those changes will prepare the next generation of *haredim* to support themselves. In the meantime, though, the government needs to phase out financial support for lifetime study by ultra-Orthodox men. This will be a slow and much-resisted transition, possible only if the state builds the bridge from the society of scholars to the society of work: it will need to give men the vocational training or higher education they need to get jobs, and pay them stipends to support their families while they study. It will have to provide job counseling, help establish small businesses, and launch a campaign to encourage employers to hire *haredim*. As long as Israel has a universal draft, a solution will be needed for service by the ultra-Orthodox, but it cannot be based on separate combat units. *Haredi* men will either have to serve in the military together with other Israelis or be required to perform civilian service.

For the country as a whole, the costs of this transition are an investment in economic growth. For the *haredim* themselves, the change will mean an end to the danger that one's children might live in subterranean storerooms in parking garages. It also promises an end to the corrupting hypocrisy of living on forced contributions from people who do not share your values. A productive *haredi* community can, if it chooses, underwrite a year or two of full-time religious study for young men and advanced study for the intellectual elite. Bitterly as ultra-Orthodox politicians and rabbis may denounce these changes, the *haredi* community will be far healthier as a result.

One area in which the state can and should continue to distinguish between Jew and non-Jew is immigration. For that reason, it is also an area in which a complete separation of state and religion will be difficult. There are no perfect solutions to this problem, but there is plenty of room for improvement over the current situation.

At independence, as I've said, the Zionist movement had implemented most of its goals and had made itself obsolete. The Jews had political independence in their historical homeland. The justifications for independence were providing a refuge from persecution for Jews, and creating a space where Jews could express their culture most fully. For those justifications to hold true, Israel had to make it possible for Jews to immigrate freely. In every other respect, the state's responsibility was toward its citizens, irrespective of ethnic identity. In immigration policy, it had a particular obligation to Jews.

That remains true, but conditions have changed drastically since 1948. The Jewish population of Israel has increased tenfold. Most other Jews in the world live in democratic Western countries. At the moment, refuge from anti-Semitism is a very marginal reason for people to immigrate to Israel, though that could change as a result of an unexpected crisis somewhere in the world. Israel still has an obligation to allow immigration of Jews who simply want to live in a country where Jews are the majority. Meanwhile, something has happened beyond the imagination of the state's founders: Israel has become safe enough and prosperous enough to attract refugees and economic immigrants who are not Jewish. Refugees from Darfur cross the Sinai from Egypt to find a haven in Israel; people from the Philippines who come on work visas to take care of elderly Israelis stay on.

Almost as unimaginable to many present-day Israelis who still think of "assimilation" as referring to Jews adopting non-Jewish culture, those non-Jewish immigrants assimilate into Israeli Jewish society. Their children grow up speaking Hebrew and go to schools where they learn Jewish history. Israel desperately needs an immigration policy that includes Jewish repatriation but is wider than that.

I do not pretend to have a full policy in mind. I do believe that Jewish history and basic humanity require giving preference to the Darfuri refugee over economic immigrants. On a wall at Yad Vashem, the Holocaust museum in Jerusalem, appears a quotation from an Australian official that demonstrates the world's indifference to Jewish refugees on the eve of the genocide: "Australia cannot do more. . . . As we have no racial problem, we are not desirous of importing one." Jewish memory demands that we do not repeat such callousness.

As for Jewish repatriation, it requires giving priority to

two overlapping groups of people: Jews and people perse-cuted as Jews. In the latter group, someone with one paternal Jewish grandparent and no particular sense of being Jewish might conceivably face discrimination or even death threats because of her neighbors' racial anti-Semitism somewhere in the world. She should be allowed entry even at a lower level of danger than normally necessary to qualify for asylum. If the same person wants to move from Azerbaijan to Israel only to improve her standard of living, she should get in line with the other economic immigrants. This distinction re-quires amending the Law of Return, which in its current form grants automatic entry to anyone with one Jewish grandparent.

The more difficult problem is who qualifies as a Jew. This is where the state cannot avoid religious issues. Most secular Jews retain a sense that "Jewish" implies religious as well as ethnic identity. Most religious Jews still think of Jew as a tribe, not just a faith community.

A classic Israeli Supreme Court case demonstrates the complexity. In 1962, a Catholic monk known as Brother Daniel—or by his given name, Oswald Rufeisen—de-manded to be recognized under the Law of Return. Rufeisen had been born as a Jew in Poland. During the Holocaust, he was hidden in a convent, began reading the New Testament, converted to Catholicism, and eventually became a monk. He later came to Israel and sought citizenship as a Jew. Un-der religious law, *halakhah*, he had a case: in *halakhah*, some-one born a Jew always remains a member of the tribe; accepting another faith is a sin, but it doesn't cancel one's Jewishness.

The court, however, ruled that the Law of Return was civil law, and that the word *Jew* in it had to be understood in its everyday meaning as used by Israelis (by which the justices clearly meant Hebrew-speaking Israelis, which is to say, Jews). And even for the most secular, postreligious Israeli, someone who actively converted to another religion ceased being a Jew. Therefore, Brother Daniel was not a Jew. Note the ironies: The court rejected religious law. It insisted on a civil definition. Yet the civil definition of Jewish ethnicity contained a religious element.

Similarly, the everyday meaning of *Jew* in Hebrew includes converts to Judaism as Jews, adopted members of the ethnic group. That certainly does not mean the Israeli on the street accepts the current state rabbinate as the arbiter of valid conversion—or that the Israeli on the street has carefully formulated for himself or herself what conversion entails. The common denominator of imprecise answers would probably include giving up one's previous faith, practicing Judaism in some way, and—if living outside Israel—belonging to some kind of Jewish community. Conversion cannot be something undergone purely to immigrate to Israel for economic reasons. An immigration policy must include a more precise definition, and not leave the matter to the discretion of suspicious government clerks, and certainly not to state-salaried clerics. That definition will include religious elements, meaning that the state will have to occasionally make decisions about religious identity. This is messy, contradictory, and unavoidable, and should be the maximum extent of government involvement in religion.

If a non-Jewish Israeli citizen decides to convert to Judaism, on the other hand, there is no reason it should concern the government. More widely, the distinction between Jew and non-Jew may be a factor in immigration policy, but from the moment someone receives an immigrant visa, the distinction should no longer matter. There should be one process of naturalization, applying equally to Jews, to economic immigrants, and to non-Israeli spouses of citizens, including the Nablus-born husband of an Arab citizen of Israel.

What of Palestinian return? The logic of a two-state arrangement is that Jews express self-determination in the Jewish state and have the right of repatriation to it; likewise, ethnic Palestinians must have the right of repatriation to the new Palestinian state—not to Israel.

This does not erase the need for Israel to recognize—for the sake of justice and of reconciliation—that its creation was a disaster for the Palestinians. Israeli actions were a major reason for that disaster, even if it occurred during a war imposed on Israel. As part of a peace agreement, Israel may well agree to the symbolic return of a small number of the descendants of refugees. More important, it should help in the resettlement of Palestinians within their new state. But translating the Palestinian right of return into a prerogative for millions of Palestinians to return to the pre-1948 homes of their families would create the same disastrous consequences that I have described for a one-state "solution." It would also displace millions of present-day Jews who had no role in the events of the Nakba.

A last point about repatriation: Israel should accept Jewish immigrants, but the national project of seeking out immigrants is another example of continuing to pursue outdated goals and values. The early Zionist belief in "negating the Diaspora" has passed its expiration date. The Diaspora is not disappearing, Israel is not underpopulated, and demographic anxiety about preserving a Jewish majority should fade away after Israel's borders are restored.

This is just part of an overdue rethinking of Israel's relation with the Diaspora, especially with American Jewry. In the past, many American Jews thought of Israel as a replacement for the lost Jewish "old country" of Eastern Europe—and therefore imagined it as a country-sized shtetl, impoverished and about to be overcome by Islamic Cossacks. The image has served Jewish fund-raisers and hawkish Israeli politicians seeking Diaspora support, but it is profoundly ahistorical. It ignores Israel's transformation into a developed country, its military strength, and its opportunities for peacemaking—some of which have been seized, and some squandered.

A realistic and fruitful relationship between Israel and Diaspora Jewry should not be based on fear of physical destruction. What Israel, especially a reestablished Israel, offers the Diaspora is a place where the public arena is largely Jewish: where the language of newspapers, of edgy experimental novels, and of nightclubs is Hebrew; where everyone gets off work for Jewish holidays and one does not feel out of place celebrating them; where the standards of physical beauty are shaped by how Jews look; where "assimilation" properly refers to Ghanaian immigrants holding their church services on Saturday; and where the question of whether being Jewish has anything to do with religion is a natural part of the national debate.

What Diaspora Jews should give Israel—now, immediately, without waiting—is a reminder that we were strangers in Egypt, in Russia and Germany, even in America. They can remind Israelis of the urgency that the minority experience gives to liberal values. They can support organizations in Israel, as they do in the Diaspora, that advocate human rights and the separation of religion and state. They can help fund institutions that teach Judaism as it deserves to be taught, as a faith that deepens respect for every human being. Instead of pretending that Israel is the country they want it to be, or giving up on it because it is not, they can help make it that country.

The greatest responsibility, though, naturally falls on Israelis, on us who live here.

History is not an inevitable process, of redemption or of decay. It is not written in advance. In fact, even the past is constantly being rewritten. The choices that Israel makes now will determine whether its beginnings are remembered as the birth of a failed state or of a successful democracy.

The changes I've described—ending the occupation, guaranteeing full equality, separating state and synagogue—require a much smaller revolution than did the establishment of the country. They are not only possible, but also essential to Israel's future.

We can allow Israel to continue unmaking itself, or we can choose to remake it.

ACKNOWLEDGMENTS

Writing this book has been a journey with many guides.

At the start of my search for sources, I was fortunate to benefit from the suggestions of Menachem Friedman, Yehudah Mirsky, Kimmy Caplan, Nahum Karlinsky, Avi Raz, Avi Bareli, Paul Scham, and Shlomo Fischer, all of whom were generous with their time and expertise. Dror Etkes shared his wide knowledge and documentation of the settlement enterprise, along with his encouragement and unflagging energy. Hagit Ofran of Peace Now's Settlement Watch team and Nir Shalev of Bimkom likewise provided vital background on settlements, planning procedure, and land law. Attorneys Michael Sfard and Shlomy Zecharia not only gave me vital background on the complex legal situation in the West Bank but also access to the documentary record of key litigation. Busayna Dabit of the New Israel Fund–Shatil Mixed Cities Project provided background and access to activists in Akko and Jaffa.

Shira Robinson was kind enough to share her dissertation on the Israeli military government in the first years of the state. Miriam Billig helped me with her research articles on settlement, and Jonathan Fine gave me added insights on his doctoral research on the transition from British rule to an independent state in 1948.

I am grateful to David Kretzmer and Theodor Meron for their incisive explanations of international humanitarian law. Yaron Ezrahi, as always, set me off in new directions with his insights into Israeli politics and culture. Ze'ev Bauer, Stuart Cohen, Louise Fischer, Daniel Gottlieb, Lev Grinberg, Yehudit Karp, Menachem Klein, Ronald Krebs, Yagil Levy, Michael Melchior, Arye Naor, Moshe Negbi, Gretchen Peters, Yosseph Shilhav, Shlomo Tikochinski, Avigail Yinon, and other scholars gave of their time and knowledge. A. Rashied Omar, Mustafa Abu Sway, and David Cook were quick to assist me with their knowledge of Islamic texts. Naturally, I am solely responsible for how I chose to interpret the ideas and information that have been shared with me so generously.

Documentary evidence is the bedrock of historical research. My access to previously classified papers on settlement in the occupied territories from the Israel Defense Forces Archive was the result of a suit before the High Court of Justice, in which I was represented by attorney Avner Pinchuk of the Association for Civil Rights in Israel. Avner's unstinting work on the case lasted nearly six years. I am deeply appreciative of his dedication and of ACRI's support.

I am also grateful for the assistance of the staff at the Israel State Archives, the Knesset Archives, the Menachem

Begin Heritage Center Archives, the Israel Defense Forces' memorial library for fallen soldiers, the Registrar of Non-profit Organizations (Rasham Ha'amutot), and the Hebrew University Law Library. In my research for this book and previous projects I have benefited from the collections in the archives in a number of settlements, including Neveh Tzuf, Ofrah, Kfar Etzion, and Merom Golan. Einat Hurvitz of the Israel Religious Action Center gave me access to legal correspondence regarding the funding of the Od Yosef Hai yeshivah, and Matti Friedman shared the documents he uncovered in his investigation of land claims at Migron. Peter Demant's collection of early Gush Emunim documents continued to yield fascinating information. My research assistant, Anna Reznikovski, was invaluable in sorting through published sources of information.

To add to the written material, I interviewed people who have been involved in the events described in this book and experts who have followed those events closely. I have also used interviews conducted over many years of reporting. In a few cases, there are reasons to withhold interviewees' names; otherwise, they are listed in the bibliography. I am thankful to all who shared their time with me.

Sharon Ashley and Ronnie Hope, my former colleagues at the *Jerusalem Report*, read the manuscript as I wrote, and their comments reminded me of what a pleasure it was to work with them. Sometimes I was sensible enough to take their suggestions.

I am thankful to my agent, Lisa Bankoff, and to my editor, Tim Duggan, at HarperCollins, whose support has been essential.

Most important, this book would not have been possible without the enormous patience of my children, Yehonatan, Yasmin, and Shir-Raz—and most of all, without the help, encouragement, wisdom, and love of my wife, Myra Noveck.

—*Jerusalem, January 2011*

NOTES

Abbreviations

Acc	Accessed
Admoni ms.	Admoni, Yehiel, "Asor Shel Shikul Da'at: Hahityashvut Me'ever Lekav Hayarok, 1967–1977," author's manuscript. Listed by year and page.
BCA	Menachem Begin Heritage Center Archives
CA	Civil Appeals
DC	Demant Collection—early Gush Emunim documents collected by Peter Robert Demant
DK	*Divrei Haknesset* (Knesset Record)
Doc.	Document
Diss.	Dissertation
HCJ	High Court of Justice
IDFA	Israel Defense Forces Archive
ISA	Israel State Archive
KMA	Hakibbutz Hame'uhad Archive
LPS	Labor Party Secretariat
MGA	Merom Golan Archive
MER	*Middle East Record*
NARA	National Archives and Records Administration
NTA	Neveh Tzuf Archive
OA	Ofrah Archive
PS	Protected source, material provided on condition of anonymity
RNPO	Registrar of Nonprofit Organizations, Israel
YAOH	Yigal Allon Oral History. Listed by interview and page number
YLE	Yad Levi Eshkol
YTA	Yad Tabenkin Archive

Israeli press coverage listed by newspaper and date, with further details on articles of particular significance. Headlines are normally in the original language, except for items I received in translation. Article and book titles are in the original language, with English translations when provided by the publisher. Hebrew publishers often do not provide place of publication. Where the publisher gave only the Hebrew date, the civil date is in brackets.

I. The Road to Elisha

2 **mockery of the rule of law:** Talia Sasson, *Havat Da'at (Beina'im) Benose Ma'ahazim Bilti Murshim* (Opinion Concerning Unauthorized Outposts) (Jerusalem: 2005). Details on Elisha are in appendix 1:22. Slightly different numbers of outposts have been reported elsewhere, as a function of how the particular writer defines what constitutes an outpost and when the outpost effort began.

3 **"as all the others combined":** Ya'akov Halevi Filber, *Ayelet Hashahar* (Jerusalem: Haskel, 5728 [1967–68]): 33.

3 **"part of the redemption of Israel":** Yitzhak Nissim, interview.

4 **page of premilitary academies:** "Mekhinot Kdam Tzvai'ot," www.aka.idf.il/giyus/general/?CatID=23072&DocID=25015, acc. 21 Sept. 2010.

4 **third or more of its budget:** RNPO, financial reports of Mekhinah Toranit Kdam Tzvait Elisha. In the years 2003–2007, the ministry's share of the academy's budget varied between 33 and 64 percent.

4 **and in its officer corps:** B., "Mekomam Shel Hovshei Hakipot Bapikud Hatakti Shel Tzahal," *Ma'arakhot* 432 (2010): 50–57.

4 **"all the rabbis say not to":** Interview, Elisha student, name withheld.

5 **"maintaining a democratic façade":** Oren Yiftachel, *Ethnocracy: Land and Identity Politics in Israel/Palestine* (Philadelphia: University of Pennsylvania Press, 2006): 3.

6 **Jews eighteen to one in Palestine:** Benny Morris, *1948: The First Arab-Israeli War* (New Haven, Conn.: Yale University Press, 2008): 2.

7 **"an act of aggression":** Arab Higher Committee Delegation communication of 6 Feb. 1948, quoted in United Nations Palestine Commission, *First Special Report to the Security Council*, 16 Feb. 1948, unispal.un.org/UNISPAL.NSF/5ba47a5c6cef541b802563e000493b8c/fd f734eb76c39d6385256c4c004cdba7, acc. 26 Sept. 2010.

7 **both descriptions are true:** On the construction of the contrasting Israeli and Palestinian narratives, see Ahmad H. Sa'di and Lila Abu-Lughod, eds., *Nakba: Palestine, 1948, and the Claims of Memory* (New York: Columbia University Press, 2007); and Benny Morris, ed., *Making Israel* (Ann Arbor: University of Michigan Press, 2007).

7 **"irrespective of religion, race or sex":** "The Declaration of the Establishment of the State of Israel," 14 May 1948, www.mfa.gov.il/MFA

Peace+Process/Guide+to+the+Peace+Process/Declaration+of+Establish
ment+of+State+of+Israel.htm, acc. 26 Sept. 2010.

8   **the Accidental Empire:** Gershom Gorenberg, *The Accidental Empire:
Israel and the Birth of the Settlements, 1967–1977* (New York: Times
Books, 2006).

9   **from 116,000 to 300,000:** Dror Etkes, "Gidul Ha'ukhlusiah Hayehudit
Bagadah Hama'aravit Uretzu'at Azzah," March 11, 2003, summary of
Central Bureau of Statistics figures; Central Bureau of Statistics, "Population of Localities 30.06.2010 (Provisional Data)," www.cbs.gov.il/pop
ulation/new_2010/table1.pdf, acc. 22 Nov. 2010.

9   **are now in ultra-Orthodox schools:** Dan Ben-David, ed., *State of the
Nation Report—Society, Economy and Policy 2009* (Jerusalem: Taub
Center for Social Policy Studies in Israel, 2009), 160, taubcenter.org.il/
tauborgilwp/wp-content/uploads/E2009_Report_Education_System_
Domestic_Perspective_Chapter.pdf, acc. 27 Sept. 2010.

11 **"treat humans as humans":** Avishai Margalit, *On Compromise and Rotten
Compromises* (Princeton, N.J.: Princeton University Press, 2010): 54–61.

11 **genesis have grown harsher:** See Gershom Gorenberg, "The War to
Begin All Wars," *New York Review of Books*, 28 May 2009.

12 **"sustained an entire world":** Mishnah, Sanhedrin 4:5, text according to
the Parma and Budapest manuscripts, via jnul.huji.ac.il/dl/talmud/
mishna/selectmi.asp, acc. 23 Dec. 2010.

12 **to "pursue justice":** See Deuteronomy 16:18–20.

13 **"its institutions by a secular state":** Yeshayahu Leibowitz, *Judaism, Human Values and the Jewish State* (Cambridge, Mass.: Harvard University
Press, 1992): 176.

13 **to soil or to human institutions:** Leibowitz 218, 225–27.

II. *Remember the* Altalena

15 **"We shall act decisively":** ISA 7312/27-Alef, Yisrael Galili to David
Ben-Gurion. The note is dated 0800 20.6 (20 June 1948), but the events
described match the following morning. See Uri Brenner, *Altalena: Me-
ḥḳar Medini Utzva'i* (Altalena: A Political and Military Study) (Tel Aviv:
Hakibbutz Hame'uhad, 1978): 134ff.; ISA Provisional Government
minutes, 20 June 1948: 51–58.

16 **"legitimate use of force":** Max Weber, "Politics as a Vocation," in *Essays
in Sociology*, trans. Hans H. Gerth and C. Wright Mills (New York:
Oxford University Press, 1946), via www.ne.jp/asahi/moriyuki/abu
kuma/weber/lecture/politics_vocation.htm, acc. 31 Jan. 2010.

16 **Hundreds of Irgun members:** Brenner, *Altalena* 124, estimates that
there were 500 to 600 Irgun members and supporters on the beach, but
cites Irgun chief operations officer Amichai Faglin as suggesting there
may have been thousands.

17   **present-day kingdom of Jordan:** Arye Naor, *Eretz Yisrael Hashlemah: Emunah Umdiniut* (Greater Israel: Theology and Policy) (Haifa: University of Haifa/Zmora-Bitan, 2001): 71–86.

17   **by the vote or the gun:** Yonathan Shapira, *Leshilton Behartanu: Darkah Shel Tnu'at Haherut—Hesber Sotziologi-Politi* (Chosen to Command: The Road to Power of the Herut Party—A Socio-Political Interpretation] (Tel Aviv: Am Oved, 1989): 9–10.

17   **with Nazi Germany against Britain:** Morris, *1948*, 29. On the world stage, Lehi was also the last organization to identify itself as "terrorist." David C. Rapoport, "The Four Waves of Rebel Terror and September 11," *Anthropoetics* 8.1 (Spring/Summer 2002).

17   **rejected the U.N. partition plan:** Naor, *Eretz Yisrael Hashlemah* 93.

18   **arms-buying efforts also failed:** Shlomo Nakdimon, *Altalena* (Jerusalem: Edanim, 1978): 54–57; Brenner, *Altalena* 34, 66.

18   **the accord said:** ISA 7312/27-Alef, Galili to Ben-Gurion, 20 June 1948; Brenner, *Altalena* 44–48; Nakdimon, *Altalena* 114–15; Peter Medding, *The Founding of Israeli Democracy, 1948–1967* (New York: Oxford University Press, 1990): 19–20; David Ben-Gurion, *Medinat Yisrael Hamehudeshet* (Tel Aviv: Am Oved, 1969): 145–46.

18   **en route from Marseilles:** ISA 7312/27-Alef, Galili to Ben-Gurion, 20 June 1948.

19   **arms smuggling in the past:** Brenner, *Altalena* 105–11; Nakdimon, *Altalena* 158–71, 464; ISA 7312/27-Alef, Galili to Ben-Gurion.

19   **"a relation of equals":** ISA 7312/27-Alef, Galili to Ben-Gurion; ISA Provisional Government minutes, 22 June 1948, 3–4.

20   **"what they will do tomorrow":** ISA Provisional Government minutes, 20 June 1948, 51–58.

20   **next morning and afternoon:** ISA 7312/27-Alef, Galili to Ben-Gurion, 21 June 1948, 8:00 a.m.; Brenner, *Altalena* 123–28, 134–36; Nakdimon, *Altalena* 202. Galili wrote the ultimatum; Dan Evan, commander of the Alexandroni Brigade, signed it.

20   **join the forces on the beach:** Brenner, *Altalena* 146. Cf. ISA Provisional Government minutes, 20 June 1948, 54.

20   **former Lehi men:** Brenner, *Altalena* 149–51, 160–61; cf. ISA 7312/27-Alef, Galili to Ben-Gurion, 21 June 1948, afternoon.

21   **into men running for cover:** Nakdimon, *Altalena* 229–30; Brenner, *Altalena* 163–64.

21   **panic, not casualties:** Brenner, *Altalena* 165–66, 170–71.

21   **the climactic act of Irgun defiance:** On the significance of moving the confrontation to Tel Aviv, see Natan Yanai, *Mashberim Politi'im Biyisrael: Tekufat Ben-Gurion* (Jerusalem: Keter, 1982): 33–34.

21   **Home Guard:** Hebrew: *Heyl mishmar*.

21   **the Ritz Hotel:** Brenner, *Altalena* 199–202.

22   **"proletarian hegemony in Zionism":** Yanai, *Mashberim Politi'im Biyis-*

rael 39–40; Anita Shapira, *Yigal Allon: Aviv Heldo* (Igal Allon: Spring of His Life) (Tel Aviv: Hasifriah Hahadashah, 2004): 220.

22 **began jumping overboard:** Brenner, *Altalena*, 216–30; Shapira, *Yigal Allon* 344–47.

23 **not to use their weapons:** *Hamashkif*, 24 June 1948: 1. Death toll: Brenner, *Altalena* 240.

23 **final ultimatum to disband:** Medding, *Founding of Israeli Democracy* 22; Ben-Gurion, *Medinat Yisrael*, 285.

23 **the extremely reluctant willingness:** Ilana Tsur, dir., *Altalena* (1994).

23 **Ben-Gurion dissolved the Palmah:** Yoav Gelber, *Lamah Perku Et Ha-palmah* (Tel Aviv: Schocken, 1986); Yanai, *Mashberim Politi'im Biyisrael* 38–46.

23 **to serve in separate units:** Ze'ev Drori, *Bein Emunah Letzava: Gedud Hanahal Haharedi—Sikkuim Vesikkunim* (Between Faith and Military Service: The Haredi Nahal Battalion) (Jerusalem: Floersheimer Institute for Policy Studies, 2005): 12.

25 **"precious beyond all value":** *Hamashkif*, 24 June 1948: 1.

25 **responsible for killing Jews:** Shapira, *Yigal Allon* 348–49. Hewing to the Irgun narrative, Benjamin Netanyahu has described the *Altalena* affair as a "dramatic exception to the absence of Jewish political murder." Benjamin Netanyahu, *A Place Among the Nations: Israel and the World* (New York: Bantam, 1993): 444, note 29.

25 **possess military power:** Yanai, *Mashberim Politi'im Biyisrael* 25.

26 **sufficient condition for democracy:** See Lev Luis Grinberg, *Politics and Violence in Israel/Palestine: Democracy Versus Military Rule* (New York: Routledge, 2010): 15. Against Von Clausewitz and others, Grinberg asserts that violence is not a continuation of politics, but its opposite.

26 **The Greek Civil War:** Tony Judt, *Postwar: A History of Europe since 1945* (London: William Heinemann, 2005): 32–35.

26 **"within a given territory":** Weber, "Politics."

26 **who is being governed:** Grinberg, *Politics and Violence* 1.

27 **deference to Britain's Arab allies:** Arab Higher Committee Delegation communication of 6 Feb. 1948, quoted in United Nations Palestine Commission, *First Special Report*; Morris, *1948* 65–74.

27 **responsibility for Arab ones:** ISA 2196/14-Gimel, doc. 8B, Report on Activities of the Nahariyah District Administration.

28 **West Bank of the Jordan River:** Zeev Tsur, *Mipulmus Hahalukah Ad Tokhnit Allon* (From the Partition Dispute to the Allon Plan) (Ramat Efal, Israel: Tabenkin Institute, 1982): 73–74; Shapira, *Yigal Allon* 444–48; YAOH, 7:10.

28 **"armed prophet of the Whole Land":** Haim Gouri, interview.

28 **The motion failed:** Yoel Marcus, "Boker Tov, Ehud," *Haaretz*, 5 Dec. 2003, www.haaretz.co.il/hasite/spages/368874.html, acc. 9 Oct. 2010.

29   **by voting no confidence:** Hok Hama'avar, 1949; Medding, *Founding of Israeli Democracy* 32–34.

30   **the case ever since:** "Haknesset Harishonah," www.knesset.gov.il/his tory/heb/heb_hist1_s.htm, acc. 10 Oct. 2010.

30   **a low-priced political bargain:** Medding, *Founding of Israeli Democracy* 44–53, 82–84; Tom Segev, *1949: The First Israelis* (New York: Metropolitan, 1998): 282; Shapira, *Yigal Allon* 464.

31   **all power in Mapai's hands:** "The prime minister wants to eliminate the influence of parties in the army, leaving [only] the influence of his own party." Menachem Begin, DK, 7 Feb. 1950: 738; Medding, *Founding of Israeli Democracy* 47, 134ff.; Lev Luis Grinberg, *Hahistadrut Me'al Lakol* (The Histadrut above All) (Jerusalem: Nevo, 1993): 94.

31   **fulfillment of Jewish history:** Eliezer Don Yehiya, *Mashber Utmurah Bemedinah Hadashah: Hinukh, Dat Upolitikah Bama'avak Al Ha'aliyah Hagdolah* (Crisis and Change in a New State: Education, Religion and Politics in the Struggle over the Absorption of Mass Immigration in Israel) (Jerusalem: Yad Ben-Zvi, 2008): 57.

31   **four party-run systems:** Hok Limmud Hovah, 1949.

31   **after the first ones:** A full description of the education crisis is given in Don Yehiya, *Mashber Utmurah.*

32   **Kol Ha'am (Voice of the People):** This discussion of *Kol Ha'am* is based on HCF 53/73, 53/87; Pnina Lahav, *Judgment in Jerusalem: Chief Justice Simon Agranat and the Zionist Century* (Berkeley: University of California Press, 1997): 107–12; David Kretzmer, *The Occupation of Justice: The Supreme Court of Israel and the Occupied Territories* (Albany: SUNY Press, 2002); Moshe Negbi, interview.

35   **founded after 1945:** Medding, *Founding of Israeli Democracy* 3–4.

35   **Sharon did suggest a coup:** Amir Oren, "Mehkar Betzahal: Sharon Dibber Im Rabin Be-'67 Al 'Tfisat Hashilton Bidei Hatzava Kedei Lekabel Hahlatah' Letzet Lemilhamah," *Ha'aretz,* November 16, 2004: 1.

36   **"the past is a fiction":** Jacob Katz, "Orthodoxy in Historical Perspective," *Studies in Contemporary Judaism* 2 (1986): 4; cf. Michael Silber, "The Emergence of Ultra-Orthodoxy: The Invention of a Tradition," in *The Uses of Tradition: Jewish Continuity in the Modern Era,* ed. Jack Wertheimer (New York: Jewish Theological Seminary, 1992): 23.

36   **assumption into a question:** Menachem Friedman, *Hahevrah Haharedit: Mekorot, Megamot Vetahalikhim* (Jerusalem: JIIS, 1991): 1–3; Katz, "Orthodoxy in Historical Perspective" 3–7; Silber, "Emergence of Ultra-Orthodoxy" 24–25.

36   **separation from other Jews:** Katz, "Orthodoxy in Historical Perspective" 5–8; Friedman, *Hahevrah* 6–10.

37   **personal affairs as well:** Binyamin Baron, "Ve'ein Shi'ur Rak Hatorah Hazot," *Eretz Aheret* 39 (September–October 2007): 57–58.

38 **especially in Poland and Germany:** Katz, "Orthodoxy in Historical Perspective" 9–12; Friedman, *Hahevrah* 6–9, 26ff.

38 **"vanish in the foreseeable future":** Friedman, *Hahevrah* 2; Menachem Friedman, interview.

39 **an arm of the government:** Menachem Friedman, "The Structural Foundations for Religio-Political Accommodation in Israel: Fallacy and Reality," in *Israel: The First Decade of Independence*, ed. S. Ilan Troen and Noah Lucas (Albany: SUNY Press, 1995): 67ff.

39 **creating a state school system:** Hok Hinukh Mamlakhti, 1953.

40 **not to prepare them for it:** Don Yehiya, *Mashber Utmurah* 463–64; Menachem Friedman, interview.

40 **the secular-religious split:** Medding, *Founding of Israeli Democracy* 90–91.

40 **"in the palm of its hand":** Leibowitz, *Judaism* 115.

40 **"disappear off the face of the earth":** Amos Oz, *A Tale of Love and Darkness*, trans. Nicholas de Lange (London: Vintage, 2005): 271–73.

41 **"a mechanical majority":** DK, 7 Feb. 1950: 738.

41 **"rights of the individual":** DK, 7 Feb. 1950: 734.

42 **separate synagogue and state:** DK, 7 Feb. 1950: 744; Medding, *Founding of Israeli Democracy* 40.

42 **suppressing Judaism—frightened them:** Menachem Friedman, "'Al Hanissim'—Prihato Shel 'Olam Hatorah' (Hayeshivot Vehakollelim) Biyisrael," in *Yeshivot Uvatei Midrashot*, ed. Emanuel Etkes (Jerusalem: Merkaz Shazar, 2006): 431–42.

42 **no consensus wide enough:** DK, 14 Feb. 1950: 796–98.

42 **"aspire to a totalitarian regime":** DK, 20 Feb. 1950: 816–18.

43 **Poland, Latvia, Italy, or Germany:** DK, 14 Feb. 1950: 796–98.

43 **slaves to slave states:** U.S. Constitution, art. 4, sec. 2.

43 **shopkeepers into workers:** DK, 7 Feb. 1950: 735.

43 **cede Jewish claims:** DK, 7 Feb. 1950: 739.

44 **assigned to the Arab state:** Morris, *1948* 52–53; Benny Morris, *The Birth of the Palestinian Refugee Problem Revisited* (Cambridge: Cambridge University Press, 2004): 13.

44 **"of its Palestinian population":** Rashid Khalidi, *The Iron Cage: The Story of the Palestinian Struggle for Statehood* (Boston: Beacon, 2007): 126.

45 **not wanted there:** Judt, *Postwar* 31–32. Three hundred thirty-two thousand Jewish DPs in fact immigrated to Israel by 1953; another 165,000 went elsewhere.

45 **necessary Jewish majority:** Uzi Benziman and Atallah Mansour, *Dayarei Mishneh* (Subtenants) (Jerusalem: Keter, 1992): 14.

45 **citizenship in the Arab state:** United Nations Special Committee on Palestine, Report to the General Assembly, 3 Sept. 1947, chap. VI, unispal.un.org/unispal.nsf/0/07175de9fa2de563852568d3006e10f3, acc. 17 Oct. 2010.

46   Jews living outside the state: "M. Shertok to D. Ben-Gurion," 30 Oct.
      1947, in Yehoshua Freundlich and Zvi Ganin, *Political Documents of the
      Jewish Agency: January–November 1947* (Jerusalem: Hasifriya Hazionit,
      1996): doc. 441.

46   1923 as a positive precedent: Morris, *Birth Revisited* 47.

46   accepted by "pragmatic" statesmen: Judt, *Postwar* 25–28.

46   the evidence is missing: Morris, *Birth Revisited* 60.

47   budget needed to pay them: Jonathan Fine, *Kakh Noladnu* (The Birth
      of a State) (Jerusalem: Carmel, 2009): 33–58.

47   sixteen Jewish and eight Arab: "Memshal Hamedinah Bimdinah
      Ha'ivrit: Hatza'ah Lemivneh Hamahlakot, Manginonan Vetaktzivei-
      hen," ISA 41/121/19-Gimel, www.archives.gov.il/ArchiveGov/itemDe
      tails.aspx?ID=41.0.1.436, acc. 22 Nov. 2009.

48   Deir Yassin outside Jerusalem: Morris, *1948* 116–28.

48   status quo ante was unthinkable: "Meeting, M. Shertok, E. Epstein - G.
      Marshall, R. Lovett, D. Rusk," 8 May 1948, in *Political and Diplomatic
      Documents, December 1947–May 1948*, ed. Gedalia Yogev (Jerusalem:
      State of Israel and WZO, 1979): doc. 483; Louise Fischer, *Moshe Sharett:
      Rosh Hamemshalah Hasheni: Mivhar Te'udot Mepirkei Hayav 1894–1965*
      (Moshe Sharett: The Second Prime Minister: Selected Documents,
      1894–1965) (Jerusalem: State of Israel, 2007): 348.

49   into a choice: Morris, *1948* 298–301; Morris, *Birth Revisited* 588–89.

49   same territory beforehand: Hillel Cohen, *Good Arabs: The Israeli Secu-
      rity Services and the Israeli Arabs, 1948–1967*, trans. Haim Watzman
      (Berkeley: University of California Press, 2010): 1–2; Morris, *1948*
      407, 411. Benziman and Mansour, *Dayarei Mishneh* 15–16, give the
      number of abandoned villages as 346; Morris, *Birth Revisited* xvi–xx,
      lists 389.

50   would be citizens: Hok Ha'ezrahut, 1952; David Kretzmer, *The Legal
      Status of Arabs in Israel* (Boulder, Colo.: Westview, 1990): 36–39.

50   Palestinian Arabs who had left: Cf. Shira Nomi Robinson, *Occupied
      Citizens in a Liberal State: Palestinians under Military Rule and the Colo-
      nial Formation of Israeli Society, 1948–1966* (Ph.D. diss., Stanford Uni-
      versity, 2005): 53–54.

50   the right to immigrate: Hok Hashvut, 1950.

51   for the Jewish people: Kretzmer, *Legal Status* 61.

51   slowed the buying effort: Benziman and Mansour, 158; Tom Segev,
      One Palestine, Complete: Jews and Arabs under the British Mandate (New
      York: Metropolitan, 2000), 273–75.

52   holding property rights: Kretzmer, *Legal Status* 49–50, 69; Samuel
      Fleischacker, "Collective Ownership," 13 Oct. 2008, normblog.typepad
      .com/normblog/2008/10/a-cool-hour-on-the-israel-palestine-conflict
      -6-by-samuel-fleischacker.html, acc. 13 Oct. 2008.

52   anyone who had left his home: Hok Nikhsei Nifkadim, 1950.

52   records from the time show: "Taibe," ISA 3098/14-Gimel; Hussein
      Jbarah and Abd al-Aziz Abu Isba Maswari, interview.
52   75,000 Arab citizens: Kretzmer, *Legal Status* 57; Cohen, *Good Arabs*
      96.
53   lease to non-Jews: Kretzmer, *Legal Status* 60–63.
53   for all state services: Benziman and Mansour, *Dayarei Mishneh* 33, 43.
53   flooded with Jewish immigrants: Grinberg, *Hahistadrut* 93, 115.
53   party interests was glaring: Cohen, *Good Arabs* 11ff., 41–45, 61–64,
      129–31, 139ff.
54   "of a colonial administration": Robinson, *Occupied Citizens* 7.
54   "the ruling Mapai party": Robinson 83.
54   a level playing field: Grinberg, *Hahistadrut* 93–94; Cohen, *Good Arabs*
      207–8.
55   struggle against the government: "When they fired the cannon, I gave
      the order, 'No!' Today I give the order, 'Yes!' . . . If need be, I will resume
      the war. . . . This will be a difficult war, lasting years. We will again
      separate from our children and our families." Menachem Begin, speak-
      ing at a demonstration in Jerusalem, 7 Jan. 1952, www.begincenter.org.
      il/uploads/Shilumim.pdf, acc. 21 Oct. 2010.
55   Bialik and Shaul Tchernichovsky: Hussein Jbarah and Abd al-Aziz
      Abu Isba Maswari, interview.

III. The Capital of Lawlessness

56   freedom-of-information request: Capt. Tzidki Maman to Yehezkel
      Lein, B'Tselem, 12 Aug. 2007, www.btselem.org/Download/2007
      0812_Letter_from_civil_administration_about_ofra.pdf, acc. 18 Oct.
      2009.
57   over 500 buildings: Interior Ministry, "Sakh Hakol Toshavei Yosh,"
      June 2007, e-mail from ministry spokesperson; Nir Shalev et al., *The
      Ofrah Settlement: An Illegal Outpost* (Jerusalem: B'Tselem, 2008): 13.
57   privately owned by Palestinians: Spiegel Report, www.haaretz.co.il/
      hasite/images/printed/P300109/uriib.mht, acc. 30 Apr. 2009. The name
      is unofficial and refers to the report's author, Brig. Gen. (reserves) Ba-
      ruch Spiegel. For background on the report, see Daniel Kurtzer, "Be-
      hind the Settlements," *American Interest*, Spring 2010: 7–9; Uri Blau,
      "Secret Israeli Database Reveals Full Extent of Illegal Settlement,"
      Ha'aretz, 1 Feb. 2009, www.haaretz.com/hasen/spages/1060043.html,
      acc. 30 Apr. 2009. According to *Ha'aretz* editor Dov Alfon (interview),
      the newspaper received the report as part of the large quantity of mate-
      rial leaked by former soldier Anat Kam.
57   synonymous with the settlement effort: For a full description of Ofrah's
      founding, see Gorenberg, *Accidental Empire* 306, 311–18, 328, 351–52.
      Additional documents showing Shimon Peres's role, in violation of

Yitzhak Rabin's instructions and in contrast to Peres's public statements, are found in IDFA 1510/1989/492. The documents were declassified following my petition to the High Court of Justice against the IDF Archives.

58 **Palestinians in the early 1980s:** Gershom Gorenberg, *The End of Days: Fundamentalism and the Struggle for the Temple Mount* (New York: Free Press, 2000): 116–18, 132–37.

58 **"without permission of the owner":** "Bneh Beitkha Be'ofrah," 29 Apr. 1976, OA. The settlers originally squatted in an abandoned Jordanian army base, and believed that title to the land had passed to the Israeli government, which had not given them permission to build on it. However, the Jordanian government never completed the process of expropriating the land. It became state property only when the Israeli military commander of the area issued an expropriation order in November 1977, after Menachem Begin replaced Yitzhak Rabin as prime minister and altered settlement policy. The expropriation order violated Israel's own interpretation of the Jordanian law on expropriation, which was still in force in the West Bank. That interpretation barred taking private land for an Israeli settlement. See Shalev et al., *Ofrah Settlement* 20–23.

58 **"greatest triumphs over adversity":** Jared Diamond, *Collapse: How Societies Choose to Fail or Succeed* (New York: Viking, 2004): 275.

59 **mining, logging, and ranching:** Diamond 211–76, 432–34.

60 **into muscular farmers:** Theodore Herzl, *Altneuland*, book 2, www.59 .org.il/en/resources/view.asp?id=1600, acc. 13 Apr. 2004, describes Jewish children in Europe as "pale, weak, timid." Cf. Arthur Hertzberg, ed., *The Zionist Idea: A Historical Analysis and Reader* (New York: Atheneum, 1973): pt. 5. Describing European Jews, early Zionist writers unconsciously repeated anti-Semitic stereotypes.

60 **"rent between ourselves and Nature":** A. D. Gordon, "People and Labor," in Hertzberg, *Zionist Idea* 374.

60 **marking the national homestead:** Tsur, *Mipulmus Hahalukah* 31; Yehiel Admoni, *Asor Shel Shikul Da'at: Hahityashvut Me'ever Lekav Hayarok, 1967–1977* (Decade of Discretion: Settlement Policy in the Territories, 1967–1977) (Makhon Yisrael Galili Leheker Hakoah Hamagen/Yad Tabenkin/Hakibbutz Hame'uhad, 1992): 17; Arnon Lammfromm and Hagai Tsoref, eds., *Levi Eshkol: Rosh Hamemshalah Hashlishi* (Levi Eshkol: The Third Prime Minister—Selected Documents, 1895–1969) (Jerusalem: Israel State Archives, 2002): 239ff.

61 **and the first half of 1967:** Zeev Tsur, *Hakibbutz Hame'uhad Beyishuvah shel Ha'aretz* (The Hakibbutz Hameuchad in the Settlement of Eretz Yisrael), vol. 4, *1960–1980* (Yad Tabenkin/Hakibbutz Hame'uhad, 1986): 52; Admoni, *Asor Shel Shikul Da'at* 11, 17–18.

61 **"war would be a disaster":** Arnan Azaryahu, interview. Azaryahu, who

died in 2008, was known for decades only by his nickname, Sini (China-man).

62 **"that neither side wanted":** Avi Shlaim, *The Iron Wall: Israel and the Arab World* (New York: W. W. Norton, 2001): 236.

62 **was unprepared for battle:** Shlomo Gazit, *Peta'im Bemalkodet: Shloshim Shnot Mdiniut Yisrael Bashtahim* (Trapped) (Tel Aviv: Zmora-Bitan, 1999): 15; Eitan Haber, *Hayom Tifrotz Milhamah* (Today War Will Break Out: The Reminiscences of Brig. Gen. Israel Lior) (Tel Aviv: Edanim/Yediot Aharonot, 1987): 147; Shlomo Lahat, interview.

62 **expected a one-front war:** Shlaim, *Iron Wall* 236–43.

62 **rolled to the waterway:** Michael B. Oren, *Six Days of War: June 1967 and the Making of the Modern Middle East* (New York: Oxford University Press, 2002): 259; NARA RG 59 Central Files 1967–69, POL 28 Jerusa-lem, Tel Aviv cable 4019.

62 **the entire West Bank:** Lammfromm and Tsoref, *Levi Eshkol* 557–58; Shlaim, *Iron Wall* 245.

62 **ordered an invasion:** Oren, *Six Days of War* 195, 278–80; Lammfromm and Tsoref, *Levi Eshkol* 559.

62 **sending his troops farther:** YAOH 2:22.

63 **"the gains of the war":** Azaryahu, interview.

63 **intoxicated secular Jews:** A. Ben-Ami, ed., *Hakol: Gvulot Hashalom Shel Eretz Yisrael* (Hakol: The Peace Frontiers of Israel) (Tel Aviv: Madaf, 1967).

64 **cooperate in a diplomatic solution:** Foreign Relations of the United States (FRUS) 19:49; Lammfromm and Tsoref, *Levi Eshkol* 579.

64 **Arab birth rate was higher:** Israeli population: Central Bureau of Statis-tics, *Statistical Abstract of Israel 2003*, www1.cbs.gov.il/shnaton54/st02_01.pdf, acc. 14 July 2004. Note: 1967 figures include Arab nonciti-zen residents of annexed East Jerusalem. Postwar Israeli estimates of the population of the occupied territories went as high as 1.5 million (ISA 153.8/7921/2-Alef, doc. 331). Later documents (ISA 153.8/7921/3-Alef), including October 1967 census figures for West Bank and Gaza, lead to an approximate total of 1.1 million. The discrepancy is due in part to refugees leaving the West Bank during and after the war.

64 **had fallen in 1948:** David E. Eisenstadt, *Hatmurot Bigvulot Ha'ironiim (Municipaliim) shel Yerushalayim, 1863–1967* (The evolution of Jerusa-lem's municipal boundaries, 1863–1967) (MA thesis, Bar Ilan Univer-sity, Ramat Gan, 1998): 121, 130–51; David Eisenstadt, interview.

64 **citizenship on another's citizens:** Uzi Benziman, *Yerushalayim: Ir Lelo Homah* (Jerusalem: City without a Wall) (Tel Aviv: Schocken, 1973): 203–5.

64 **annexing the land:** In legal terms, the annexation was effected by ex-tending Israeli Jerusalem's city limits and applying Israeli law to the new areas of the city. The word *annexation* was not used, with the hope of

reducing international backlash. At the time, the State Department instructed the U.S. ambassador in Israel to inform the Israeli government that international law forbade not just unilateral annexation, but also changes in local law of occupied territory, with the exception of changes needed for military purposes (NARA RG59 Central Files 1967–69, POL27 ARAB-ISR, cable 218573). At an Israeli cabinet meeting on 10 Sept. 1967, justice minister Ya'akov Shimshon noted, "In relation to Jerusalem, we strode with our eyes wide open and violated the Geneva Conventions in the clearest possible fashion, on a one-time basis." Reuven Pedatzur, *Nitzahon Hemukhah: Mdiniut Memshelet Eshkol Bashtahim Le'ahar Milhemet Sheshet Hayamim* (The Triumph of Embarrassment: Israel and the Territories after the Six-Day War) (Tel Aviv: Bitan/Yad Tabenkin, 1996): 195. A leading Israeli scholar of international law, Tel Aviv University law professor Yoram Dinstein, argued in his classic 1970 article, "Tzion Bemishpat Beinle'umi Tipadeh," *Hapraklit* 27 (1971): 5–11, that Israel lacked any basis in international law for annexing East Jerusalem unilaterally. However, Dinstein's article came in response to an Israeli Supreme Court ruling that East Jerusalem had in fact been annexed by Israel's actions in 1967. The court thereby undercut the claim made for diplomatic purposes that extending the municipal limits was not intended as annexation.

64 **"and Israel's security needs":** YTA 15 Galili/2/3/115; Pedatzur, *Nitzahon Hemukhah* 55–56.

65 **to protect the straits:** ISA 43/7234/7-Alef, doc. 287.

65 **"the dowry comes the bride":** ISA 153.8/7920/7-Alef, Eshkol speech to Ihud Hakvutzot Vehakibbutzim, 22 Nov. 1967.

65 **"not be citizens of Israel":** ISA Cabinet minutes, 19 June 1967, 65.

65 **and few of the people:** ISA Cabinet minutes, 19 June 1967, 41–50; ISA 153.8/7921/2-Alef, doc. 192; YAOH 7:22.

65 **decided not to decide:** YAOH 3:20–21.

66 **"done with the Zionist enterprise":** ISA Cabinet minutes, 19 June 1967, 39–40.

66 **"every colonial regime":** Leibowitz, *Judaism* 226.

66 **"say in the same breath":** LPS, 9 Nov. 1972, 33–35.

67 **"will not be printed":** YTA, 15 Allon/17/4, 30 Oct. 1967.

67 **a democracy—its borders:** David Newman, "The Territorial Politics of Exurbanization," *Israel Affairs* 1.1 (Aug. 1996): 74–77.

67 **only 37 percent could draw:** Larisa Fleishman and Ilan Salomon, "Lashe'elah 'Heikhan Hakav Yarok?' Hateshuva 'Ma Zeh Hakav Hayarok," *Alpaim* 29 (2005): 26–52.

69 **contiguous Palestinian state:** Yossi Alpher, "Sharon's Coercion, Arafat's Fantasies," *bitterlemons*, 2 Dec. 2001, www.bitterlemons.org/previous/bl101201ed4.html, acc. 24 Nov. 2010; Yossi Alpher, interview; Jim Hoagland, "Sharon Sees Time Ripe to Regain Defense Post," *Washington*

Post, 7 Nov. 1988, A25. Sharon's idea of fingers dividing Palestinian land dates back to his time as head of the IDF's Southern Command. Ariel Sharon, with David Chanoff, *Warrior: An Autobiography* (New York: Touchstone, 2001), 251–58; Yair Douer, *Lanu Hamaggal Hu Herev II* (Our Sickle Is Our Sword: Nahal Settlements from 1967 until 1992) (Ministry of Defense and Yad Tabenkin, 1997): 220.

69 **"ended up on the Jewish side":** Aluf Benn, "Behitnahaluyot Yesh Element Shel Zmaniut," *Haaretz,* 4 Apr. 2004.

70 **jobs for the unemployed:** Admoni, *Asor Shel Shikul Da'at*, 23–24; YAOH 6:11–12; MGA 502-10-01-01, Rafael Ben-Yehudah's diary; KMA, Mazkirut Hakibbutz Hame'uhad, box 15, book 90; KMA 5/26/1, Mo'etzet Hakibbutz Hame'uhad decisions, 23–24 June 1967; *Alei Golan* 32 (16 July 1968): 2–4; *Alei Golan* 185 (30 June 1972); *Merom Golan: Reshit* (Merom Golan: 1977): 2–10; Yehudah Harel, "Meharamah Hasurit Leramat Hagolan," author's ms.; Vardina Shnurman, "Esrim Vehamesh Shanim Le'ahar Quneitra," *Eretz Hagolan*, 15 May 1997, 12–14; Tsur, *Mipulmus Hahalukah* 85; Naor, *Eretz Yisrael Hashlemah* 43; Eytan Sat, Yehudah Harel, Gershon Meinrat, and Carmel Bar, interviews.

71 **Division received its budget:** Yehiel Admoni, interview; Peter Robert Demant, *Ploughshares into Swords: Israeli Settlement Policy in the Occupied Territories, 1967–1977* (Ph.D. diss., Universiteit van Amsterdam, 1988): 205.

71 **Porat sent the guns:** Porat, interview. Yehiel Admoni, in Admoni ms. 76:36, describes Zevulun Hammer citing the incident in the cabinet meeting of 9 May 1975; Admoni, treating the incident as well known, comments that moving army-issue guns from Kfar Etzion to Hebron "violated all instructions and directions concerning use of weapons provided to settlements."

72 **approval of a ministerial committee:** The first cabinet decision requiring cabinet approval for establishing settlements was made on 1 Oct. 1967; see Pedatzur, *Nitzahon Hemukhah* 201. Sasson, *Havat Da'at* (Beina'im) *Benose Ma'ahazim Bilti Murshim* (Opinion Concerning Unauthorized Outposts) (Jerusalem, 2005): 55–58, describes subsequent decisions reaffirming this requirement, and stresses that it has legal force.

72 **did not become a settlement:** IDFA 1510-89-491, 28 April 1975, 29 April, 1975; YTA 15Galili/2/2/52, 29 April, 1975.

72 **refurbishing the Jordanian buildings:** IDFA 1510-89-491, 22 May 1975, 3 June 1975, 8 June 1975, 19 June 1975, 23 June 1975, 10 July 1975. Declassified in response to my High Court of Justice suit against the IDF Archives.

72 **the Israeli electricity grid:** Admoni ms. 75:23; Moshe Netzer, *Mishoreshav: Sippur Haim* [Life Story] (Ministry of Defense, 2002): 292.

73 **under Orthodox pressure:** Porat, interview; *Yediot Aharonot*, *Ha'aretz*, and *Jerusalem Post*, 28 Sept. 1967.

73 **settlements that fell in 1948:** ISA 153.8/7921/2A, doc. 317; ISA

153.8/7921/3A, doc. 289–91, with unnumbered cover notes; ISA 153.8/7920/7A, docs. 5–69, 8–67; YLE 5/31; Pedatzur, *Nitzahon Hemukhah*, 33, 190.

73 **"provisions of the Fourth Geneva Convention":** ISA 153.8/7921/3-Alef. Legal opinion numbered as doc. 289–91, with unnumbered cover notes, which show that Meron's memorandum was forwarded to Defense Minister Dayan and Justice Minister Shapira.

74 **"the same opinion today":** Donald Macintyre, "Secret Memo Shows Israel Knew Six Day War Was Illegal," *Independent on Sunday*, 26 May 2007, www.independent.co.uk/news/world/middle-east/secret-memo-shows-israel-knew-six-day-war-was-illegal-450410.html, acc. 26 May 2007. In an interview with CNN correspondent Christiane Amanpour for the documentary special *God's Jewish Warriors*, aired 21 Aug. 2007, Meron again stressed that legally, "you cannot settle your population in occupied territories." transcripts.cnn.com/TRANSCRIPTS/0708/22/cp.01.html, acc. 28 August 2007.

74 **be a Nahal position:** Cabinet discussion: Admoni, *Asor Shel Shikul Da'at* 51–53; Pedatzur, *Nitzahon Hemukhah* 186, 193–94; Lammfromm and Tsoref, *Levi Eshkol* 576–77. Press: *Davar, Hatzofeh, Ha'aretz, Hayom, Jerusalem Post, Lamerhav, Ma'ariv, Yediot Aharonot*, 28 Sept. 1967. Diplomats: YLE 5/31, cable 676.

74 **tells the real story:** IDFA 2845/1997/46/32. Declassified in response to my HCJ suit against the IDF Archives. Gazit's official position was coordinator of government activities in the territories.

75 **"contravenes international conventions":** ISA 153.8/7920/7-Alef, doc. 60, 15 Oct. 1968.

76 **"forced transfer of [its] civilians":** Ministry of Foreign Affairs, "Israel's Settlements—Their Conformity with International Law," Dec. 1996, www.mfa.gov.il/mfa/go.asp?MFAH0dgj0, acc. 1 Nov. 2010. The statement, like nearly every legal defense of the settlements in the past twenty years, cites Eugene Rostow's letter to the *American Journal of International Law* 84 (July 1990): 717–23. Rostow, who served as undersecretary of state for political affairs in the Johnson administration, presented the same arguments in two articles in the *New Republic*, published on 23 April 1991 and 21 Oct. 1991. Settlement advocates' frequent citation of Rostow's position obscures how unusual it is among authorities on international law. At the time Rostow served as undersecretary, the State Department warned Israel that settlements violated the Geneva Convention. NARA RG 59, Central Files 1967–69, POL 27 ARAB-ISR, CA-7122, "Israeli Settlements in Occupied Territory."

76 **settlement by the occupying power:** Kretzmer, *Occupation of Justice* 77. See notes there for key sources on legality of settlement.

76 **occupation do not apply:** Meir Shamgar, who was IDF judge advocate-

general (chief legal officer) in 1967, and later became chief justice of the Israeli Supreme Court, made this argument in 1971, when he was Israel's attorney general. He, in turn, cited Hebrew University professor Yehudah Blum. Meir Shamgar, "The Observance of International Law in the Administered Territories," *Israel Yearbook on Human Rights* 1 (1971): 262–65. The Israeli Foreign Ministry statement cited above ("Israel's Settlements—Their Conformity with International Law," December 1996) alludes to this position. Kretzmer, *Occupation of Justice* 33–34, details the holes in this argument.

76 **sovereignty over occupied territory:** Stephen M. Boyd, "The Applicability of International Law to the Occupied Territories," *Israel Yearbook on Human Rights* 1 (1971): 258–61.

76 **"demographic, social status quo":** Meron, interview. Cf. Boyd, "Applicability."

76 **mandate is still in force:** Ministry of Foreign Affairs, "Israel's Settlements"; Yehuda Zvi Blum, "Tzion Bemishpat Beinle'umi Nifdetah," *Hapraklit* 27 (1971): 315–24. I note that while the Israeli Supreme Court has never ruled on the legality of settlement as such, the status of the League of Nations mandate arose in its ruling allowing evacuation of the Gaza Strip settlements, HCJ 1661/05. One justice, Edmund Levy, wrote a dissent arguing that the right of settlement throughout Mandatory Palestine remained in force. The other ten justices did not accept this view. elyon1.court.gov.il/files/05/610/016/a20/05016610.a20.HTM, acc. 1 Nov 2010.

77 **promulgated on July 2, 1967:** Yuval Ginbar, *On the Way to Annexation: Human Rights Violations Resulting from the Establishment and Expansion of the Ma'aleh Adumim Settlement* (Jerusalem: B'tselem, 1999): 13, and n. 44 there.

77 **extended the emergency regulation:** Hok Leha'arakhat Tokpan shel Takanot Sha'at Herum (Aveirot Bashtahim Hamuhzakim—Shiput Ve'ezrah Mishpatit), 1967.

78 **settlers were allowed to vote:** MER 5:345ff. In 1969, nine polling stations were set up to serve approximately one thousand Israelis living in the West Bank and Golan Heights. The election law was only formally changed the following year.

78 **granted National Insurance coverage:** Hok Leha'arakhat Tokpan shel Takanot Sha'at Herum (Yehudah Vehashomron Vehevel Aza—Shiput Be'averot Ve'ezrah Mishpatit), 1977, amended text, www.takdin.co.il/search/NetisUtils/srvrutil_getdoc.aspx?path=/nepsdoc/2L3aqN5HJJ4WmD3WkLL14BcXqRMm0/TSLH048.UPD.html, acc. 5 Jan. 2010.

78 **had reached 81,000:** Central Bureau of Statistics, *Statistical Abstract of Israel 2010*, table 2:7.

78 **gave settlers health insurance:** Hok Leha'arakhat Tokpan shel Takanot Sha'at Herum, 1977, amended text.

78 **the councils' jurisdiction:** Orders 783 and 892, in *Dinei Hamoatzot*

Hamekomiot Vehamoatzot Ha'eizoriot Be'eizor Yehudah Veshomron (Interior Ministry, 1996).

79   **for the Gaza Strip:** Ginbar, *On the Way to Annexation* 16, n. 59.

79   **negotiations were about to start:** William B. Quandt, *Peace Process: American Diplomacy and the Arab Israeli Conflict since 1967* (Washington, D.C.: Brookings Institution/University of California, 1993): 326–29, 341, 446–48, 472–73.

79   **as if they were residents:** For example, a 1984 addition extended various laws on personal status to settlements, including the law on the legal age of marriage. The order states that if the couple's residence is the West Bank, the law will apply "as if it were in Israel." *Dinei Hamoatzot Hamekomiot*, 281.

79   **equality before the law:** Kretzmer, *Occupation of Justice* 27; Kretzmer, interview.

80   **eighth of the total area:** Yehezkel Lein, *Land Grab: Israel's Settlement Policy in the West Bank* (Jerusalem: B'Tselem, 2002), states that by 1972, Israel had identified 687 square kilometers of the West Bank as state land, out of a total land area of 5,640 square kilometers.

80   **the 1907 Hague Regulations:** Regulations concerning the Laws and Customs of War on Land (The Hague, 18 October 1907), Article 55, www.icrc.org/ihl.nsf/FULL/195, acc. November 2, 2010.

80   **to create permanent change:** Shlomo Gazit, who served as coordinator of government activities in the territories in the first years of the occupation, states succinctly in his 1999 study of the occupation, *Peta'im Bemalkodet* (Trapped) (Tel Aviv: Zmora-Bitan, 1999): 245, "Israeli settlements in the territories were, without a doubt, a purpose that was not temporary."

81   **after the Six-Day War:** Lein, *Land Grab* 58–59.

81   **settlement of Ma'aleh Adumim:** Gershom Gorenberg, "Failure Written in West Bank Stone," *Washington Post*, 30 Sept. 2008. After a long freedom-of-information legal battle, Israeli activist Dror Etkes obtained details on the expropriation from the Civil Administration in the West Bank. A map of the area can be accessed via southjerusalem.com/settlement-and-occupation-historical-documents/.

81   **one of the three largest:** As of July 2008, the Interior Ministry listed 34,989 residents registered as living in Ma'aleh Adumim.

81   **expropriation only for public use:** Hague Regulations, article 46; Lein, *Land Grab* 60–61.

81   **temporarily for military purposes:** Hague Regulations, article 52.

81   **which has to guard them:** Newman, "Territorial Politics" 66–69.

82   **the court's jurisdiction:** Kretzmer, *Occupation of Justice* 1–2, 19–21; Moshe Negbi, *Kevalim Shel Tzedek: Bagatz Mul Hamemshal Hayisraeli Bishtahim* (Justice under Occupation: The Israeli Supreme Court versus the Military Administration in the Occupied Territories) (Jerusalem: Cana, 1981): 12–18.

82   **"supervision of military bodies":** Shamgar, interview.

82   **"dubious legal arguments":** Kretzmer, *Occupation of Justice* 3.

82   **returned the land to its owners:** HCJ 390/79; Kretzmer, *Occupation of Justice* 85–89; Negbi, *Kevalim Shel Tzedek* 50–68.

83   **the state in the first place:** The explanation of West Bank land law here is meant only as a brief overview. Sources include Eyal Zamir, *Admot Medinah Biyehudah Vehashomron: Skirah Mishpatit* (State Land in Judea and Samaria: The Legal Status) (Jerusalem: JIIS, 1985); Raja Shehadeh, *Occupier's Law: Israel and the West Bank* (Washington, D.C.: Institute for Palestine Studies, 1985): 15–49; Plia Albeck, "Hashimush Bekarka'ot Biyehudah Uveshomron Letzorekh Hahityashvut Hayehudit," in *Ha'aliyah El Hehar: Hahityashvut Hayehudit Hamithadeshet Biyehudah Veshomron* (Ascent to the Mountains: Renewal of Jewish Settlement in Judea and Samaria), ed. Avraham Shvut (Jerusalem: Sifriat Beit El, 2002): 221–31; Lein, *Land Grab* 47–64; Benn, "Behitnahaluyot Yesh Element Shel Zmaniut"; State Comptroller, Report 56a (2005): 190–95; Shlomo Zecharia, interview; Nir Shalev, correspondence.

84   **until private ownership was proven:** Albeck, "Hashimush" 226.

84   **"holy about the Green Line":** Benn, "Behitnahaluyot Yesh Element Shel Zmaniut."

85   **this should be kept secret:** Moshe Glick to Plia Albeck, 28 Aug. 1990; Plia Albeck to Coordinator of Government Activities in the Territories, 16 Nov. 1990; Plia Albeck to Coordinator of Government Activities in the Territories, 8 Nov. 1992. The correspondence was revealed by counsel for the Fund for Redemption of the Soil and Green Park, a Canadian development company, in response to a High Court of Justice petition (HCJ 8414/05) by residents of the Palestinian village of Bilin against the route of the Israeli security fence through their land. The fence route was intended to allow continued development of the Modi'in Illit settlement; Green Park was one of the developers. Green Park and the Fund claimed that the Fund had bought the land for the development and that they had a vested interest in it. See Shaul Arieli and Michael Sfard, *Homah Umehdal: Gader Hahafradah—Bitahon O Hamdanut* (The Wall of Folly) (Tel Aviv: Sifrei Aliyat Hagag, 2008): 346–52.

86   **development on Palestinian property:** Spiegel Report.

86   **the theft take place:** The Peace Now Settlement Watch report, "Illegal Construction in the Settlements: The List of Demolition Orders," 4 Dec. 2007, based on information provided by the Civil Administration, states that the Civil Administration opened 3,449 files against illegal construction in settlements in the preceding decade. The Civil Administration actually razed only 107 structures; another 171 were taken down by the offenders. However, these figures include building that is illegal for a variety of reasons. The report does not indicate how many of the files deal with construction on stolen property.

86   **a strongly worded, despairing report:** Yehudit Karp, *Hakirat Hashadot Neged Yehudim Biyehudah Veshomron* (Justice Ministry, 1982).

88   **he served three:** *Ha'aretz*, 2 May 1990, 15 Aug. 1990.

88   **example of schizophrenic justice:** On the underground affair, see Gorenberg, *End of Days* 116–18, 132–37.

88   **that she sought:** The "Shamgar I" report on the 1994 massacre in Hebron lists the virtually same problems in law enforcement, twelve years after the Karp Report. *Vaadat Hahakirah Le'inyan Hatevah Bime'arat Hamakhpelah Behevron: Din Veheshbon* (Jerusalem, 1994).

88   **protecting Israelis, not Palestinians:** Yehudit Karp, interview.

90   **participation in modern society:** Menachem Klein, *Bar-Ilan: Akademiah, Dat Vepolitikah* (Bar-Ilan University between Religion and Politics) (Jerusalem: Magnes, 1998), 139.

90   **live in religious kibbutzim:** Danny Rubinstein, *Mi Lashem Elai: Gush Emunim* (On the Lord's Side: Gush Emunim) (Tel Aviv: Hakibbutz Hame'uhad, 1982); Yisrael Harel, interview; *Zra'im*, Iyar 5727 (May–June 1967): 9–12.

91   **more than seriously studied:** Avraham Yitzhak Hacohen Kook, *Orot* (Jerusalem: Mossad Harav Kook, 5753 [1992–93]): 9, 83–85, 102–4, 121–23; Aviezer Ravitzky, *Haketz Hameguleh Umedinat Hayehudim* (Messianism, Zionism, and Jewish Religious Radicalism) (Tel Aviv: Am Oved, 1993): chap. 3.

91   **"power—conquering the Land":** Speech given by Tzvi Yehudah Kook on the night of Israeli Independence Day, May 14, 1967. Transcribed by students, it was published as "Mizmor Yod-Tet Shel Medinat Yisrael," in various formats, including Ben-Ami, *Hakol* 65–75.

91   **"no complete redemption":** Ya'akov Halevi Filber, *Ayelet Hashahar* (Jerusalem: Haskel, 5728 [1967–68]): 32.

92   **"commandment of settling the Land":** Filber 32.

92   **deep in occupied territory:** Newman, "Territorial Politics" 65–66.

93   **settlers and ultranationalist faith:** David Newman, ed., *The Impact of Gush Emunim: Politics and Settlement in the West Bank* (London: Croom Helm, 1985): 20.

93   **as a "community settlement":** OA 6/5, "Doh Tzevet Hahityashvut Shel Gush Emunim" (Gush Emunim Settlement Team Report), autumn 1975, 12, identifies Ofrah as a community settlement (*yishuv kehilati*), before other Gush Emunim settlements were established. David Newman and Leviah Applebaum, "Hakfar Vehayishuv Hakehilati Mera'ayon Lemetzi'ut," in Shvut, *Ha'aliyah El Hehar* 157–58, states that the concept was developed that year by planner Uzi Gdor.

94   **"closed" and "homogenous":** OA 6/5, "Doh Tzevet Hahityashvut Shel Gush Emunim," 7–11; DC 145, *Tochnit-Av Lehityashvut Yehudit Biyehudah Veshomron* (Master Plan for Jewish Settlement in Judea and Sa-

maria), an early, undated Gush Emunim plan for widespread settlement in the West Bank, adopts the Ofrah outline in its entirety.

94 **criterion for membership:** NTA Hakamat Hayishuv 1977, doc. 29, Hakamat Hayishuv 1978, doc. 36, Hakamat Hayishuv 1979, doc. 20. According to one early Ofrah settler, families asking to join the community had to commit themselves to observe the Sabbath and to "family purity," the religious rules prohibiting sexual intercourse during menstruation.

94 **boarding schools in settlements:** DC 145 17. The plan endorses an existing trend: Yeshivot had already been established in the Etzion Bloc and Kiryat Arba.

95 **up to 20 percent:** HCJ 11163/03, sec. 20; Eyal Hareuveni, *By Hook and by Crook: Israeli Settlement Policy in the West Bank* (Jerusalem: B'Tselem, July 2010): 42.

95 **nearly twice as much:** Central Bureau of Statistics, *Statistical Abstract of Israel 2010*, table 12:14. (The Israeli population as counted in CBS figures reflects the blurring of borders: it is the sum of all people living in pre-1967 Israel, annexed East Jerusalem, and the Golan, plus Israeli settlers living in the West Bank.)

96 **"be an Arab government":** Lea Sklar, interview.

IV. Children of the Hills

98 **"fruit of the land":** Numbers 12:30.

98 **"a time to uproot":** Ecclesiastes 3:2.

98 **"forgotten their Jewish identity":** Handbill found on 28 Oct. 2009. The lack of an author's name is presumably intended to hinder a police investigation.

99 **here-and-now inhabitants:** Genesis 13:7. The rabbinic gloss appears in *Breshit Rabba* 40:7, and in Rashi's commentary on Genesis 13:7.

99 **adultery into a ritual:** Gershom Scholem, *The Messianic Idea in Judaism* (New York: Schocken, 1971): 109–14. In *Sabbatai Sevi: The Mystical Messiah* (Princeton, N.J.: Princeton University Press, 1973): 387, 669–71, 880, Scholem also brings testimony that Shabtai Tzvi himself encouraged his wife to attempt to seduce another man, and that he engaged in intercourse with a boy while wearing phylacteries.

99 **tribal, as religious doctrine:** Aviezer Ravitzky, *Haketz Hameguleh: Umedinat Hayehudim* (Messianism, Zionism, and Jewish Religious Radicalism) (Tel Aviv: Am Oved, 1993): 188–90.

100 **"holiness into the world":** "Ha'atar Shel Shvut Ami," http://svotamy.fav.co.il/index.php , acc. 16 Nov. 2010.

100 **harvested and stolen:** "35 Tree Vandalism Cases in 6 Weeks," 31 Oct. 2010, joint statement by the Association of Civil Rights in Israel, B'Tselem, Rabbis for Human Rights, and Yesh Din.

101 **lack Jewish consciousness:** This list is taken partly from Roi Sharon,

Amir Rappaport, and Amit Cohen, "No Man's Land," *Ma'ariv*, 11 Aug. 2008: B8.

102 **to make the arrangements:** Itai Zar, interview. Tadia Sasson, *Havat Da'at (Beina'im) Benose Ma'ahazim Bilti Murshim* (Opinion Concerning Unauthorized Outposts) (Jerusalem, 2005), appendix 1:16, identifies the land as private, belonging to Far'ata residents, adding that the military appeals committee approved registering it in the name of Har Vegai, a company owned by Moshe Zar. The description implies that Far'ata residents unsuccessfully challenged Zar's claim before the Israeli committee. As of 2005, when Sasson wrote her report, Zar had not submitted the land survey needed to complete the registration. In 2009, Itai Zar told me registration had yet to be completed.

102 **pattern of the outposts:** Sharon never regained consciousness after his 2006 stroke; Hever has not granted interviews for years. Amana, legally registered as a cooperative, is not required to make its financial papers public. *Ha'aretz* military correspondent Amos Harel reported, "Officers well versed in the twisted process of setting up an outpost believed that in the vast majority of the cases, Sharon was an active partner in formulating the plans, as well as selecting the location and the timing." *Ha'aretz*, 16 May 2003, www.haaretz.com/print-edition/news/inquiry-into-dummy-outpost-reveals-a-complex-picture-1.9961, acc. 27 May 2003. On Hever's role, see Sara Leibovich-Dar, "Ma'ahazei Zambish," *Ha'aretz*, 10 July 2002, www.haaretz.co.il/hasite/pages/ShArtPE.jhtml?itemNo=185396, acc. 15 June 2010.

102 **illegal several times over:** Sasson, *Havat Da'at*, appendix 1:16.

102 **main settler leadership body:** Ynet, 20 Oct. 2002, www.ynet.co.il/articles/0,7340,L-2189016,00.html, www.ynet.co.il/articles 0,7340,L-2/191134,00.html, acc. 15 Nov. 2010. Over the years, Havat Gilad has been the locus of several other confrontations between settlers and security forces.

102 **only by religious law:** Itai Zar, interview.

104 **"force, might and beatings":** "Israel Declines to Study Rabin Tie to Beatings," *New York Times*, 12 July 1990.

104 **stopped by military means:** Yaakov Perry, interview.

106 **collaborators with the Nazis:** Nachum L. Rabinovitch, "Generals, Jews and Justice," *Jerusalem Post*, 27 Dec. 1993. In "Pekudah Bilti Hukit," *Gilyon Rabbanei Yesha* 18 (25 Iyar 5754 [6 May 1994]), Rabinovitch compared government evacuation of settlers to the Nazi Nuremberg Laws. Rabinovitch's yeshivah belongs to the *hesder* program, in which young men alternate between religious studies and shortened military service (see chap. 5 below). The yeshivah continues to receive funding from the Education Ministry; see www.tmichot.gov.il, acc. 21 Nov. 2010.

106 **capital punishment for blasphemy:** Nachum L. Rabinovitch, *Gilyon Rabbanei Yesha* 28 (Tishrei 5756 [Sept.–Oct. 1995]): 2–3. The medieval

texts, it should be noted, refer to a court-imposed punishment, not to an act by an individual zealot. After the assassination, Rabinovitch was questioned on suspicion of inciting to murder, but was not charged. Yair Sheleg, "Et Hakesher Harabbani Lo Hakru," *Haaretz*, 3 Nov. 2005, www.haaretz.co.il/hasite/pages/ShArtSR.jhtml?itemNo=641407, acc. 21 Nov. 2010.

106 **"asunder before their eyes"**: Dan Be'eri, "Shuv Ha'Saison' Bapetah," *Nekuda*, March 1994: 22–26.

107 **as a hero and martyr**: Gershom Gorenberg, *The End of Days: Fundamentalism and the Struggle for the Temple Mount* (New York: Free Press, 2000), 203–8.

107 **law student Yigal Amir**: The Jerusalem Report Staff, *Shalom Friend: The Life and Legacy of Yitzhak Rabin* (New York: Newmarket, 1996): 226.

107 **"to love all Jews"**: Jerusalem Report Staff, *Shalom Friend* 247.

108 **concrete mixers worked overtime**: Deborah Sontag, "Barak's Ministry Outpaces Netanyahu's on New Settlements," *New York Times*, 28 Sept. 1999, www.nytimes.com/1999/09/28/world/barak-s-ministry-outpaces-ne tanyahu-s-on-new-settlements.html, acc. 7 July 2009; Benny Morris, "Camp David and After: An Exchange (1. An Interview with Ehud Barak)," *New York Review of Books*, 13 June 2002, www.nybooks.com/articles/ar chives/2002/jun/13/camp-david-and-after-an-exchange-1-an-interview-wi/, acc. 18 Jan. 2006. Morris paraphrases Ehud Barak as saying he "allowed the expansion of existing settlements in part to mollify the Israeli right, which he needed quiescent as he pushed forward toward peace."

108 **from 116,000 to 198,000**: Dror Etkes, "Gidul Ha'ukhlusiah Hayehudit Bagadah Hama'aravit Uretzu'at Azzah," 11 March 2003 summary of Central Bureau of Statistics figures.

108 **surely figures as one factor**: See Deborah Sontag, "Quest for Mideast Peace: How and Why It Failed," *New York Times*, 26 July 2001; Hussein Agha and Robert Malley, "Camp David: The Tragedy of Errors," *New York Review of Books*, 9 Aug. 2001.

109 **areas of East Jerusalem**: Central Bureau of Statistics, "Population of Localities 30.06.2010 (Provisional Data)," www.cbs.gov.il/population/ new_2010/table1.pdf, acc. 22 Nov. 2010; B'Tselem, "Ha'ukhlusia Bahit-nahaluyot Bagadah Hama'aravit Lefi Shanim," www.btselem.org/He brew/Settlements/Settlement_population.xls, acc. 27 Sept. 2010.

109 **"what portion . . . is allocated"**: State Comptroller, Report 54b (2003): 309.

109 **"than the [Mordechai] Vanunu affair"**: Gershom Gorenberg, "Settlement Flurry," *Jerusalem Post*, 3 Dec. 1986.

110 **an unnatural cash stimulant**: Dror Tzaban, *Omdan Helki Shel Taktzivei Memshalah Hamufnim Lehitnahaluyot Bagadah Hama'aravit Ubiretzu'at Azzah Veshel Tiktzuv Ha'odef Bishnat 2001*, January 2001; Hareuveni, *By Hook and by Crook: Israeli Settlement Policy in the West Bank* (Jerusalem:

B'Tselem, July 2010): 37–47; Yehezkel Lein, interview; Gershom Gorenberg, "At What Price," *Mother Jones*, July–August 2003: 42–49.

111   **livelihood of one's choice:** Hok Yesod: Kvod Ha'adam Veheruto, 1992; Hok Yesod: Hofesh Ha'isuk, 1992.

111   **contradicted a basic law:** CA 6821/93, *Bank Mizrahi v. Migdal Kfar Shitufi*, www.nevo.co.il/Psika_Word/elyon/PADI-NH-4-221-L.doc,acc.22 Nov. 2010.

111   **receiving the largest benefits:** HCJ 116/03; Hareuveni, *By Hook and by Crook* 38–39; Yehudit Karp, "I-Tziut Hamedinah Lefiskei Shel Batei Hamishpat," letter to Attorney General Yehudah Weinstein (undated, received by Weinstein 7 Feb. 2010).

112   **the breakdown is classified:** Tzaban, *Omdan*; Dror Tzaban, interview.

112   **"in the post-1967 era":** Shlomo Swirski, *The Burden of Occupation: The Cost of the Occupation to Israeli Society, Polity and Economy, 2008 Update* (Tel Aviv: Adva Center, 2008): 61.

113   **to the prophet Muhammad:** Ahmad Agbariya, interview, citing the hadith, "Mamuna said: 'O Messenger of Allah! Inform us about Bayt Al-Maqdis [Jerusalem]!' He said: 'It is the land where people will be gathered and resurrected [on the Day of Judgement]. Go and pray in it, for a prayer in it is the equivalent of a thousand prayers in other [mosques].' " (The hadith appears in the classic collections Abu Dawud, Sunan 467; Ibn Majah, Sunan 147; Ahmad Ibn Hanba, Musnad 6/463; Al-Bayhaqi, Sunan 2/441. My thanks to Mustafa Abu Sway, A. Rashied Omar, and David Cook for locating the material.)

113   **Intifada had been ignited:** I deliberately stress the deaths following Sharon's visit as more inflammatory than the visit itself. In Oct. 2000, a senior Israeli security official, speaking on condition of anonymity, told me it would have been better to schedule Sharon's visit for the beginning of the week rather than a Thursday, allowing time for Palestinian anger to dissipate before Friday prayers. The official did not mention the police failure to learn from previous incidents at the Mount that nonlethal crowd control methods were vital.

113   **However spontaneous its eruption:** The 2001 Mitchell Report states, "We were provided with no persuasive evidence that . . . the PA planned the uprising." George J. Mitchell et al., *Sharm El-Sheikh Fact-Finding Committee Report, 30 April 2001* (Washington, D.C.: U.S. Department of State, 2001), 2001–2009.state.gov/p/nea/rls/rpt/3060.htm. The debate on the issue continues.

113   **over 65,000 Palestinians:** B'Tselem, "27 Sept. '10: 10 Years to the Second Intifada—Summary of Data," www.btselem.org/English/Press_Releases/20100927.asp, acc. 22 Nov. 2010.

114   **"fingers" of Israeli settlement:** See sources at **contiguous Palestinian state**, p. 264 above.

114   **"Israeli" side of the fence:** "Revised Route of the Security Fence Accord-

ing to the Government Decision of April 30, 2006," www.seamzone.mod. gov.il/Pages/eng/seamzone_map_eng.htm, acc. 28 Sept. 2006.

114 **separated from their farmlands:** Yehezkel Lein, *Behind the Barrier: Human Rights Violations as a Result of Israel's Separation Barrier* (Jerusalem: B'Tselem, 2003), gave initial estimates of 11,700 Palestinians on the west side of the barrier, 128,500 Palestinians in enclaves surrounded by the barrier, and 72,200 separated from their farmland and dependent on Israeli permits to pass through gates to cultivate their crops. The fence route was subsequently altered in response to High Court of Justice decisions and political developments, altering these numbers but not eliminating the issues.

114 **an Israeli-Palestinian border:** Dany Tirza, interview.

114 **"border of the state of Israel":** Yuval Yoaz, "Justice Minister: West Bank Fence Is Israel's Future Border," *Ha'aretz*, 1 Dec. 2005.

114 **both sides of the fence:** Tirza, interview; www.seamzone.mod.gov.il/ Pages/Heb/mivne.htm, acc. 23 Nov. 2010.

115 **at the closed gate:** Abdulkarim Ayoub Ahmed, interview.

115 **"won't be a diplomatic process":** Ari Shavit, "Beshem Marsho," *Ha'aretz*, 8 Oct. 2004, www.haaretz.co.il/hasite/pages/ShArtPE. jhtml? itemNo=486151, acc. 24 Aug. 2005.

115 **600 residents:** Interior Ministry listing of Israeli population in "Judea, Samaria and Gaza," communicated July 21, 2005.

116 **burn before the holiday:** *Ha'aretz*, 22 Apr. 2005, www.haaretz.co.il/ hasite/pages/ShArtPE.jhtml?itemNo=568351, acc. 26 Aug. 2005.

116 **"It will not be":** *Arutz Sheva Hadashot*, 23 June 2005, www.inn.co.il/ News/News.aspx/115887, acc. 24 Nov. 2010.

116 **crops were harvested:** "Keren Ma'amin Vezore'a," www.group.co.il/ donation/katifund/CreditInput.asp?type=zore, acc. 26 Aug. 2005; Nadav Shragai, "Hodshayim Lifnei Hahitnatkut, Alafim Samim Kaspam Al Keren 'Ma'amin Vezore'a,'" *Ha'aretz*, 17 June 2005.

116 **orange six-pointed stars:** "Disengagement Timeline," www.haaretz. com/hasen/pages/ShArtDisengagement.jhtml?itemNo=614898, acc. 22 Aug. 2005.

117 **over sacred soil:** *Ma'ariv, Yediot Aharonot,* 19–21 July 2005.

117 **philosopher Avishai Margalit:** Avishai Margalit, *On Compromise and Rotten Compromises* (Princeton, N.J.: Princeton University Press, 2010): 57.

117 **doubt, self-castigation, failure:** See, for instance, Hagai Huberman, "Hakhi Rehok She'efshar," *Eretz Binyamin*, Feb. 2008, www.binyamin. org.il/?CategoryID=537&ArticleID=1060, acc. 21 Aug. 2008.

118 **law-abiding for "Jews":** This is a brief summary of interviews and informal conversations over five years. See also Gershom Gorenberg, "Religious Zionists Facing Deep Rifts after Evacuation of Amona Outpost," *Forward*, 10 Feb. 2006; Gershom Gorenberg, "Religious Zionists Feel

Anger, Alienation as Israel's Political Map Shifts Leftward," *Forward*, 5 May 2006; Meron Rapoport, "Me'akhshav Zeh Yehudim Mul Yisrae- lim," *Ha'aretz*, 6 Jan. 2006; Nahum Barnea, "The Neighbor's Winery," *Yediot Aharonot*, 28 Aug. 2009; Nahum Barnea, "Wallerstein: I Was Si- lent for Too Long," *Yediot Aharonot*, 12 Jan. 2010.

118   **Yitzhar near Nablus:** The yeshivah was originally located at Joseph's Tomb inside Nablus.

118   **after a plea bargain:** Eitan Felner and Roly Rozen, *Law Enforcement on Israeli Civilians in the Occupied Territories* (Jerusalem: B'Tselem, 1994): 17, 62; Gershom Gorenberg and Myra Noveck, "West Bank Settlers Go on a Rampage," *Middle East Times*, 6–12 June 1989: 1. The killing oc- curred on 29 May 1989. Three weeks later, on 20 June 1989, one of the same students from Od Yosef Hai opened fire on Palestinian workers waiting for rides on Gehah Highway outside Tel Aviv. Gershom Goren- berg and Myra Noveck, "Underground Determined to Thwart Peace Efforts," *Middle East Times*, 4–10 July 1989: 3; "Jews at Slain Settler's Funeral Call Shamir 'Traitor,'" *New York Times*, 21 June 1989, www .nytimes.com/1989/06/21/world/jews-at-slain-settler-s-funeral-call- shamir-traitor.html, acc. 2 Jan. 2011.

119   **"total travesty of justice":** Alan Cowell, "An Israeli Mayor Is Under Scrutiny," *New York Times*, 6 June 1989, query.nytimes.com/gst/full- page.html?res=950DE1DD1631F935A35755C0A96F948260&scp=1&sq =Yitzhak%20Ginsburg&st=cse, acc. 2 Jan. 2011.

119   **mass murderer of Hebron:** "Yeshivat Od Yosef Hai Berashut Harav Yitzhak Ginsburg Shlita," www.odyosefchai.org.il, acc. 25 Nov. 2010. Eulogy originally published in 1994 as a pamphlet by Ginsburgh, *Ba- ruch Hagever: Hamesh Mitzvot Klaliot Shehen Hebetim Pnimi'im Bema'asehu Shel Hakadosh Rav Baruch Goldstein, Hashem Yikom Damo*, and republished in Michael Ben-Horin, ed., *Baruch Hagever: Sefer Zi- karon Lekadosh Dr. Baruch Goldstein* (Jerusalem: Yehudah, 5755 [1994– 95]). See also Ehud Sprinzak, *Brother against Brother: Violence and Extremism in Israeli Politics from Altalena to the Rabin Assassination* (New York: Free Press, 1999): 268–71.

119   **grow up to harm us:** Yitzhak Shapira and Yosef Elitzur, *Torat Hamelekh: Dinei Nefashot Ben Yisrael Le'amim* (Hamakhon Hatorani Sheleyad Yeshivat Od Yosef Hai, 5710 [2009]): 17–27, 158–98.

120   **caused national controversy:** RNPO, financial reports of Beit Hamid- rash Od Yosef Hai; "Perut Tmikhot," via www.tmichot.gov.il, acc. 25 Nov. 2010. Shapira and Elitzur were arrested and questioned in the summer of 2010 on suspicion of inciting racism and violence, but were released and have not been charged as of this writing.

120   **the number of its students:** In 2010, the Education Ministry budgeted 1,279,318 shekels ($342,705) for Od Yosef Hai but actually transferred only 945,368 shekels ($254,318). The Welfare Ministry, which provided

Od Yosef Hai with 92,352 shekels in 2009 ($23,484), did not give it funding in 2010. www.tmichot.gov.il, acc. 25 Nov. 2010. The letters from attorney Einat Hurvitz of the Israel Religious Action Center to the directors-general of the Education Ministry and Welfare Ministry are dated 8 Apr. 2010. A letter of 8 Aug. 2010 from Education Ministry director-general Shimshon Shoshani to IRAC states funding for Od Yosef Hai is under review "following your letter." (Correspondence provided by IRAC.) However, on 5 Jan. 2011, the Education Ministry's spokesperson, responding in writing to my questions, said the suspension followed an inspection showing that the yeshivah had fewer students than it had reported. The Welfare Ministry spokesperson wrote on the same date that funding was suspended because "the results of an audit showed need for additional examination."

121 **after marrying Yitzhak:** Sasson, *Havat Da'at*, appendix 1:31, and the Spiegel Report, www.haaretz.co.il/hasite/images/printed/P300109/uri ib.mht, acc. 30 Apr. 2009, give the founding date as October 1998. In late 2009, however, Skali said that she and her husband had been there ten years. Hagit Ofran, Peace Now Settlement Watch, lists the founding date as "early 1999." Hagit Ofran, "Outpost List," e-mailed 24 Nov. 2010.

121 **never been approved by the government:** Sasson, *Havat Da'at*, appendix 1:31; Ofran, "Outpost List." Sasson lists the Housing Ministry outlay on "infrastructure" and "public buildings" as 800,000 shekels. The exchange rate has fluctuated; giving an exact dollar amount is not possible.

122 **suspected of attacking Palestinians:** Lior Yavne, *A Semblance of Law* (Tel Aviv: Yesh Din, 2006): 117–21.

123 **sewage lines to classrooms:** Ronny Goldschmidt, interview.

123 **remove those outposts:** Office of the Spokesman, Department of State, *A Performance-Based Roadmap to a Permanent Two-State Solution to the Israeli-Palestinian Conflict*, 30 Apr. 2003.

123 **her report is incomplete:** Talia Sasson, interview.

124 **hiding the ministry's role:** Sasson, *Havat Da'at* 113–14, 139, 149.

124 **fictitiously designated outposts:** Sasson, *Havat Da'at* 24, 113, 125–30.

124 **neighborhoods of older ones:** Sasson, *Havat Da'at* 125–26, 129–30; "Hityahasut Hahativah Lehityashvut Behistadrut Hatzionit Ha'olamit Lehavat Da'at (Beina'im) Benose Ma'ahazim Bilti Murshim," 2005: 15, provided by the WZO Settlement Division. Appendix 8 of this document is Avigdor Lieberman's letter of 10 Feb. 1997 to Sallai Meridor, head of the Settlement Division. Lieberman describes "neighborhoods" of existing settlements built at a distance from them and having their own communal organization, and instructs him to treat them as separate settlements. Sasson accurately assesses the letter as evidence that labeling outposts as neighborhoods of existing settlements was a deliberate fiction. The specific "neighborhoods" listed by Lieberman were

established before the wave of outposts, but the instruction was applied as a general rule for such "neighborhoods."

125 **by Israel's own standards:** Sasson, *Havat Da'at* 63–66.

125 **guide government officials:** Sasson, interview.

125 **began under Netanyahu:** Sasson, *Havat Da'at*, appendix 1, lists several outposts apparently established during Rabin's term. Sasson also included in her report several settlements established illegally before the Rabin government's freeze on settlement planning—that is, before the government's public position was that no new settlements would be established.

125 **land in peace negotiations:** Wallerstein, interview; Nadav Shragai, "Ma'ahaz Ve'od Ma'ahaz—Kakh Yotzrim Bagadah 'Retzef Hityashvut' Yehudi," *Ha'aretz*, 6 Sept. 2004, www.haaretz.co.il/hasite/pages/ShArt .jhtml?itemNo=474206, acc. 2 Nov 2009.

126 **to Palestinian Authority rule:** Wye River Memorandum, www.state .gov/www/regions/nea/981023_interim_agmt.html, acc. 26 Nov. 2010.

126 **"will be in their hands":** "Provocative Words Raise Mideast Tensions," CNN, www.cnn.com/WORLD/meast/9811/15/mideast.wrap/, acc. 11 Mar. 2003; "Briefing by Foreign Minister of the State of Israel Ariel Sharon, National Press Club, Washington, D.C., December 7, 1998," www.israel-mfa.gov.il/mfa/go.asp?MFAH08su0, acc. 11 Mar. 2003.

126 **interaction between two states:** Menachem Klein, *The Shift: Israel-Palestine from Border Struggle to Ethnic Conflict* (London: Hurst, 2010): 119.

126 **approval or building permits:** Sasson, *Havat Da'at*, appendix 1:43, states that Amonah was established in 1995, on private Palestinian land. Ofran, "Outpost List," dates it to 1997.

127 **a row of houses:** Yifat Ehrlich, interview; on-the-ground observations.

127 **end of the ridge:** Sasson, *Havat Da'at*, appendix 1:43. The houses were photographed by Peace Now Settlement Watch director Dror Etkes repeatedly in early 2005.

127 **housing minister Effie Eitam:** Sasson, *Havat Da'at* 139–68. Sasson states that the decision on buying the mobile homes was made in 2002 or early 2003, and that she was informed that Eitam made the decision. I note that Eitam became housing minister on March 3, 2003, so there may be a discrepancy in the timing.

127 **state land to outposts:** Sasson *Havat Da'at* 22, 27–31, 40–41, 161–68.

127 **was far from completing:** Sasson, interview.

128 **"setting up unauthorized outposts":** Sasson, *Havat Da'at* 148.

128 **did not find evidence:** Sasson, interview; Uri Glickman, "Sharon Lo Kashur Lehakamat Hama'ahazim," www.nrg.co.il/online/1/ART/866 /799.html, acc. 24 Nov. 2010.

128 **to pore over maps:** Amos Harel, "Mofaz Makshiah Et Yahaso Lema'ahazim, Sharon Megabeh Otam," *Ha'aretz*, 16 May 2003, news .walla.co.il/?w=//388380, acc. 27 May 2003.

128 **where to build outposts:** Shragai, "Ma'ahaz Ve'od Ma'ahaz." Quoting unnamed settlers, Shragai also describes how Sharon, as infrastructure minister under Netanyahu, instructed them in subterfuges to establish an outpost on what he regarded as a strategic hilltop.

128 **overlooking the Jordan River:** See sources at **contiguous Palestinian state,** p. 264; "Ma'ahazim Mekashrim Ben Hitnahaluyot Biyehudah Veshomron" (map), www.haaretz.co.il/hasite/images/daily/D0609 04/map_maahazim.jpg, acc. 24 Nov. 2010; "Degem Hashlitah Haterritorialit Bagadah Hama'aravit," map (Jerusalem: Peace Now, 2005).

128 **only about 4,000 people:** Ofran, "Outpost List."

129 **with Western culture:** Ehrlich, interview.

129 **began families in the outposts:** Etti Borstein, "Noar Hagva'ot: Ben Hemshekhiut Lemered," www.articles.co.il/article/4793, acc. 21 May 2009; Hanoch Daum, "Dor Hakipot Hagruziniot," *Nekuda*, October 1999, 12–15; Yisrael and Noa Ariel, interview; Skali, interview; Zar, interview; anonymous interviewees at outposts.

129 **not surprisingly, are rare:** Yavne, *Semblance*, 42, 45, 47, 83, 103–6, 108–10, 112–20; Shifra Elbaz-Rivkin, "Haguru. Zakai," *Hatzofeh*, Jan. 2005, www.hazofe.co.il/web/katava6.asp?id=41175, acc. 20 Nov. 2010; "Beit Hamishpat Zikah Et Avri Ran," *Arutz Sheva*, 16 Jan. 2006, www .shechem.org/interact/publish/article_204.shtml, acc. 20 Nov. 2010.

130 **the state promised to remove:** HCJ 6357/05, "Atirah Letzav Al Tnai Vetzav Benayim," www.peacenow.org.il/data/SIP_STORAGE/ files /1/1151.doc, acc. 8 Feb. 2006; "Hahahlatah," 8 Aug. 2005, elyon1.court .gov.il/files/05/570/063/R07/05063570.r07.pdf, acc. 8 Feb. 2006.

130 **the houses were razed:** *Ynet*, 1 Feb. 2006, www.ynetnews.com/ articles/1,7340,L-3209023,00.html, www.ynet.co.il/articles/0,7340,L-32 09281,00.html, acc. 1 Feb. 2006; Israeli Radio reports, 1 Feb. 2006.

131 **"Connect to Torah":** Gershom Gorenberg, "Religious Zionists Facing Deep Rifts after Evacuation of Amona Outpost," *Forward*, 10 Feb. 2006.

131 **ardor for outposts:** State Comptroller, Report 54b, 305–74, and Report 56a, 187–99; PS letter from M. Mazuz to cabinet members, 30 May 2006.

131 **razed new buildings:** E.g., the demolition of a house at the Negohot outpost in Nov. 2009. Efrat Weiss, "Soldiers Again Protest Settlement Evacuation," *Ynet*, 16 Nov. 2009, www.ynetnews.com/articles/0,7340,L-3805871,00.html, acc. 16 Nov. 2009.

131 **"We've never heard":** Sasson, interview.

132 **manufactured reasons not to act:** E.g., HCG 9051/05, Peace Now petition asking for demolition of illegal houses in the outposts of Hayovel and Hareshah, elyon1.court.gov.il/files/05/510/090/32n/05090510.32n. htm; HCG 3008/06, petition by Peace Now against the outposts Ramat Gilad, Givat Asaf, Ma'aleh Rehavam, Mitzpeh Lakhish, and Givat Haro'eh, elyon1.court.gov.il/files/06/080/030/P09/06030080.p09 .pdf;HCJ 8887/06; HCJ 9060/08.

132   **forty years after he died:** Matti Friedman, "West Bank Land Deal Leads to California," Associated Press, 19 Dec. 2008. A copy of the notarized document, in my possession, states that "Abdel-Latif Hassaan Sumarin" signed it on 12 Feb. 2004. The purported signature of the notary, D. K. Shaw, looks nothing like his signature on a document filed with the clerk-recorder of Orange County, California. A document issued by a Palestinian Authority sharia court in 1998—also in my possession—certifies that Abdel Latif Sumarin died in 1961.

132   **IDF to remove Migron:** HCJ 8887/06, "Atirah Lematan Tzav al Tnai," www.peacenow.org.il/data/SIP_STORAGE/files/0/2510.doc, acc. 16 Mar. 2009.

132   **the state's lawyer wrote:** HCJ 8887/06, "Teguvah Mikdamit Mita'am Hameshivim 1-4," 17 Dec. 2006, www.peacenow.org.il/data/SIP_STORAGE/files/8/2638.pdf, acc. 16 Mar. 2009.

132   **nearby settlement of Adam:** HCJ 8887/06, "Tatzhir Teshuvah Mita'am Hameshivim 1-4," 1 Feb. 2009, www.peacenow.org.il/data/SIP_STORAGE/files/0/3990.pdf, acc. 16 Mar. 2009.

132   **not shy in saying so:** Roni Genad, interview.

133   **Migron stayed in place:** HCJ 8887/06, "Hahahlatah," 15 Mar. 2010, elyon1.court.gov.il/files/06/870/088/n38/06088870.n38.pdf, acc. 10 Nov. 2010.

133   **"nothing is ever done":** *Ynet*, 15 Sept. 2010, www.ynet.co.il/articles/0,7340,L-3954705,00.html, acc. 11 Nov. 2010. The case is HCJ 9060/08, elyon1.court.gov.il/files/08/600/090/n13/08090600.n13.pdf, acc. 24 Nov. 2010.

133   **powerless to protect human rights:** In a February 2010 letter to Attorney General Yehudah Weinstein, former deputy attorney general Yehudit Karp listed a series of Supreme Court decisions that the government had failed to implement. Karp, "I-Tziut Hamedinah."

134   **"backbone of the army":** Sasson, interview.

V. Disorderly Conduct

135   **Moshe Botavia said no:** Details of the Botavia case are taken primarily from the military appeals court ruling, A144/06, and the Supreme Court ruling, PCA 5716/08. Botavia refused to be interviewed.

136   **"values that he has grown up on":** Hagit Rotenberg, "Ga'avat Yehidah," *Besheva*, 22 Dec. 2005, www.inn.co.il/Besheva/Article.aspx/5220, acc. 14 Nov. 2010.

138   **a universal draft:** Hok Sherut Bitahon, 1949.

138   **"one's ability to fight":** Motti Golani, interview.

139   **leadership and prominence:** Yagil Levy, "The Case of the al-Aqsa Intifada: The Linkage between Israel's Military Policies and the Military's Social Composition," *American Behavioral Scientist* 51.11 (2008): 1578; Yonathan Shapiro, *Illit Lelo Mamshikhim* (An Elite without Successors:

Generations of Political Leaders in Israel) (Tel Aviv: Sifriat Poalim, 1984): 128–44; Yagil Levy, *Mitzava Ha'am Letzava Haperiferiot* (From "People's Army" to "Army of the Peripheries") (Jerusalem: Carmel, 2007): 39–45.

139 **old ethic of self-sacrifice:** Yaron Ungar, *Gvulot Hatziut Vehasarbanut Lapekudah Hatzva'it* (Jerusalem: Knesset, Merkaz Hamehkar Vehameda, 2010); Yesh Gvul, www.yeshgvul.org/about_e.asp, acc. 12 June 2002; Gershom Gorenberg, "The Thin Green Line," *Mother Jones*, Sept.–Oct. 2002.

140 **new program for Orthodox men:** Drori, *Bein Emunah Letzava* (Between Faith and Military Service: The Haredi Nahal Battalion) (Jerusalem: Floersheimer Institute for Policy Studies, 2005): 14–15; Yagil Levy, "Yeshivot Bli Hesder," *Ynet*, 14 July 2005, www.ynet.co.il/articles/0,7340,L-3112445,00.html, acc. 15 Aug. 2010; Menachem Klein, *Bar-Ilan: Akademiah, Dat Vepolitikah* (Bar-Ilan: University between Religion and Politics) (Jerusalem: Magnes, 1998): 141–43. The first *hesder* yeshivah, Kerem Beyavneh, was established in the 1950s, and an initial arrangement with the army began in 1959 as part of Nahal. The formal beginning of the *hesder* as an independent program, however, came only in 1965.

141 **promoted religious radicalism:** Drori, *Bein Emunah Letzava* 14–15; Stuart A. Cohen, "Dilemmas of Military Service in Israel: The Religious Dimension," *Tora u-Madda Journal* 12 (2004): 9; Klein, *Bar-Ilan*, 141–44; B., "Mekomam Shel Hovshei Hakipot Bapikud Hatakti Shel Tzahal," *Ma'arakhot* 432 (2010): 50–57; Eliezer Don Yehiya, "The Book and the Sword: The Nationalist Yeshivot and Political Radicalism in Israel," in *Accounting for Fundamentalisms: The Dynamic Character of Movements*, ed. Martin E. Marty and R. Scott Appleby (Chicago: Fundamentalism Project, University of Chicago Press, 1994): 271–90; Moshe Moskovic private papers, 7 July 1968 letter from Col. Dan Hiram to commander of Judea and Samaria Area and 11 Nov. 1968 letters to students and parents of Har Etzion Yeshivah; ISA 153.8/7920/7A, docs. 216–17; YLE 5/31, 3 Sept. 1968; Moshe Moskovic, interview; M. Menahem, "Hayeshivah El Mul Hakotel," *Zra'im*, Nisan 5728 (Mar.–Apr. 1968): 6–7.

141 **for top combat units:** "Toldot Hamekhinah," www.bneidavid.org/show_item.asp?levelId=62596; "Mekhinah Kdam Tzva'it," www.bneidavid.org/show_item.asp?levelId=62601&itemId=9, acc. 1 Dec. 2010.

142 **secular society to the Orthodox:** Hagai Huberman, "Kumtah Srugah," *Besheva,* 8 July 2004, www.inn.co.il/Besheva/Article.aspx/3010, acc. 7 Dec. 2010.

142 **preparing motivated soldiers:** Matti Friedman, "The Thirteenth Year," *Jerusalem Report*, 15 Dec. 2003: 18.

142 **there were thirty-six:** "Mekhinot Kdam Tzva'iot," cms.education.gov.il/EducationCMS/Units/Mechinot_Kdam/Odot/skira.htm, acc. 1 Dec., 2010.

142 **graduates of religious schools:** Stuart A. Cohen, interview; B., "Mekomam" 50–57.

143 **"people and the Land":** *Yossi,* privately published memorial book for Sgt. Yosef Weinstock: 142–43; "Sgt. Yosef Weinstock," www.izkor.gov .il/HalalView.aspx?id=514375, acc. 11 Aug. 2010.

143 **"martyrs" worthy of emulation:** See, for example, *Or Hame'ir,* privately published memorial booklet for First Sgt. Meir Shenwald, 2–3; "First Sgt. Meir Shenwald," www.izkor.gov.il/HalalView.aspx?id=514285, acc. 11 Aug. 2010.

143 **officers were Orthodox:** B., "Mekomam" 50–57. Since the army does not keep figures on how many recruits are Orthodox, the author of the article used statistics on graduates of Orthodox high schools as the best available substitute.

144 **or of the Bnei David academy:** Lilach Shoval, "Golani Hoveshet Kippah," *Yisrael Hayom,* 6 Jan. 2010: 11.

144 **of Israel's Jewish population:** *Bamahaneh,* 1 Oct. 2010: 8, 51–53; Central Bureau of Statistics, *Statistical Abstract of Israel 2010,* table 2:7.

144 **twice their proportion:** Stuart A. Cohen, "Tensions between Military Service and Jewish Orthodoxy In Israel: Implications Imagined and Real," *Israel Studies* 12.2 (2007): 104; B., "Mekomam."

146 **"into a black flag":** Itai Haviv, interview.

147 **"Tomorrow the objection":** HCJ 7622/02.

147 **return fugitive slaves:** F. N. Mono, *The Drinking Gourd* (New York: Harper & Row, 1970).

148 **became a national issue:** The issue had briefly arisen earlier, before the IDF dismantled bases in order to withdraw from six West Bank cities at the end of 1995 under the Oslo II accord on expanded Palestinian autonomy. In July 1995 fifteen rabbis, including ex–chief rabbi Avraham Shapira and the deans of several *hesder* yeshivot, issued a ruling against dismantling the bases. After the pullout, army officials said they did not knew of any soldiers who had refused orders. However, according to one of the *hesder* rabbis who signed the ruling, the army avoided assigning *hesder* units to dismantling bases. The role of graduates of premilitary academies in the army was still small at the time. See "Psak Halakhah Be'inyan Seruv Pekudah," www.yeshiva.org.il/midrash/ shiur.asp?id=1978, acc. 12 Dec. 2010; *Ha'aretz,* 12 July 1995; Peter Hirschberg, "Soldiers Ignore Rabbis' Ban on W. Bank Pullout," *Jerusalem Report,* 25 Jan. 1996: 4.

148 **"Heaven doesn't want this":** Rabbi Aharon Trop, "Gerush Yehudim Zo Averah," *Besheva,* 15 Oct. 2004 (actual publication was on 14 Oct.), www.inn.co.il/Besheva/Article.aspx/3396, acc. 1 Dec. 2010.

148 **"forbidden for any Jew":** "Isur Hishtatfut Be'akirat Yishuvim Uma'ahazim," 29 Tishrei 5765 (15 Oct. 2010), rotter.net/User_files/fo rum/gil/41716f560ab30a49.pdf, acc. 1 Dec. 2010.

148 **twenty-four *hesder* soldiers:** Arik Bender, "63 Sarbanim Bizman Hahitnatkut," *NRG,* 7 Sept. 2005, www.nrg.co.il/online/1/ART/980/911

.html, acc. 9 June 2010. An earlier report appearing in *Bamahaneh*, 23 Aug. 2005, said 163 soldiers disobeyed orders during the preparations and implementation of the disengagement, creating reason to question Halutz's figures.

148 **than with the disengagement:** Cohen, "Tensions" 103–26; Cohen, "Dilemmas" 12.

148 **peace since the 1980s:** Menahem Rahat, "Nikra'im Bein Harabbanim," *NRG*, 25 Oct. 2004, www.nrg.co.il/online/1/ART/804/492.html, acc. 24 Nov. 2010.

150 **"the tent of Torah":** Avihai Ronski, "Seruv Leseruv Pekudah," *Besheva*, 28 May 2003, www.inn.co.il/Besheva/Article.aspx/1597, acc. 16 Dec. 2009.

150 **carrying out such orders:** Shlomo Aviner, "Seruv Lo! Motivatzia Gam Lo!" *She'ilat Shlomo*, www.havabooks.co.il/article_ID.asp?id=65 (original publication date, according to secondary reports, was in late Oct. 2004), acc. 24 Nov. 2010.

150 **nine of the Ten Commandments:** Shlomo Aviner, "Aseret Hadibrot Lamegaresh," *She'ilat Shlomo*, www.havabooks.co.il/article_ID.asp?id=62 (original publication date, according to secondary reports, was 11 July 2005), acc. 24 Nov. 2010.

151 **"carry out this mission":** Moshe Hagar, interview.

151 **"none carried out orders":** Yitzhak Nissim, interview.

151 **avoided carrying them out:** Hagit Rotenberg, "Hasarbanim: Hasippur Ha'amiti," *Besheva*, 6 Oct. 2005, www.inn.co.il/Besheva/Article.aspx/4963, acc. 9 Mar. 2009.

151 **total police force in Israel:** Anat Bashan, "Dakat Ha-90," *Korim Meah*, 9 Aug. 2005: 3, www.police.gov.il/meida_laezrach/pirsomim/KitveiEt/Documents/daka90.pdf, acc. 17 Nov. 2009. In a 19 Nov. 2009 statement, the Israel Police spokesperson's office informed me that the total strength of the Israel Police, including the paramilitary Border Police, was then 26,848.

151 **contingent numbered 15,000:** Stuart Cohen, "Tensions" 108.

152 **opt out of army service:** Yagil Levy, "The Embedded Military: Why Did the IDF Perform Effectively in Executing the Disengagement Plan?" *Security Studies* 16.3 (2007): 402–3; Amos Harel, "Nisayon Halehimah Im Hapalistinaim Umispar Hadati'im Hagavo'ah—Hotzi'u Hativat Golani Mima'agalei Hapinui," *Ha'aretz*, 17 June 2005, www.haaretz.co.il/hasite/pages/ShArt.jhtml?itemNo=589104, acc. 12 Dec. 2009; Cohen, "Tensions" 109; Rotenberg, "Hasarbanim," reports a case of Orthodox women soldiers refusing orders.

152 **return to sovereign Israel:** As of June 2009, over 65,000 Israelis lived east of the security fence. See "Hagadah Hama'aravit," www.peacenow.org.il/sites/default/files/SHeb_WBSide%20June%202009.pdf, acc. 1 Dec. 2009.

153   **Od Yosef Hai yeshivah:** RNPO, request to register Od Yosef Hai as a nonprofit organization, 4 Apr. 1983.

153   **illegal outpost outside Itamar:** Sasson, *Havat Da'at* 101, 123, appendix 1:23.

154   **religious law took precedence:** Gilad Shenhav, "Rav Tzva'i Hadash," *NRG*, 27 Mar. 2006, www.nrg.co.il/online/1/ART1/065/860.html, acc. 21 July 2009.

154   **of educating the army:** Off-the-record interviews with IDF soldiers and education officers.

154   **"a desecration of God's name":** *Lekhu Lahamu Belahmi* (Harabbanut Hatzva'it, 2009).

155   **"prevent harm" to noncombatants:** "Hakod Ha'eti Shel Tzahal," dover .idf.il/IDF/About/Purpose/Code_Of_Ethics.htm, acc. 14 July 2009.

155   **"blurring of values":** Yuval Freund, "Kotzer Ruah Veruah Gedolah," *Toda'ah Yehudit Letzahal Menatze'ah*, published by the Army Rabbinate for the Sabbath of 24 Jan. 2009.

155   **were really at war:** Avihai Ronski, lecture at the dedication of a Torah scroll, 12 Nov. 2009, www.karnash.co.il/contentManagment/uploaded-Files/audioGallery/R.RONSKY_sefertora.wma, acc. 16 Nov. 2009.

156   **price to enemy civilians:** *Operation Cast Lead* (Breaking the Silence, 2009), hosting-source.bronto.com/11522/public/Breaking_the_Silence_-_Operation_Cast_Lead_report_-_ENG.pdf, acc. 15 July 2009.

157   **"the army of destruction":** "'Lo Lehitgayyes Letzahal Aharei Hagerush,'" *Arutz Sheva Hadashot*, 10 Nov. 2005, www.inn.co.il/News/News .aspx/129397, acc. 1 Dec. 2010.

158   **"welfare office for Palestinians":** Itai Zar, interview.

159   **unsure what they'd do:** Keren Levi, *Tfisat Hazehut Hakollectivit Al Markiveiha Hashonim Bekerev Noar Dati Leumi* (The collective identity of religious Zionist youth and its relation to the willingness to serve in the Israeli army and to obey the law) (MA thesis, Bar-Ilan University, 2009).

159   **alumni have become officers:** "Toldot Hamekhinah," www.bneidavid .org/show_item.asp?levelId=62596, acc. 1 Dec. 2010.

160   **"Letter to Youth":** Eli Sadan, "Lehosif Or—Igeret Lano'ar," www .bneidavid.org/VF/ib_items/334/%D7%9C%D7%94%D7%95%D7%A1 %D7%99%D7%A3%20%D7%90%D7%95%D7%A8.pdf, acc. 24 Mar. 2009.

160   **"will not be given":** Eliezer Melamed, *Revivim* 2 (Jerusalem: Makhon Har Brakhah, 5768 [2007–8]): 299–300, 321–22.

160   **in the Kfir Brigade:** *Ha'aretz*, 18 Nov. 2009.

160   **twenty days in the stockade:** *Ma'ariv, Ynet, Ha'aretz*, 23–26 Oct. 2009.

161   **removed from combat duty:** *Ma'ariv, Ynet, Yediot Aharonot*, Israel Radio, 16–18 Nov. 2009.

161   **from the *hesder* program:** *Ma'ariv, Ha'aretz*, and *Ynet*, 13 Dec. 2009.

162   **"absolutely, *he shouldn't do it*":** "Sugiah Behesder," *Olam Katan*, 23 Tevet 5770 (9 Jan. 2010): 4–5.

VI. The Labor of the Righteous Is Done by Others

164   **of secular Zionist ideology:** Amos Oz, *A Tale of Love and Darkness*, trans. Nicholas de Lange (London: Vintage, 2005): 15–16.

165   **changing in the 1950s:** Menachem Friedman, *Hahevrah Haharedit: Mekorot, Megamot Vetahalikhim* (Jerusalem: JIIS, 1991): 1, 63, 121.

166   **and find work:** Friedman, interview; Menachem Friedman, "'Al Hanissim': Prihato Shel 'Olam Hatorah' (Hayeshivot Vehakollelim) Biyisrael," Emanuel Etkes, ed., *Yeshivot Uvatei Midrashot* (Jerusalem: Merkaz Shazar, 2006): 431–42; Joseph [Yosseph] Shilhav and Menachem Friedman, *Hitpashtut Tokh Histagrut: Hakehillah Haharedit Biyerushalayim* (Growth and Segregation: The Ultra-Orthodox Community of Jerusalem) (Jerusalem: Jerusalem Institute for Israel Studies, 1985): 50–52.

166   **necessarily more limited:** Limited, but not absent. Ultra-Orthodox communities, presumably using the political leverage of a block vote, have gained some preferential funding, despite the separation of religion and state in the United States. An example: the U.S. Department of Housing and Urban Development actively seeks minority contractors for certain projects. The minorities entitled to such affirmative action include "Black Americans, Hispanic Americans, Native Americans, Asian Pacific Americans, Asian Indian Americans, and *Hasidic Jewish Americans*" [emphasis added]. Dept. of Housing and Urban Development, *Procurement Handbook for Public Housing Agencies (7460.8 rev-2)*, chap. 15 and app. 1, www.hud.gov/offices/adm/hudclips/handbooks/pihh/74608/, acc. 30 Jan. 2011.

166   **ultra-Orthodox men at work:** Alex Levac, "Anashim Be'avodah," occasional photographic series appearing in section B of *Ha'aretz*, 29 Aug.–5 Oct. 2000. On the wider issues of *haredi* revival in the West, see Haym Soloveitchik, "Rupture and Reconstruction: The Transformation of Contemporary Orthodoxy," in *Jews in America: A Contemporary Reader*, ed. Roberta Rosenberg Farber and Chaim I. Waxman (Hanover, N.H.: Brandeis University Press, 1999): 320–76.

167   **ultra-Orthodoxy was vanishing:** Hok Limmud Hovah, 1949; ISA 21/11-Kaf, Knesset Education Committee minutes, 29 June 1949, 27 July 1949, and 24 Aug. 1949.

168   **7,000 to 24,000 pupils:** Friedman, *Hahevrah Haharedit* 56, 67.

168   **receive funding from the state:** Hok Hinukh Mamlakhti, 1953.

168   **rabbis substituting for parents:** Friedman, interview; Friedman, *Hahevrah Haharedit* 70–72.

168   **and their secular rivals:** Friedman, interview; Friedman, "'Al Hanissim'" 431–42.

169   **to 4,700 in 1968:** Naomi Mei-Ami, *Giyyus Talmidei Yeshivot Letzahal Vehok Dehiyat Sherut Letalmidei Yeshivot Shetoratam Umanutam (Hok Tal)* (Jerusalem: Knesset, Merkaz Hamehkar Vehameda, 2007): 3.

169   **and other general studies:** Binyamin Baron, "Ve'ein Shi'ur Rak Hatorah Hazot," *Eretz Aheret*, Sept.–Oct. 2007: 64; Friedman, "'Al Hanissim'" 431–42; interviews with *haredi* informants requesting anonymity.

169   **son was a full-time student:** Bezalel Cohen, interview; Yosseph Shilhav, interview; anonymous *haredi* informants, interviews.

169   **age twenty became the standard:** Shilhav and Friedman, *Hitpashtut* 50–52.

170   **"in [religious] practice and belief":** Moshe Scheinfeld, "Veheshiv Lev Avot El Banim," *Diglenu*, Nissan 5714 (April–May 1954), quoted in Friedman, "'Al Hanissim.'"

170   **a product of modernity:** Friedman, *Hahevrah Haharedit* 80–87.

170   **claiming to be old-time religion:** Laurence J. Silberstein, ed., *Jewish Fundamentalism in Comparative Perspective: Religion, Ideology and the Crisis of Modernity* (New York: New York University Press, 1993): 27–55.

171   **"the great *halakhic* innovators":** Lawrence Kaplan, "The Hazon Ish: Haredi Critic of Traditional Orthodoxy," in *The Uses of Tradition: Jewish Continuity in the Modern Era*, ed. Jack Wertheimer (New York: Jewish Theological Seminary, 1992): 145–73.

171   **be accepted without question:** Lawrence Kaplan 168.

172   **rubble of Eastern Europe:** Soloveitchik 320–76; Menachem Friedman, "The Lost Kiddush Cup: Changes in Ashkenazic Haredi Culture—A Tradition in Crisis," in Wertheimer, *Uses of Tradition* 175–86; Shlomo Tikochinski, interview.

172   **of a working laity:** Friedman, "'Al Hanissim'" 431–42; Friedman, *Hahevrah Haharedit* 80–87; Baron, "Ve'ein Shi'ur" 57–59.

174   **pillars that supported:** Bezalel Cohen, interview; anonymous *haredi* informants, interviews.

174   **Eastern European Jewish life:** Arye Naor, interview; Shilhav, interview.

174   **religious and budgetary issues:** KA 0523, coalition agreement between the Likud, the National Religious Party, and Yehadut Hatorah-Agudat Yisrael, 19 June 1977.

175   **other ultra-Orthodox educational institutions:** BCA ADA_00053500, coalition agreement between the Likud, the National Religious Party, Yehadut Hatorah-Agudat Yisrael, and Tenuat Mesoret Yisrael, 4 Aug. 1981.

175   **honor of Jewish women:** Naor, interview.

175   **passing the 40,000 mark:** Mei-Ami, *Giyyus*, 3.

176   **got a cash infusion:** National Insurance Institute, *Riva'on Statisti*, Apr.–June 2010, 105; Naor, interview; Esther Toledano et al., *The Effect of Child Allowances on Fertility* (Jerusalem: National Insurance Institute, 2009): 5–7; Dan Ben-David, *Israel's Labor Market: Today, in the Past and in Comparison with the West* (Jerusalem: Taub Center for Social Policy Studies in Israel, 2010): 237.

176 **long-term impact:** Naor, interview.

176 **barely supervised by the state:** "Kol Haknasot," www.knesset.gov.il/
history/heb/heb_hist_all.htm, acc. 15 Sept. 2009; Gershom Gorenberg,
"Hot Shas," *New Republic,* 25 Jan. 1999: 11–13; Naor, interview; Friedman, *Hahevrah Haharedit* 175ff. Ultra-Orthodox strength in the elections of 1996, 1999, and 2003 was partly a function of the electoral
system used in those years, in which voters cast one vote for prime
minister and a separate vote for a party in parliament. Shas, in particular, benefited from this system.

177 **9 percent of Israeli Jews:** Daniel Gottlieb, *Ha'oni Vehahitnahagut Beshuk Ha'avodah Bahevrah Haharedit* (Poverty and Labor Market Behavior in the Ultra-Orthodox Population in Israel) (Jerusalem: Van
Leer Institute, 2007): 12. There are higher estimates of the *haredi*
population. See, for instance, Norma Gurovich and Eilat Cohen-
Kastro, *Haharedim: Tifroset Geografit Umefayanim Demografiim,
Hevratiim Vekhalkaliim Shel Ha'ukhlusiah Haharedit Biyisrael, 1996–
2001* (Ultra-Orthodox Jews: Geographic Distribution and Demographic, Social and Economic Characteristics of the Ultra-Orthodox
Jewish Population in Israel) (Jerusalem: Central Bureau of Statistics,
2004): 80, which estimates that there were 550,000 *haredim* in Israel
in 2002.

177 **seven children in her lifetime:** Toledano, *Effect of Child Allowances* 9,
calculates the TFR (total fertility rate) for *haredi* women in 2001–2 as
7.24, and for other Israeli Jewish women as 2.13.

177 **stipends for large families:** National Insurance Institute, *Riva'on
Statisti,* April-June 2010, 91; Ben-David, *Israel's Labor Market* 237–38.
Sharon's coalition consisted of the Likud, Labor, and the militantly
secularist Shinui party.

177 **small drop in childbearing:** Toledano, *Effect of Child Allowances* 9.

177 **deepening the social crisis:** Na'amah Tzifroni and Bambi Sheleg, "Ani
Hared Me'od Legoral Hayehadut Haharedit," *Eretz Aheret,* Aug.–Sept.
2007: 25; Bezalel Cohen, interview.

178 **65 percent in 2008:** Ben-David, *Israel's Labor Market* 233.

178 **occupation of adult men:** Gottlieb, *Ha'oni Vehahitnahagut* 11, using figures from the Central Bureau of Statistics. In a 26 Dec. 2010 statement,
the Education Ministry spokesperson said 70,000 men were receiving
ministry stipends as *kollel* students. It is unlikely that the discrepancy in
figures is due to an increase of nearly 15,000 students in two years. At
least part of the discrepancy may be due to fraudulent listing of students,
including men who are working off the books while registered as *kollel*
students.

178 **among ultra-Orthodox women:** Ben-David, *Israel's Labor Market* 242.
In 2008, less than half of ultra-Orthodox women in the 35–54 age
bracket were employed.

178   **two-thirds of ultra-Orthodox families:** Miri Endewald et al., *2008: Poverty and Social Gaps, Annual Report* (Jerusalem: National Insurance Institute, 2009): 1, 15.

178   **aged four or less:** Gottlieb, *Ha'oni Vehahitnahagut* 13.

178   **ultra-Orthodox institutions in 2009:** Nachum Blass, *Israel's Educational System: A Domestic Perspective* (Jerusalem: Taub Center for Social Policy Studies in Israel, 2010): 165.

181   **no alternative for divorce:** Religious jurisdiction over marriage and divorce applies to other faith communities in Israel. *Sharia* courts, for instance, control divorce among Muslims. A particularly extreme consequence is that Catholic couples have no legal path to divorce.

181   **posts with their appointees:** Friedman, interview.

181   **Jewish law to solve the problem:** Center for Women's Justice, "The Problem and Our Solutions," www.cwj.org.il/the-problem-and-our-solutions, acc. 1 Dec. 2010.

182   **Jewishness into those frames:** Avi Sagi and Zvi Zohar, *Transforming Identity: The Ritual Transformation from Gentile to Jew—Structure and Meaning* (London: Continuum, 2007); Zvi Zohar, interview.

182   **annul her conversion:** Sagi and Zohar, *Transforming Identity* 252–63; Zohar, interview. Regulations on conversion by Chief Rabbi Shlomo Amar in 2006, in his role as head of the rabbinical courts, describe the process for annulling conversion—itself a radical concept—though without describing the grounds for doing so. Shlomo Amar, "Klalei Hadiun Bevakashot Legiur," 17 Shvat 5766 (15 Feb. 2006).

183   **in fact, converted properly:** Susan Weiss et al., *The Interrogation of the Convert "X" by the Israeli Rabbinic Courts* (Jerusalem: Center for Women's Justice, 2010); Zohar, interview.

183   **alliances with the ultra-Orthodox:** After the 1999 election, Ehud Barak also included *haredi* parties in his coalition. However, that election took place under the two-ballot system. While Barak won a majority in the vote for prime minister, the ultra-Orthodox and right-wing parties had a majority in parliament.

184   **five seats in parliament:** The Communist-led Hadash list draws most but not all of its support from Arab voters, and always includes a Jew in its Knesset delegation.

184   **ultra-Orthodox can charge more:** The theoretical basis for this discussion is Philip D. Straffin, "Topics in the Theory of Voting" (Boston: Birkhauser, 1980): 1–17.

184   **but hardly sufficient:** Interview, anonymity requested.

185   ***haredim* into the settlement enterprise:** Shilhav, interview; Eliahu Naeh, interview. Immanuel, a settlement designated entirely for ultra-Orthodox residents, was established earlier, but failed to attract large numbers of settlers.

185   **$50,000 interest-free mortgage:** Anonymous interviews, Beitar Illit.

185   **settlement population outside East Jerusalem:** Central Bureau of Statistics, "Population in Municipalities and Local Councils," www.cbs .gov.il/ishuvim/ishuv2009/table7.xls, acc. 1 Dec. 2010. Modi'in Illit had 46,200 residents and Beitar Illit 35,000. The municipality of Beitar Illit gave slightly higher figures, listing 36,757 residents as of 18 Oct. 2010 in a printout given to me by the municipal spokesman.

185   **aged four or under:** Central Bureau of Statistics, "Modi'in Illit," www .cbs.gov.il/publications/local_authorities2007/pdf/552_3797.pdf, acc. 29 Dec. 2010. The precise proportion, as of 2007, was 28.9 percent. In Beitar Illit, as of 18 Oct. 2010, 28.1 percent of residents were age five or under, according to the municipality. See previous note.

186   **"further to the extreme":** Shilhav, interview.

187   *haredi* **education succeeds:** Yosef Rozovsky and Eran Ben-Porat, interviews.

188   **"sealed it hermetically":** Tikochinski, interview; Bezalel Cohen, *Economic Hardship and Gainful Employment in Haredi Society in Israel: An Insider's Perspective* (Jerusalem: Floersheimer Institute for Policy Studies, 2006): 32.

188   **help** *haredim* **do that:** Naomi Darom, "Haredim Lefarnasatam," *The Marker*, 27 May 2010: 30–34; Bezalel Cohen, interview; Shilhav, interview.

189   **getting a mainstream job:** Bezalel Cohen, *Economic Hardship* 50.

189   **meager** *kollel* **salary:** Bezalel Cohen, *Economic Hardship* 48–50.

189   **"economy of the next world":** Friedman, interview.

189   **state ignored the first one:** HCJ 10296/02 (judgment delivered 11 Aug., 2004); HCJ 4805/07 (judgment delivered 27 July 2008).

189   **only teach religious subjects:** Hok Mosdot Hinukh Tarbutiim Yihudiim, 2008.

191   **to understand human complexity:** The debate over what an education in humanities should include and how it should be conducted is much too wide to sum up here. For a brief introduction, see Martha C. Nussbaum, *Not for Profit: Why Democracy Needs the Humanities* (Princeton, N.J.: Princeton University Press, 2010).

191   **moral complexity of everyday life:** Joshua Gutoff, private communication.

192   **yeshivah students sign up:** Drori, *Bein Emunah Letzava* 26–41, 51–78; Ze'ev Drori, interview; interviews with soldiers and officers in Netzah Yehudah.

193   **to keep religious commandments:** Drori, *Bein Emunah Letzava* 75.

193   **"[defending] the Jewish people":** Drori, interview; Lt. Col. Dror Spiegel, interview.

193   **"historical and divine decree":** Lt. Ariel Eliahu, interview.

194   **"ideological and political credo":** Drori, interview.

194   **soldiers in that bind:** Drori, interview; Spiegel, interview.

VII. Importing the Revolution

197 **immigrants to join them:** Benny Morris, *1948: The First Arab-Israeli War* (New Haven, Conn.: Yale University Press, 2008): 164–66; Johayna Saifi, interview; ISA 2196/14-Gimel, document 8B, Report on Activities of the Nahariyah District Administration.

197 **martyrs of the Israeli right:** Tom Segev, *One Palestine, Complete: Jews and Arabs under the British Mandate* (New York: Metropolitan, 2000): 457; Shimon Cohen, "Hayom Ha'azkarah Le'Shnei Eliahu,'" *Arutz Sheva*, 27 Mar. 2007, www.inn.co.il/News/News.aspx/160911, acc. 12 Jan 2010. In 2009, Education Minister Gideon Sa'ar of the Likud launched a new educational unit for eighth and ninth graders on "those who ascended to the gallows"—twelve members of the Irgun and Lehi who were either executed or who committed suicide in prison. They included the "two Eliahus." A ministry letter to school principals described the unit as promoting the "values of heroism, self-sacrifice and devotion to national rebirth, based on the character and actions" of the twelve. The program fit the martyrdom narrative promoted by the political heirs of the Irgun and Lehi since 1948. "Haf'alat Tokhnit Yihudit Benose Olei Hagardom," 20 Nov. 2009, cms.education.gov.il/NR/rdonlyres/125B367F-3304-4174-A710-FC61B439B5D7/104647/MictavMenahalim.doc, acc. 10 Jan. 2010; *Olei Hagardom* (Jerusalem: Education Ministry, 2009), cms.education.gov.il/NR/rdonlyres/125B367F-3304-4174-A710-FC61B439B5D7/104645/oleyGardom.pdf, acc. 10 Jan. 2010.

197 **town of Nahariyah:** Meron Rapoport, "Mitzvat Yishuv Ha'aretz Etzel Ahmad Basalon," *Ha'aretz*, 10 Oct. 2006, www.haaretz.co.il/hasite/pages/ShArtPE.jhtml, acc. 14 Oct. 2008.

197 **mosques outside the walls:** Sami Hawary, Suheila Khalil, and Suheil Omari, interviews.

198 **majority in the town:** As of 9 Dec. 2009, according to Akko municipal spokesperson Sharon Dahan, the city's population was 53,252, of whom 72 percent were Jews. The Central Bureau of Statistics gives lower figures for the total population and Jewish portion: at the end of 2009, it listed 46,300 residents, of whom 30,600—65 percent—were Jews. Central Bureau of Statistics, *Statistical Abstract of Israel 2010*, table 2.15. A 2002 Knesset report, however, listed the city's population at that time as 51,825, of whom 12,956—25 percent—were Arabs. Yossi Zulfan, *Ha'ir Akko* (Jerusalem: Knesset, Merkaz Hamehkar Vehameda, 2002).

198 **"settlement groups":** The Hebrew term I have translated as "settlement group" is *garin*, literally "seed" or "nucleus," and is the standard term for a group organized to establish a settlement or to strengthen an existing one.

198 **native of Elon Moreh:** Avishag Adari, "Te'atron Aher," *Besheva*, 13 Oct. 2008: 10; Nachshon Cohen, interview.

198   **more than eighty families:** Naftali Reznikovich, interview.

199   **"stopped the Arab encroachment":** Adari, "Te'atron."

199   **"to invade into Akko":** Sara Paparin, interview.

199   **"Akko is a Jewish city":** Nachshon Cohen, interview.

199   **"highest in the country":** "Odot Hayeshivah," www.yakko.co.il/about
       .asp, acc. 6 Jan. 2011.

199   **"power, determination and confidence":** Ori Tal, *Hametihut Bein Ye-
       hudim Le'aravim Bishkhunat Wolfson Be'akko* (Jerusalem: Knesset,
       Merkaz Hamehkar Vehameda, 2006): 3, quoting the Web page cited in
       the previous note as it appeared on 26 Oct. 2006.

199   **their military assault rifles:** Tal, "Hemetihut" 2, 4. Some soldiers are
       required to take their guns while traveling to and from their bases,
       though the IDF has reduced the number required to do so. After arriv-
       ing at his destination, the soldier must either follow strict rules on lock-
       ing up his gun or carry it with him. Some of the soldiers arriving at the
       yeshivah, therefore, had no choice but to carry their rifles. Once they
       were there, however, carrying the guns was a matter of choice. On
       changes in IDF policy on carrying guns, see Hanan Greenberg, "Ha-
       mahapekhah Nimshekhet: Anshei Keva Yistovevu Lelo Neshek," *Ynet*,
       12 Dec. 2005, www.ynet.co.il/articles/0,7340,L-3183248,00.html, acc. 29
       Jan. 2011.

200   **the peace in Wolfson:** Tal, "Hametihut" 3–4.

201   **"Akko and raised morale":** *Ynet* and *Ha'aretz*, 9–12 Oct. 2008; Ala Hle-
       hel, ed., *October 2008 in Akka (Acre): Course of Events* (Akko: Akka
       Residents Coalition, 2008), www.ittijah.org/UserFiles/File/Report-
       English.pdf, acc. 1 Dec. 2009; Elyashiv Reichner, "Garinim Birgashot
       Me'uravot," *Nekuda*, Oct. 2009: 22–26; Noam Wreshner, Ahmed Odeh,
       interviews.

202   **Beit El, Elon Moreh, and Yitzhar:** Reichner, "Garinim."

202   **connect to local Jews:** Eliyahu Mali, interview; Reichner, "Garinim."

203   **"settling in Jaffa":** Gideon Dokov, "Mitnahalim Beyaffo," 16 Iyyar 5769
       (10 May 2009), www.kipa.co.il/now/show.asp?id=32851, acc. 11 Jan.
       2011; "Proyekt Yaffo Letzibur Dati Le'umi," bemuna.co.il/project
       .asp?id=66, acc. 11 Jan. 2011. The firm describes the East Jerusalem
       project as being in the Jewish neighborhood of East Talpiot (www.be
       muna.co.il/english/project.asp?id=53), but it is actually located in the
       adjacent Palestinian neighborhood of Arab a-Sawahra. Arab and Jew-
       ish residents of Jaffa unsuccessfully challenged the Israel Lands Author-
       ity's decision to sell development rights to a firm intending to sell the
       apartments in a discriminatory manner. The Supreme Court rejected
       the suit on the grounds that it was filed after the company's sale of apart-
       ments was "an accomplished fact." Administrative Appeal 1789/10.

203   **"encourage voluntary emigration":** Uri Ariel, "Behazarah Le'akko
       Veyaffo," *Besheva*, 13 Oct. 2008: 13.

204   **the words written in it:** Sholem Asch, *God of Vengeance,* in *The Great Jewish Plays,* ed. and trans. Joseph C. Landis (New York: Avon, 1972). The play was first performed in Yiddish in 1907. When it was staged in English in New York in 1923, the cast and producer were arrested and convicted of giving an immoral performance, with the judge, identified by the *New York Times* only as "McIntyre," decrying the "desecration of the sacred scrolls of the Torah" ("'God of Vengeance' Players Convicted," *New York Times,* 24 May 1923: 1). Asch's literary reputation has survived the charge of attacking Judaism.

205   **and sold to the JNF:** David Kretzmer, *The Legal Status of Arabs in Israel* (Boulder, Colo.: Westview, 1990): 18–19, 61–66, 90–98; Yiftachel, *Ethnocracy,* 142–43; Hok Ma'amad Hahistadrut Hatzionit—Hasokhnut Hayehudit Le'eretz Yisrael, 1952.

205   **sell to well-off Jews:** Sebastian Wallerstein and Emily Silverman, *Housing Distress within the Palestinian Community of Jaffa: The End of Protected Tenancy in Absentee Ownership Homes* (Bimkom, 2009); Omar Siksek, interview; Yudit Ilany, interview.

205   **6 percent of the civil service:** Population figures from *Statistical Abstract of Israel 2010,* table 2.8, corrected by subtracting Jerusalem Arabs, most of whom are noncitizen East Jerusalem residents. Figures for Jerusalem Arabs: *Jerusalem Institute of Israel Studies, 2009–2010 Statistical Yearbook,* jiis.org/.upload/web%20C0409.xls, acc. 13 Jan. 2011. Employment figures: Ali Haider, ed., *The Equality Index of Jewish and Arab Citizens in Israel, 2008* (Jerusalem: Sikkuy, 2009): 55.

205   **larger than in Jewish schools:** Haider, *Equality Index* 41. The average for Arab classes was 29, 18 percent above the Jewish average of 24.6.

205   **almost three times larger:** Haider 45. Of Jews aged 20–34, 9 percent were enrolled in universities, compared to 3.3 percent of Arabs. The reporting method may underestimate the number of Arabs, since many Arabs start higher education at eighteen, unlike the great majority of Jewish Israelis, who first serve in the military. Factors contributing to the discrepancy may include poorer funding for schools in Arab communities, cultural bias in college-entrance testing, and the fact that Arab students must study in their second language at Israeli universities.

206   **a political transformation:** Hussein Jbarah and Abd al-Aziz Abu Isba Maswari, interviews.

206   **representation in the Knesset:** In the 1965 election, the only independent party receiving its support primarily from Arab citizens was Rakah (New Communist List), which won three seats; two other Arab parties that won a total of four seats were clients of Mapai. In 1984, two independent parties primarily supported by Arab voters won six seats. In 2009, three Arab-backed tickets won a total of eleven seats in the Knesset. "Kol Haknasot," www.knesset.gov.il/history/heb/heb_hist_all.htm, acc. 1 Dec. 2010.

207   **halfway inside the system:** Tawfik Jabareen, Dany Tirza, and Hashem Mahameed, interviews.

208   **was to exclude Arabs:** Yiftachel, *Ethnocracy* 111, 142.

208   **before the High Court of Justice:** HCJ 6698/95, ruling issued 8 Mar. 2000; Adel Ka'adan, interview; Dan Yakir, interview.

209   **"it cannot do indirectly":** HCJ 6698/95, ruling issued 8 Mar. 2000.

209   **buy a lot in Katzir:** HCJ 8060/03, petition filed 7 Sept. 2003, 194.90.30.84/hebrew-acri/article.asp?id=719, acc. 5 Jan. 2011; request for expenses, filed 1 Jan. 2006, www.acri.org.il/pdf/petitions/hit8060baqasha2.pdf, acc. 5 Jan. 2011.

209   **building their home:** "Anashim Ketanim She'asu Mahpekhot Gedolot," *The Marker,* 27 Nov. 2008, www.themarker.com/tmc/article.jhtml?ElementId=skira20081127_1041224, acc. 5 Jan. 2011.

209   **case is still pending:** HCJ 8036/07, petition filed 23 Sept. 2007 by Adalah—The Legal Center for Arab Minority Rights in Israel, the Jerusalem Open House (for LGBT rights), Mizrahi Democratic Rainbow, and others, www.adalah.org/features/land/admission-p.pdf, acc. 5 Jan. 2011; postponement of hearing, 23 Dec. 2010, elyon1.court.gov.il/files/07/360/080/n60/07080360.n60.pdf, acc. 5 Jan. 2011.

210   **danger of domestic enemies:** This section is based in part on Gershom Gorenberg, "The Minister for National Fears," *Atlantic Monthly,* May 2007. Lieberman's position on the system of government is expressed most sharply in a 2006 bill for change of the governmental system submitted by Israel Is Our Home: 17th Knesset, P1072, Hatza'at Hok Yesod: Hamemshalah, Avigdor Lieberman, et al. Under the bill, the prime minister could appoint ministers without parliamentary approval. If the Knesset approved a state of emergency, the cabinet could enact emergency regulations temporarily superseding laws—and if "the prime minister sees that the cabinet cannot be convened, and there is a pressing and vital need for emergency regulations, he may enact them." The effect of the law would be to allow the prime minister to assume dictatorial powers.

210   **total political division:** Avigdor Lieberman, interview.

210   **torture of the conspirators:** Alexey Tolstoy, *Peter the First,* trans. Tatiana Shebunina (New York: Macmillan, 1959).

210   **and began to read:** Avigdor Lieberman, interview.

211   **shattered relations with his party colleagues:** *Ha'aretz,* 12–25 Nov. 1997.

211   **"anti-Semite would invent him":** Jean-Paul Sartre, *Anti-Semite and Jew,* trans. George J. Becker (New York: Schocken, 1965): 13, 27.

212   **advocated expelling Arab citizens:** DK, 2 June 2004.

213   **"among them the United States of America":** *Tochnit Medinit Liyisrael: Matza Yisrael Beitenu* (Israel Is Our Home platform, received from party officials in 2006); Fania Kirshenbaum, interview.

213   **citizenship to non-Estonians:** Yiftachel, *Ethnocracy* 29–32.

213   **Jewish upper house in the Knesset:** Moshe Feiglin, "Tokhnit 100 Haymim," *Manhigut Yehudit*, he.manhigut.org/content/view/2457/153/, acc. 9 Nov. 2008.

213   **hard-liners fill the party ticket:** *Ha'aretz* and *Yediot Aharonot*, 9 Dec. 2008.

214   **on a two-state solution:** *Ma'ariv* and *Yediot Aharonot*, 23–24 Feb. 2009.

215   **"its Jewish and democratic values":** Hatza'at Hok Mirsham Ukhlusin, 2009, P/18/811; Hatza'at Hok Sherut Hamedinah, 2010, P/18/2792; Hatza'at Hok Hakolno'a, 2010, P/18/2307; Association for Civil Rights in Israel, *Knesset 2010 Winter Session: Expectations and Concerns*, Oct. 2009.

215   **require a loyalty oath of everyone:** *Ynet* and *Ha'aretz*, 10 Oct. 2010.

215   **economic equality, and other liberal causes:** Full disclosure: the Association for Civil Rights in Israel represented me in my High Court of Justice suit against the Israel Defense Forces Archive, and I have been a paid speaker at New Israel Fund events.

216   **invasion of Gaza in 2009:** Im Tirtzu, *Hashpa'atam Shel Irgunei Haḳeren Hahadashah Liyisrael Al Doh Goldstone*, 10 Feb. 2010, imti.org.il/Uploads/GoldstoneHE5.pdf, acc. 10 Feb. 2010. For the New Israel Fund rebuttal, see "Analysis of the Im Tirtzu Report on the New Israel Fund," www.nif.org/media-center/under-attack/lies-damn-lies-and-the-im.html, acc. 11 Feb. 2010. The official name of the UN report is *Human Rights in Palestine and Other Occupied Arab Territories: Report of the United Nations Fact-Finding Mission on the Gaza Conflict* 25 Sept. 2009 (www2.ohchr.org/english/bodies/hrcouncil/docs/12session/A-HRC-12-48.pdf, acc. 19 Oct. 2009). It is generally known by the name of the South African jurist who headed the mission, Richard Goldstone.

216   **"serves Communist interests":** Ronen Shoval, interview.

216   **"attempts to purchase its land":** Knesset votes diagrammed, 5 Jan. 2011, www.knesset.gov.il/vote/heb/Vote_Res_Map.asp?vote_id_t=15118, www.knesset.gov.il/vote/heb/Vote_Res_Map.asp?vote_id_t=15119, acc. 12 Jan. 2011.

217   **"weakening the IDF":** Video excerpts of Lieberman's widely broadcast speech of 10 Jan. 2011, at www.ynet.co.il/articles/1,7340,L-4011576,00.html, acc. 10 Jan. 2011.

217   **allegations that terror groups:** Danon's allegations are cited in a post on his website: "Beyozmat Danon: Va'adat Hakirah Baknesset Al Irgunei Smol," 6 Jan. 2011, www.dannydanon.com/he/index.php?view=article&catid=35:media&id=256:2011-01-05-21-35-05, acc. 10 Jan. 2011.

218   **racist interpretation of Judaism:** "Gilui Da'at," www.zefat.net/images/stories/10_2010/esorrav.jpg, www.bhol.co.il/article.aspx?id=22296, acc. 16 Jan. 2011; Eli Ashkenazi, "Kenes Rabbanim Lidehikat Ha'aravim Metzfat Ne'erakh Bemimun Hamedinah," *Ha'aretz*, 20 Oct. 2010, www.haaretz.co.il/hasite/spages/1194347.html, acc. 20 Oct. 2010.

218 **"match the social-cultural fabric":** Hok Letikkun Pekudat Ha'agudot Hashitufi'ot (Mispar 8), 2011. http://www.knesset.gov.il/Laws/Data/law/2286/2286.pdf, acc. 13 Apr. 2011. The law does state that a candidate must not be disqualified on the basis of his or her "race, religion, gender, nationality, handicaps, personal status, age, parental status, or sexual orientation." However, the Ka'adan case showed that it would be easy enough to disqualify a candidate by citing another criterion. By explicitly allowing disqualification based on the "social-cultural fabric" of the community, the law empties of content the ban on discrimination.

219 **"most meaningful national issues":** Yishai Friedman, "Eikh Kipah Srugah Mityashevet Al Madim Kehulim," *Olam Katan*, Rosh Hashanah 5771 (Sept. 2010): 6.

219 **"people at a very high level":** "Ani Ma'amin Shehakol Patir," *Olam Katan*, Rosh Hashanah 5771 (Sept. 2010): 6.

219 **with thirty-five recruits:** *Yediot Aharonot*, 3 Oct. 2010.

220 **"the corruption of individuals":** Yeshayahu Leibowitz, *Judaism, Human Values and the Jewish State* (Cambridge, Mass.: Harvard University Press, 1992): 225.

VIII. The Reestablishment of Israel

222 **to be a Jewish state:** To some extent, the belief in this either-or choice is a response to demands by Israeli Arab politicians and activicts that Israel transform itself from a Jewish state to a "state of all its citizens."

223 **homeland, or part of it:** Chaim Gans, *A Just Zionism: On the Morality of the Jewish State* (Oxford, England: Oxford University Press, 2008): 18–20, 25ff.

223 **in contrast to utopias:** As Emmanuel Sivan writes in his afterword to the Hebrew edition of Raymond Aron's *La Tragédie Algérienne*, "Utopias are not within reach; advancing one goal always comes at the expense of another." Raymond Aron, *Hatragediah Ha'aljirit* (The Algerian Tragedy), first published in France as *La Tragédie Algérienne*, Hebrew edition, with afterword by Emmanuel Sivan (Tel Aviv: Sifrei Aliyat Gag, 2005): 87.

224 **for which they were born too late:** Paul Berman, *A Tale of Two Utopias: The Political Journey of the Generation of 1968* (New York: W. W. Norton, 1996): 30–56, describes how the founders of the 1960s New Left were often children of Old Left activists and longed to match the heroism of their parents; they feared becoming "veterans of the cinemathèque." In a paler version, the same dynamic may connect the antiapartheid activism of the 1980s on Western campuses and some activism targeting Israel today.

228 **one-tenth of the per capita wealth:** The per capita GDP of the West Bank and Gaza Strip in 2008 was $2,900 (Central Intelligence Agency,

The World Fact Book, www.cia.gov/library/publications/the-world-fact-book/geos/we.html), and for Israel was $29,000 (www.cia.gov/library/publications/the-world-factbook/geos/is.html, both acc. 1 Jan. 2011). The figures may be distorted by including Israeli settlements as part of Israel rather than of the West Bank.

229 **stay in Israeli hands:** "Static Maps," Geneva Initiative, www.geneva-accord.org/mainmenu/static-maps/, acc. 27 Jan. 2011. Cf. the more complex border options suggested by David Makovsky et al., *Imagining the Border: Options for Resolving the Israeli-Palestinian Territorial Issue,* www.washingtoninstitute.org/pubPDFs/StrategicReport06.pdf, acc. 27 Jan. 2011. Another proposal for annexing settlements is that floated during the Sharon and Olmert governments—using the security fence as a baseline for a new border. As discussed on page 114, that line is unworkable as a border, and offers no compensation to the Palestinians for land annexed by Israel.

232 **opposition to leaving will be greatest:** International Crisis Group, "Israel's Religious Right and the Question of Settlements," *Middle East Report* 89 (20 July 2009): 2, www.crisisgroup.org/~/media/Files/Middle%20East%20North%20Africa/Israel%20Palestine/89_israels_religious_right_and_the_question_of_settlements.ashx, acc. 11 Aug. 2009.

233 **"Maybe I'll lay down my life":** Cheftziba Skali, interview.

233 **"any other level" of resistance:** Yisrael Ariel, interview.

233 **"also acted under orders":** Rabbi Nachum Rabinovitch, dean of the Birkat Moshe *hesder* yeshivah in the settlement of Ma'aleh Adumim, in a 1995 conversation with Orthodox peace activist Yitzhak Frankenthal. Frankenthal recorded the conversation. Quotations here are from a translation of the full conversation prepared in 1997 for a British court in the case of *Rabbi Rabinovitch v. Peter Halban Publishers Ltd.*

235 **four-fifths Jewish majority:** At the end of 2009, the population of Israel, including West Bank settlers and not including Palestinian residents of East Jerusalem, was 78.3 percent Jewish, 17.4 percent Arab, and 4.3 percent "other"—a category in official figures that refers to non-Jews, mainly immigrants from the former Soviet Union, who are socially part of the Jewish majority. National population figures: Central Bureau of Statistics, *Statistical Abstract 2010,* table 2.1. Arab population of Jerusalem: Jerusalem Institute of Israel Studies, *2009–2010 Statistical Yearbook,* jiis.org/.upload/web%20C0409.xls, acc. 13 Jan. 2011.

237 **Hebrew shaped by Arabic:** I am grateful to my Arabic-speaking son for his comments on this.

238 **protecting Jews from destruction:** Gans, *Just Zionism* 75–79.

239 **will have constitutional status:** I deliberately do not refer here to enacting a full written constitution, which is too often seen by jurists and scholars as a panacea for Israeli democracy. The danger exists today, as at independence, of enacting foolish compromises in order to ratify a

constitution. An example is the draft "Constitution by Consensus" proposed by the Israel Democracy Institute, a think tank (www.idi.org.il/PublicationsCatalog/Pages/Consti/index.htm, accessed 7 Jan. 2009). On one hand, the draft includes a laudable bill of rights. On the other, to assuage the right and the clerical parties, it excludes the major issues of religion and state from judicial review, gives constitutional status to the current flag and anthem, and places a version of the Law of Return in the constitution.

239 **"no greater degradation":** Yeshayahu Leibowitz, *Judaism, Human Values and the Jewish State* (Cambridge, Mass.: Harvard University Press, 1992): 176.

239 **38 percent in developed countries:** Steve Crabtree and Brett Pelham, "What Alabamians and Iranians Have in Common," *Gallup*, 9 Feb. 2009, www.gallup.com/poll/114211/Alabamians-Iranians-Common.aspx, acc. 3 Feb. 2009; Steve Crabtree, "Analyst Insights: Religiosity around the World," *Gallup*, 9 Feb. 2009, www.gallup.com/video/114694/Analyst-Insights-Religiosity-Around-World.aspx, acc. 3 Feb. 2009.

240 **religious innovation and variety:** Brenda Brasher, interview.

240 **starting with paying clergy:** Leibowitz, *Judaism* 178.

240 **to perform the ceremony:** The U.S. approach is based on a conception of a cleric performing a sacrament that creates the marriage. In Judaism, a rabbi does not perform the sacrament of marriage; the couple does that. The rabbi is present to ensure that the ceremony is performed properly. Technically speaking, the same role could be filled by someone who is not ordained.

241 **a shared foundation for identity:** The average religious Zionist parent in Israel today would object that the financial burden of paying for religious education is too great. Yet today those parents, like other Israelis, pay much of the cost of basic education: they must buy their children's textbooks, pay tutors to make up for abysmal schools, and often pay extra fees for what should be part of free education. I recommend cutting the pie differently: the state will fulfill its obligation to provide general education, and parents will pay for additional hours to pass on their religious values to their children.

242 **particular obligation to Jews:** This section draws on Gans, *Just Zionism*, chap. 5.

245 **ethnicity contained a religious element:** CA 72/62.

BIBLIOGRAPHY

Archives

Gush Etzion Archive
Israel Defense Forces Archive
Israel State Archive
Knesset Archive
Menachem Begin Heritage Center Archives
Merom Golan Archive
Midreshet Eretz Yisrael—Makhon Reshit
National Archives and Records Administration (College Park, Maryland)
Neveh Tzuf Archive
Ofrah Archive
Registrar of Nonprofit Organizations
Yad Levi Eskhol
Yad Tabenkin Archive/Hakibbutz Hame'uhad Archive

Books, Articles, and Documents

Titles are in the original language, with English translations when provided by the
publisher. Hebrew publishers often do not provide place of publication. Where the
publisher gave only the Hebrew date, the civil date is in brackets.

Admoni, Yehiel. *Asor Shel Shikul Da'at: Hahityashvut Me'ever Lekav Hayarok,
      1967–1977* (Decade of Discretion: Settlement Policy in the Territories,
      1967–1977). Makhon Yisrael Galili Leheker Hakoah Hamagen/Yad Ta-
      benkin/Hakibbutz Hame'uhad, 1992.
Allon, Yigal. Oral history. Israel State Archives 154.0/1-19/5001/19-22-Alef.
      Twenty-three interviews, conducted 1979 by the Davis Institute of the He-
      brew University.
Amar, Shlomo. "Klalei Hadiun Bevakashot Legiur." 17 Shvat, 5766 (15 Feb. 2006).
Anderson, Benedict. *Imagined Communities*. London: Verso, 2006.

Aran, Gideon. "From Religious Zionism to Zionist Religion: The Roots of Gush Emunim." *Studies in Contemporary Jewry* 2 (1986): 116–43.

Arieli, Shaul, and Michael Sfard. *Homah Umehdal: Geder Hahafradah—Bitahon O Hamdanuti* (The Wall of Folly). Tel Aviv: Sifriyat Aliyat Hagag, 2008.

Aron, Raymond. *Hatragediah Ha'aljirit* (La Tragedie Algérienne), Hebrew edition, with afterword by Emmanuel Sivan. Tel Aviv: Sifrei Aliyat Gag, 2005.

Asch, Sholem. *God of Vengeance*. In *The Great Jewish Plays*, ed. and trans. Joseph C. Landis. New York: Avon, 1972.

Association for Civil Rights in Israel. *Knesset 2010 Winter Session: Expectations and Concerns*. Oct. 2009.

B. [full name not given] "Mekomam Shel Hovshei Hakipot Bapikud Hatakti Shel Tzahal." *Ma'arakhot* 432 (2010): 50.

Bareli, Avi. *Mapai Bereishit Ha'atzma'ut, 1948–1953*. Jerusalem: Yad Yitzhak Ben-Zvi, 2007.

Baron, Binyamin. "Ve'ein Shi'ur Rak Hatorah Hazot." *Eretz Aheret*. Sept.–Oct 2007: 56–65.

Bashan, Anat. "Hadakah Hatishim." *Korim 100*, 9 Aug. 2005. www.police. gov.il/meida_laezrach/pirsomim/KitveiEt/Documents/daka90.pdf. Accessed 17 Nov., 2009.

Ben-Ami, A., ed. *Hakol: Gvulot Hashalom Shel Eretz Yisrael* [Hakol: The Peace Frontiers of Israel]. Tel Aviv: Madaf, 1967.

Ben-David, Dan. *Israel's Labor Market: Today, in the Past and in Comparison with the West*. Jerusalem: Taub Center for Social Policy Studies in Israel, 2010.

Ben-Gurion, David. *Medinat Yisrael Hamehudeshet*. Tel Aviv: Am Oved, 1969.

Ben-Horin, Michael, ed. *Baruch Hagever: Sefer Zikaron Lekadosh Dr. Baruch Goldstein*. Jerusalem: Yehudah, 5755 (1994–95).

Benziman, Uzi. *Yerushalayim: Ir Lelo Homah* (Jerusalem: City Without a Wall). Tel Aviv: Schocken, 1973.

Benziman, Uzi, and Atallah Mansour. *Dayyarei Mishneh* (Subtenants). Jerusalem: Keter, 1992.

Berman, Paul. *A Tale of Two Utopias: The Political Journey of the Generation of 1968*. New York: W. W. Norton, 1996.

Billig, Miriam, Dan Soen, and S. Sorkraut. "Bnei Dor Hahemshekh Beyishuvim Hakehillati'im Beshomron Uvinyamin Venitioteheim Bevehirat Mekom Megurim Le'aher Hanisu'im" (Second-Generation Young People in the Shomron Region and Their Place Attachment), *Mehkarei Yehudah Veshomron*, 10. Ariel, West Bank: Research Institute, College of Judea and Samaria, 2001.

Blass, Nachum. *Israel's Educational System: A Domestic Perspective*. Jerusalem: Taub Center for Social Policy Studies in Israel, 2010.

Blum, Yehuda Zvi. "Tzion Bemishpat Beinle'umi Nifdetah." *Hapraklit* 27 (1971): 315–24.

Borstein, Etti. "Noar Hagva'ot: Ben Hemshekhiut Lemered." www.articles .co.il/article/4793. Accessed 21 May 2009.

Boyd, Stephen M. "The Applicability of International Law to the Occupied Territories." *Israel Yearbook on Human Rights* 1 (1971): 258–61.

Brenner, Uri. *Altalena: Mehkar Medini Utzva'i* (Altalena: A Political and Military study). Hakibbutz Hameuchad, 1978.

Center for Women's Justice. "The Problem and Our Solutions." www.cwj.org .il/the-problem-and-our-solutions. Accessed 1 Dec. 2010.

Cohen, Bezalel. *Economic Hardship and Gainful Employment in Haredi Society in Israel: An Insider's Perspective.* Jerusalem: Floersheimer Institute for Policy Studies, 2006.

Cohen, Hillel. *Good Arabs: The Israeli Security Services and the Israeli Arabs, 1948–1967.* Trans. Haim Watzman. Berkeley and Los Angeles: University of California Press, 2010.

Cohen, Stuart A. "Dilemmas of Military Service in Israel: The Religious Dimension." *Tora u-Madda Journal* 12 (2004): 1–23.

———. "Tensions Between Military Service and Jewish Orthodoxy In Israel: Implications Imagined and Real." *Israel Studies* 12.1 (2007): 103–26.

———. "Relationships between Religiously Observant and Other Troops in the IDF: Vision Versus Reality." In *The Relationship of Orthodox Jews with Believing Jews of Other Religious Ideologies and Non-Believing Jews.* Ed. Adam Mintz. New York: KTAV, 2010.

"The Declaration of the Establishment of the State of Israel." 14 May 1948. www.mfa.gov.il/MFA/Peace+Process/Guide+to+the+Peace+Process/Declaration+of+Establishment+of+State+of+Israel.htm. Accessed 26 Sept. 2010.

Demant, Peter Robert. *Ploughshares into Swords: Israeli Settlement Policy in the Occupied Territories, 1967–1977.* Ph.D. diss., Universiteit van Amsterdam, 1988.

Diamond, Jared. *Collapse: How Societies Choose to Fail or Succeed.* New York: Viking, 2004.

Dinstein, Yoram. "Tzion Bemishpat Beinle'umi Tipadeh." *Hapraklit* 27 (1971): 5–11.

Don Yehiya, Eliezer. "The Book and the Sword: The Nationalist Yeshivot and Political Radicalism in Israel." In *Accounting for Fundamentalisms: The Dynamic Character of Movements.* Ed. Martin E. Marty and R. Scott Appleby. Chicago: Fundamentalism Project, University of Chicago Press, 1994.

———. *Mashber Utmurah Bemedinah Hadashah: Hinukh, Dat Upolitikah Bama'avak Al Ha'aliyah Hagdolah.* (Crisis and Change in a New State: Education, Religion, and Politics in the Struggle over the Absorption of Mass Immigration in Israel). Jerusalem: Yad Ben-Zvi, 2008.

Douer, Yair. *Lanu Hamaggal Hu Herev II* (Our Sickle Is Our Sword: Nahal Settlements from 1967 until 1992). Ministry of Defense and Yad Tabenkin, 1997.

Drori, Ze'ev. *Bein Emunah Letzava: Gedud Hanahal Haharedi—Sikkuim Vesikkunim* (Between Faith and Military Service: The Haredi Nahal Battalion). Jerusalem: Floersheimer Institute for Policy Studies, 2005.

Eisenstadt, David E. *Hatmurot Bigvulot Ha'ironiim (Municipaliim) shel Yerusha-*

layim, 1863–1967 (The Evolution of Jerusalem's Municipal Boundaries, 1863–1967). MA thesis, Bar-Ilan University, 1998.

Eldar, Akiva, and Idith Zertal. *Adonei Ha'aretz: Hamitnahalim Umedinat Yisrael, 1967–2004* (Lords of the Land: The Settlers and the State of Israel, 1967–2004). Tel Aviv: Kinneret, Zmora Bitan, Dvir, 2004.

Endewald, Miri, et al. *2008: Poverty and Social Gaps, Annual Report*. Jerusalem: National Insurance Institute, 2009.

Felner, Eitan, and Roly Rozen. *Law Enforcement on Israeli Civilians in the Occupied Territories*. Jerusalem: B'Tselem, 1994.

Festinger, Leon, Henry W. Riecken, and Stanley Schachter. *When Prophecy Fails*. New York: Harper & Row, 1964.

Filber, Ya'akov Halevi. *Ayelet Hashahar*. Jerusalem: Haskel, 5728 (1967–68).

Fine, Jonathan. *Meshilton Koloniali Mandatori Limedinah Ribonit: Hakamat Ma'arekhet Hamemshal Hayisraelit Ben Hashanim, 1947–1951* (From Colonial Mandatory Rule to a Sovereign State: The Establishment of the Israeli Governmental System between the Years 1947–1951). Ph.D. diss., Hebrew University, 2005.

———. *Kakh Noladnu: Hakamat Ma'arekhet Hamemshal Hayisraelit, 1947–1951* (The Birth of a State: The Establishment of the Israeli Governmental System, 1947–1951]. Jerusalem: Carmel, 2009.

Fischer, Louise. *Moshe Sharett: Rosh Hamemshalah Hasheni: Mivhar Te'udot Mepirkei Hayav 1894–1965* (Moshe Sharett: The Second Prime Minister; Selected Documents, 1894–1965). Jerusalem: State of Israel, 2007.

Fleishman, Larisa, and Ilan Salomon. "Lashe'elah 'Heikhan Hakav Yarok?' Hateshuva 'Ma Zeh Hakav Hayarok." *Alpaim* 29 (2005): 26–52.

Friedman, Menachem. *Hahevrah Haharedit: Mekorot, Megamot Vetahalikhim*. Jerusalem: JIIS, 1991.

———. "The Lost Kiddush Cup: Changes in Ashkenazic Haredi Culture—A Tradition in Crisis." In *The Uses of Tradition: Jewish Continuity in the Modern Era*. Ed. Jack Wertheimer. New York: Jewish Theological Seminary, 1992.

———. "The Structural Foundations for Religio-Political Accommodation in Israel: Fallacy and Reality." In *Israel: The First Decade of Independence*. Eds. S. Ilan Troen and Noah Lucas. Albany: SUNY Press, 1995.

———. "'Al Hanissim'—Prihato Shel 'Olam Hatorah' (Hayeshivot Vehakollelim) Biyisrael." In *Yeshivot Uvatei Midrashot*. Ed. Immanuel Etkes. Jerusalem: Merkaz Shazar, 2006.

Gans, Chaim. *A Just Zionism: On the Morality of the Jewish State*. Oxford: Oxford University Press, 2008.

Gazit, Shlomo. *Peta'im Bemalkodet: Shloshim Shnot Mdiniut Yisrael Bashtahim* (Trapped). Tel Aviv: Zmora-Bitan, 1999.

Gelber, Yoav. *Lamah Perku Et Hapalmah: Hakoah Hatzva'i Bema'avar Meyishuv Limedinah* (Why Was the Palmah Disbanded: Military Force in the Transition from a Yishuv to a State). Tel Aviv: Schocken, 1986.

"Gilui Da'at." www.zefat.net/images/stories/10_2010/esorrav.jpg. Accessed 16 Jan. 2011.

Ginbar, Yuval. *On the Way to Annexation: Human Rights Violations Resulting from the Establishment and Expansion of the Ma'aleh Adumim Settlement.* Jerusalem: B'Tselem, 1999.

Gorenberg, Gershom. *The Accidental Empire: Israel and the Birth of the Settlements, 1967–1977.* New York: Times Books, 2006.

———. "At What Price." *Mother Jones,* July–August 2003, 42–49.

———. *The End of Days: Fundamentalism and the Struggle for the Temple Mount.* New York: Oxford University Press, 2002.

———. "Hot Shas." *New Republic,* 25 Jan. 1999, 11–13.

———. "The Minister for National Fears." *Atlantic Monthly,* May 2007, 84–90.

———. "The Thin Green Line." *Mother Jones,* September–October 2002, 49–54, 90.

———. "The War to Begin All Wars." *New York Review of Books,* 28 May 2009, 38–41.

Gottlieb, Daniel. *Ha'oni Vehahitnahagut Beshuk Ha'avodah Bahevrah Haharedit* (Poverty and Labor Market Behavior in the Ultra-Orthodox Population in Israel). Jerusalem: Van Leer Institute, 2007.

Grinberg, Lev Luis. *Hahistadrut Me'al Lakol* (The Histadrut Above All). Jerusalem: Nevo, 1993.

———. *Politics and Violence in Israel/Palestine: Democracy Versus Military Rule.* New York: Routledge, 2010.

Gurovich, Norma, and Eilat Cohen-Kastro. *Haharedim: Tifroset Geografit Umefayanim Demografiim, Hevratiim Vekhalkaliim Shel Ha'ukhlusiah Haharedit Biyisrael, 1996–2001* (Ultra-Orthodox Jews: Geographic Distribution and Demographic, Social and Economic Characteristics of the Ultra-Orthodox Jewish Population in Israel). Jerusalem: Central Bureau of Statistics, 2004.

Haber, Eitan. *Hayom Tifrotz Milhamah* (Today War Will Break Out: The Reminiscences of Brig. Gen. Israel Lior). Tel Aviv: Edanim/Yediot Aharonot, 1987.

Haider, Ali, ed. *The Equality Index of Jewish and Arab Citizens in Israel, 2008.* Jerusalem: Sikkuy, 2009.

"Hakod Ha'eti Shel Tzahal." dover.idf.il/IDF/About/Purpose/Code_Of_Ethics.htm. Accessed 14 July 2009.

Hareuveni, Eyal. *By Hook and by Crook: Israeli Settlement Policy in the West Bank.* Jerusalem: B'Tselem, 2010.

Hertzberg, Arthur, ed. *The Zionist Idea: A Historical Analysis and Reader.* New York: Atheneum, 1973.

Herzl, Theodore. *Altneuland.* www.wzo.org.il/en/resources/view.asp?id=1600. Accessed 13 Apr. 2004.

Hlehel, Ala, ed. *October 2008 in Akka (Acre): Course of Events.* Akko: Akka Residents Coalition, 2008.

Human Rights in Palestine and Other Occupied Arab Territories: Report of the United Nations Fact-Finding Mission on the Gaza Conflict [Goldstone Report]. 25 Sept.

2009. www2.ohchr.org/english/bodies/hrcouncil/docs/12session/A-HRC–12–48 .pdf. Accessed 19 Oct. 2009.

International Crisis Group. "Israel's Religious Right and the Question of Settlements." *Middle East Report* 89 (20 July 2009). www.crisisgroup.org/en/regions/middle-east-north-africa/israel-palestine/089-israels-religious-right-and-the-question-of-settlements.aspx. Accessed 11 Aug. 2009.

Institute for National Security Studies. "Israel." In *Middle East Military Balance Files*. Tel Aviv: Institute for National Security Studies, 2009. www.inss.org.il/upload/(FILE)1284986151.pdf. Accessed 17 Nov 2009.

"Isur Hishtatfut Be'akirat Yishuvim Uma'ahazim." 29 Tishrei 5765 (15 Oct. 2010), rotter.net/User_files/forum/gil/41716f560ab30a49.pdf. Accessed 1 Dec. 2010.

Jerusalem Report Staff. *Shalom, Friend: The Life and Legacy of Yitzhak Rabin*. Ed. David Horovitz. New York: Newmarket, 1996.

Judt, Tony. *Postwar: A History of Europe since 1945*. London: William Heinemann, 2005.

Kaplan, Lawrence, "The Hazon Ish: Haredi Critic of Traditional Orthodoxy." In *The Uses of Tradition: Jewish Continuity in the Modern Era*. Ed. Jack Wertheimer. New York : Jewish Theological Seminary, 1992.

Karp, Yehudit. *Hakirat Hashadot Neged Yehudim Biyehudah Veshomron*. Jerusalem: Justice Ministry, 1982.

Katz, Jacob. "Orthodoxy in Historical Perspective." *Studies in Contemporary Judaism* 2 (1986): 3–17.

Khalidi, Rashid. *The Iron Cage: The Story of the Palestinian Struggle for Statehood*. Boston: Beacon, 2006.

Klein, Menachem. *Bar-Ilan: Akademiah, Dat Upolitikah* (Bar-Ilan: University between Religion and Politics). Jerusalem: Magnes, 1998.

——. *The Shift: Israel-Palestine from Border Struggle to Ethnic Conflict*. London: Hurst, 2010.

Kook, Avraham Yitzhak Hacohen. *Orot*. Jerusalem: Mossad Harav Kook, 5753 (1992–93).

Kook, Tzvi Yehudah Hacohen. *Lintivot Yisrael*. Jerusalem: Menorah, 5727 (1966–67).

Kretzmer, David. *The Legal Status of Arabs in Israel*. Boulder, Colo.: Westview, 1990.

——. *The Occupation of Justice: The Supreme Court of Israel and the Occupied Territories*. Albany: SUNY Press, 2002.

Lahav, Pnina. *Judgment in Jerusalem: Chief Justice Simon Agranat and the Zionist Century*. Berkeley: University of California Press, 1997.

Lammfromm, Arnon, and Hagai Tsoref, eds. *Levi Eshkol: Rosh Hamemshalah Hashlishi* (Levi Eshkol: The Third Prime Minister—Selected Documents, 1895–1969). Jerusalem: Israel State Archives, 2002.

Leibowitz, Yeshayahu. *Judaism, Human Values and the Jewish State*. Cambridge, Mass.: Harvard University Press, 1992.

Lein, Yehezkel. *Land Grab: Israel's Settlement Policy in the West Bank*. Jerusalem: B'Tselem, 2002.

―――. *Behind the Barrier: Human Rights Violations as a Result of Israel's Separation Barrier*. Jerusalem: B'Tselem, 2003.

Lekhu Lahamu Belahmi. Harabbanut Hatzva'it, 2009.

Levi, Keren. *Tfisat Hazehut Hakollectivit Al Markiveiha Hashonim Bekerev Noar Dati Leumi* (The Collective Identity of Religious Zionist Youth and Its Relation to the Willingness to Serve in the Israeli Army and to Obey the Law). MA thesis, Bar-Ilan University, 2009.

Levy, Yagil. "The Embedded Military: Why Did the IDF Perform Effectively in Executing the Disengagement Plan?" *Security Studies* 16.3 (2007): 382–408.

―――. *Mitzava Ha'am Letzava Haperipheri'ot* (From People's Army to the Army of the Peripheries). Jerusalem: Carmel, 2007.

―――. "The Case of the al-Aqsa Intifada: The Linkage between Israel's Military Policies and the Military's Social Composition." *American Behavioral Scientist* 51.11 (2008): 1575–89.

Makovsky, David, et al. *Imagining the Border: Options for Resolving the Israeli-Palestinian Territorial Issue*. www.washingtoninstitute.org/pubPDFs/StrategicReport06.pdf. Accessed 27 Jan. 2011.

Margalit, Avishai. *On Compromises and Rotten Compromises*. Princeton, N.J.: Princeton University Press, 2010.

"Mekhinot Kdam Tzvai'ot." www.aka.idf.il/giyus/general/?CatID=23072&DocID=25015. Accessed 21 Sept. 2010.

Medding, Peter. *The Founding of Israeli Democracy, 1948–1967*. New York: Oxford University Press, 1990.

Mei-Ami, Naomi. *Giyyus Talmidei Yeshivot Letzahal Vehok Dehiyat Sherut Letalmidei Yeshivot Shetoratam Umanutam (Hok Tal)*. Jerusalem: Knesset, Merkaz Hamehkar Vehameda, 2007.

Mitchell, George J., et al. *Sharm El-Sheikh Fact-Finding Committee Report* [Mitchell Report]. 30 Apr. 2001. Washington, D.C.: U.S. Department of State, 2001. 2001–9. state.gov/p/nea/rls/rpt/3060.htm.

Melamed, Eliezer. *Revivim*. Vol. 2. Jerusalem: Makhon Har Brakhah, 5768 (2007–8).

Merom Golan: Reshit. Merom Golan, Golan Heights, 1977.

Middle East Record. Vols. 3–5 (1967–69). Tel Aviv: Israel Oriental Society, Reuven Shiloah Research Center.

Morris, Benny. *The Birth of the Palestinian Refugee Problem Revisited*. Cambridge: Cambridge University Press, 2004.

―――, ed. *Making Israel*. Ann Arbor: University of Michigan Press, 2007.

―――. *1948: The First Arab-Israeli War*. New Haven, Conn.: Yale University Press, 2008.

Nakdimon, Shlomo. *Altalena*. Jerusalem: Edanim, 1978.

National Insurance Institute. *Riva'on Statisti*. National Insurance Institute, April–June 2010.

Naor, Arye. *Eretz Yisrael Hashlemah: Emunah Umdiniut* (Greater Israel: Theology and Policy). Haifa: University of Haifa/Zmora-Bitan, 2001.

Navon, Yitzhak. *Be'emunato Yihiyeh: Leḳet Dvarim Al David Ben-Gurion*. Sdeh Boker: Hamakhon Lemoreshet Ben-Gurion, 1998.

Negbi, Moshe. *Kevalim Shel Tzedeḳ: Bagatz Mul Hamemshal Hayisraeli Bishtahim* (Justice under Occupation: The Israeli Supreme Court versus the Military Administration in the Occupied Territories). Jerusalem: Cana, 1981.

Netzer, Moshe. *Netzer Mishoreshav: Sippur Haim* (Life Story). Ministry of Defense, 2002.

Newman, David. "The Territorial Politics of Exurbanization." *Israel Affairs* 1.1 (1996): 61–85.

Newman, David, ed. *The Impact of Gush Emunim: Politics and Settlement in the West Bank*. London: Croom Helm, 1985.

Nussbaum, Martha C. *Not for Profit: Why Democracy Needs the Humanities*. Princeton, N.J.: Princeton University Press, 2010.

Olei Hagardom. Jerusalem: Education Ministry, 2009.

Operation Cast Lead. Breaking the Silence, 2009.

Oren, Michael B. *Six Days of War: June 1967 and the Making of the Modern Middle East*. New York: Oxford University Press, 2002.

Or Hame'ir. Privately published memorial booklet for First Sgt. Meir Shenwald. Undated.

Oz, Amos. *A Tale of Love and Darkness*. Trans. Nicholas de Lange. London: Vintage, 2005.

Peace Now Settlement Watch Team. *Aveirah Goreret Aveirah: Bniyat Hahitnahaluyot Al Karḳa'ot Beva'alut Pratit Palestinit* (Breaking the Law—One Violation Leads to Another: Israeli Settlement Building on Private Palestinian Property). Jerusalem: Peace Now, 2006.

———. *Illegal Construction in the Settlements: The List of Demolition Orders*. Jerusalem: Peace Now, 2007.

Pedatzur, Reuven. *Nitzahon Hemukhah: Mdiniut Memshelet Eshḳol Bashtahim Le'ahar Milhemet Sheshet Hayamim* (The Triumph of Embarrassment: Israel and the Territories After the Six-Day War). Tel Aviv: Bitan/Yad Tabenkin, 1996.

"Psak Halakhah Be'inyan Seruv Pekudah." www.yeshiva.org.il/midrash/shiur .asp?id=1978. Accessed 12 Dec. 2010.

Quandt, William B. *Peace Process: American Diplomacy and the Arab Israeli Conflict since 1967*. Washington, D.C.: Brookings Institution/University of California, 1993.

Rapoport, David C. "The Four Waves of Rebel Terror and September 11." *Anthropoetics* 8.1 (2002). www.anthropoetics.ucla.edu/archive/ap0801.pdf. Accessed 18 Jan. 2006.

Ravitzky, Aviezer. *Haḳetz Hameguleh Umedinat Hayehudim* (Messianism, Zionism and Jewish Religious Radicalism). Tel Aviv: Am Oved, 1993.

Regulations Concerning the Laws and Customs of War on Land. The Hague: 18 October 1907. www.icrc.org/ihl.nsf/FULL/195. Accessed 2 Nov. 2010.

Robinson, Shira Nomi. *Occupied Citizens in a Liberal State: Palestinians under Military Rule and the Colonial Formation of Israeli Society, 1948–1966.* Ph.D. diss., Stanford University, 2005.

Rubinstein, Danny. *Mi Lashem Elai: Gush Emunim* (On the Lord's Side: Gush Emunim). Tel Aviv: Hakibbutz Hame'uhad, 1982.

Sa'di, Ahmad H., and Lila Abu-Lughod, eds. *Nakba: Palestine, 1948, and the Claims of Memory.* New York: Columbia University Press, 2007.

Sagi, Avi, and Zvi Zohar. *Transforming Identity: The Ritual Transformation from Gentile to Jew—Structure and Meaning.* London: Continuum, 2007.

Sagi, Nana, ed. *Political Documents of the Jewish Agency.* Vol. 2, *January–November 1947.* Jerusalem: Hasifriya Haziyonit, 1998.

Sartre, Jean-Paul. *Anti-Semite and Jew.* Trans. George J. Becker. New York: Schocken, 1965.

Sasson, Talia. *Havat Da'at (Beina'im) Benose Ma'ahazim Bilti Murshim* (Opinion Concerning Unauthorized Outposts). Jerusalem, 2005.

Scholem, Gershom. *The Messianic Idea in Judaism.* New York: Schocken, 1971.

———. *Sabbatai Sevi: The Mystical Messiah.* Princeton, N.J.: Princeton University Press, 1973.

Schwar, Harriet Dashiell, ed. *Foreign Relations, 1964–1968.* Vol. 19, *Arab-Israeli Crisis and War, 1967.* Washington, D.C.: U.S. Government, 2004.

Segev, Tom. *1949: The First Israelis.* New York: Metropolitan, 1998.

———. *One Palestine, Complete: Jews and Arabs under the British Mandate.* New York: Metropolitan, 2000.

Shalev, Nir, et al. *The Ofrah Settlement: An Illegal Outpost.* Jerusalem: B'Tselem, 2008.

Shamgar, Meir. "The Observance of International Law in the Administered Territories." *Israel Yearbook on Human Rights* 1 (1971): 262–65.

Shamgar, Meir, et al. *Vaadat Hahakirah Le'inyan Hatevah Bime'arat Hamakhpelah Behevron: Din Veheshbon.* Jerusalem, 1994.

Shapira, Anita. *Yigal Allon: Aviv Heldo* (Igal Allon: Spring of His Life). Tel Aviv: Hasifriah Hahadashah, 2004.

Shapira, Yitzhak, and Yosef Elitzur. *Torat Hamelekh: Dinei Nefashot Ben Yisrael Le'amim.* Hamakhon Hatorani Sheleyad Yeshivat Od Yosef Hai, 5770 (2009).

Shapiro, Yonathan. *Illit Lelo Mamshikhim: Dorot Manhigim Bahevrah Hayisraelit* (An Elite without Successors: Generations of Political Leaders in Israel). Tel Aviv: Sifriat Poalim, 1984.

———. *Leshilton Behartanu: Darkah Shel Tnu'at Haherut—Hesber Sotziologi-Politi* (Chosen to Command: The Road to Power of the Herut Party—A Socio-political Interpretation). Tel Aviv: Am Oved, 1989.

Sharon, Ariel, with David Chanoff. *Warrior: An Autobiography.* New York: Touchstone, 2001.

Shehadeh, Raja. *Occupiers Law: Israel and the West Bank.* Washington, D.C.: Institute for Palestine Studies, 1985.

Shilhav, Joseph [Yosseph], and Menachem Friedman. *Hitpashtut Tokh Histagrut: Hakehillah Haharedit Biyerushalayim* (Growth and Segregation: The Ultra-Orthodox Community of Jerusalem). Jerusalem: Jerusalem Institute for Israel Studies, 1985.

Shilhav, Yosseph. *Ultra-Orthodoxy in Urban Governance.* Jerusalem: Floersheimer Institute for Policy Studies, 1998.

Shlaim, Avi. *The Iron Wall: Israel and the Arab World.* New York: W. W. Norton, 2001.

Shvut, Avraham, ed. *Ha'aliyah El Hehar: Hahityashvut Hayehudit Hamithadeshet Biyehudah Veshomron* (Ascent to the Mountains: Renewal of Jewish Settlement in Judea and Samaria). Jerusalem: Sifriat Beit El, 2002.

Silber, Michael. "The Emergence of Ultra-Orthodoxy: The Invention of a Tradition." In *The Uses of Tradition: Jewish Continuity in the Modern Era.* Ed. Jack Wertheimer. New York: Jewish Theological Seminary, 1992.

Silberstein, Laurence J., ed. *Jewish Fundamentalism in Comparative Perspective: Religion, Ideology and the Crisis of Modernity.* New York: New York University Press, 1993.

Soloveitchik, Haym. "Rupture and Reconstruction: The Transformation of Contemporary Orthodoxy." In *Jews in America: A Contemporary Reader.* Eds. Roberta Rosenberg Farber and Chaim I. Waxman. Hanover, N.H.: Brandeis University Press, 1999: 320–76.

The Spiegel Report [on Israeli Settlements]. www.haaretz.co.il/hasite/images/printed/P300109/uriib.mht. Accessed 30 Apr. 2009.

Sprinzak, Ehud. *Ish Hayashar Be'einav: Illegalism Behevrah Hayisraelit* (Every Man Whatsoever Is Right in His Own Eyes: Illegalism in Israeli Society). Tel Aviv: Sifriat Poalim, 1986.

———. *Brother against Brother: Violence and Extremism in Israeli Politics from Altalena to the Rabin Assassination.* New York: Free Press, 1999.

Stern, Elezar. *Masa Kumtah: Nivutim Begovah Ha'einayim* (Navigations). Tel Aviv: Miskal, 2009.

Straffin, Philip D. *Topics in the Theory of Voting.* Boston: Birkhauser, 1980.

Swirski, Shlomo. *The Burden of Occupation: The Cost of the Occupation to Israeli Society, Polity and Economy, 2008 Update.* Tel Aviv: Adva Center, 2008.

Tal, Ori. *Hametihut Bein Yehudim Le'aravim Bishkhunat Wolfson Be'akko.* Jerusalem: Knesset, Merkaz Hamehkar Vehameda, 2006.

Toledano, Esther, et al. *The Effect of Child Allowances on Fertility.* Jerusalem: National Insurance Institute, 2009.

Tolstoy, Alexey. *Peter the First.* Trans. Tatiana Shebunina. New York: Macmillan, 1959.

Tsur, Ilana, dir. *Altalena.* Documentary film. 1994.

Tsur, Zeev. *Mipulmus Hahalukah Ad Tokhnit Allon* [From the Partition Dispute to the Allon Plan]. Ramat Efal: Tabenkin Institute, 1982.

———. *Hakibbutz Hame'uhad Beyishuvah shel Ha'aretz* (The Hakibbutz Hameuchad in the Settlement of Eretz Yisrael). Vol. 4, *1960–1980.* Yad Tabenkin/Hakibbutz Hame'uhad, 1986.

Tzaban, Dror. *Omdan Helki Shel Taktzivei Memshalah Hamufnim Lehitna-haluyot Bagadah Hama'aravit Ubiretzu'at Azzah Veshel Tiktzuv Ha'odef Bi-shnat 2001*. Prepared for Peace Now, 2002.

Ungar, Yaron. *Gvulot Hatziut Vehasarbanut Lapekudah Hatzva'it*. Jerusalem: Knesset, Merkaz Hamehkar Vehameda, 2010.

United Nations Palestine Commission. *First Special Report to the Security Council: The Problem of Security in Palestine*. 16 Feb. 1948. unispal.un.org/UNISPAL.NSF/5b a47a5c6cef541b802563e000493b8c/fdf734eb76c39d6385256c4c004cdba7. Accessed 26 Sept. 2010.

United Nations Special Committee on Palestine. *Report to the General Assembly*. 3 Sept. 1947. unispal.un.org/unispal.nsf/0/07175de9fa2de563852568d3006e 10f3. Accessed 17 Oct. 2010.

Wallerstein, Sebastian, and Emily Silverman. *Housing Distress within the Palestinian Community of Jaffa: The End of Protected Tenancy in Absentee Ownership Homes*. Bimkom, 2009.

Weber, Max. "Politics as a Vocation." *Essays in Sociology*. Trans. Hans H. Gerth and C. Wright Mills. New York: Oxford University Press, 1946. www.ne.jp/asahi/moriyuki/abukuma/weber/lecture/politics_vocation.html. Accessed 31 Jan. 2010.

Weiss, Susan, et al. *The Interrogation of the Convert "X" by the Israeli Rabbinic Courts*. Jerusalem: Center for Women's Justice, 2010.

World Zionist Organization Settlement Division. "Hityahasut Hahativah Lehityashvut Behistadrut Hatzionit Ha'olamit Lehavat Da'at (Beina'im) Benose Ma'ahazim Bilti Murshim," May 2005.

Yanai, Natan. *Mashberim Politi'im Biyisrael: Tekufat Ben-Gurion*. Jerusalem: Keter, 1982.

Yavne, Lior. *A Semblance of Law*. Tel Aviv: Yesh Din, 2006.

Yiftachel, Oren. *Ethnocracy: Land and Identity Politics in Israel/Palestine*. Philadelphia: University of Pennsylvania Press, 2006.

Yogev, Gedalia, ed. *Political and Diplomatic Documents, December 1947–May 1948*. Jerusalem: State of Israel and WZO, 1979.

Yossi. Privately published memorial book for Sgt. Yosef Weinstock. Undated.

Zamir, Eyal. *Admot Medinah Biyehudah Vehashomron: Skirah Mishpatit* (State Land in Judea and Samaria: The Legal Status). Jerusalem: JIIS, 1985.

Zulfan, Yossi. *Ha'ir Akko*. Jerusalem: Knesset, Merkaz Hamehkar Vehameda, 2002.

Newspapers, Journals, and News Sites

Alei Golan, Kibbutz Merom Golan
Arutz Sheva Hadashot (inn.co.il)
Bamahaneh, Tel Aviv
Besheva
bitterlemons (bitterlemons.org)
CNN (cnn.com)
Davar, Tel Aviv

Eretz Binyamin (binyamin.org.il)
Forward, New York
Gallup (gallup.com)
Ha'aretz/The Marker, Tel Aviv
Hamashkif, Tel Aviv
Hatzofeh, Tel Aviv
Hayom, Tel Aviv
Jerusalem Post
Jerusalem Report
Kipah (kipa.co.il)
Lamerhav, Tel Aviv
Ma'ariv, Tel Aviv
Nekuda, Jerusalem
News from the Shomron (shechem.org)
New York Review of Books
New York Times
NRG (nrg.co.il)
Olam Katan
Walla (news.walla.co.il)
The Washington Post
Yediot Aharonot, Tel Aviv
Yisrael Hayom, Tel Aviv
Ynet (ynet.co.il)
Zra'im

Other Web Sites

Atar Hatmikhot (Finance Ministry): tmichot.gov.il
Bemuna: bemuna.co.il
Bnei David—Eli: bneidavid.org
B'Tselem: btselem.org
Central Bureau of Statistics: cbs.gov.il
Central Intelligence Agency: cia.gov
Danny Danon: dannydanon.com
Education Ministry: cms.education.gov.il
Geneva Initiative: geneva-accord.org
Im Tirtzu: imti.org.il
Israel's Security Fence: seamzone.mod.gov.il
Jerusalem Institute of Israel Studies: jiis.org
The Knesset: knesset.gov.il
Manhigut Yehudit: he.manhigut.org
Menachem Begin Heritage Center: begincenter.org.il
Ministry of Foreign Affairs: mfa.gov.il
New Israel Fund: nif.org

Peace Now: peacenow.org.il
She'ilat Shlomo: havabooks.co.il
Shvut Ami: svotamy.fav.co.il
State Comptroller: mevaker.gov.il
U.S. State Department: state.gov
Yeshivat Hahesder Akko: yakko.co.il
Yeshivat Od Yosef Hai: odyosefchai.org.il
Yizkor: izkor.gov.il

Laws (Israel)

Dinei Hamoatzot Hamekomiot Vehamoatzot Ha'eizoriot Be'eizor Yehudah
    Veshomron, 1996
Hok Ha'ezrahut, 1952
Hok Hama'avar, 1949
Hok Hashvut, 1950
Hok Hinukh Mamlakhti, 1953
Hok Leha'arakhat Tokpan Shel Takanot Sha'at Herum (Aveirot Bashtahim
    Hamuhzakim—Shiput Ve'ezrah Mishpatit), 1967, 1977
Hok Limmud Hovah, 1949
Hok Ma'amad Hahistadrut Hatzionit—Hasokhnut Hayehudit Le'eretz Yis-
    rael, 1952
Hok Mosdot Hinukh Tarbutiim Yihudiim, 2008
Hok Nikhsei Nifkadim, 1950
Hok Sherut Bitahon, 1949
Hok Yesod: Hofesh Ha'isuk, 1992
Hok Yesod: Kvod Ha'adam Veheruto, 1992

Legal Cases (Israel)

A144/06, *Chief Army Prosecutor v. Capt. Moshe Peretz Botavia Gonen*
Administrative Appeal 1789/10, *Esther Saba et al. v. Israel Lands Authority et al.*
CA 72/62, *Oswald Rufeisen v. Minister of the Interior*
CA 6821/93, *Bank Mizrahi v. Migdal Kfar Shitufi*
HCJ 73/53, *Kol Ha'am v. Minister of the Interior*
HCJ 390/79, *Duweikat et al. v. Government of Israel et al.*
HCJ 6698/95, *Aadel and Iman Ka'adan v. Israel Lands Authority et al.*
HCJ 7622/02, *David Zonshein et al. v. Judge-Advocate General*
HCJ 10296/02, *Union of Teachers in High Schools, Seminaries and Colleges v.
    Minister of Education*
HCJ 8060/03, *Aadel and Iman Ka'adan v. Israel Lands Authority et al.*
HCJ 11163/03, *Higher Monitoring Committee for Arab Affairs et al. v. Prime Min-
    ister of Israel*
HCJ 1661/05, *Hof Aza Regional Council et al. v. Knesset et al.*

HCJ 6357/05, *Peace Now et al. v. Minister of Defense et al.*
HCJ 8414/05, *Yassin v. Government of Israel et al.*
HCG 9051/05, *Peace Now et al. v. Minister of Defense et al.*
HCG 3008/06, *Peace Now et al. v. Minister of Defense et al.*
HCJ 8887/06, *Yussuf Musa Abed a-Razek al-Nabut et al. v. Minister of Defense et al.*
HCJ 4805/07, *Israel Religious Action Center v. Ministry of Education et al.*
HCJ 8036/07, *Fatina Ebriq Zubeidat et al. v. The Israel Land Administration et al.*
HCJ 9060/08, *Nadmi Hassan Muhammad Salman et al. v. Minister of Defense et al.*
PCA 5716/08, *Chief Army Prosecutor v. Capt. Moshe Botavia*

Interviews

Aasi, Samir	14 Dec. 2009
Abou Shehadeh, Sami	8 July 2010
Admoni, Yehiel	12 Dec. 2003
Agbariya, Ahmad	8 July 1999
Ahmed, Abdulkarim Ayoub	2 Jan. 2008
Alfon, Dov	14 Apr. 2010
Alpher, Yossi	21 Feb. 2002
Ariel, Noa	28 Oct. 2009
Ariel, Yisrael	28 Oct. 2009
Azaryahu, Arnan (Sini)	5 Nov. 2003
Bar, Carmel	3 Nov. 2003
Bareli, Avi	3 Sept. 2009
Bauer, Ze'ev	14 Sept. 2009
Ben-Porat, Eran	27 Oct. 2009
Ben-Shushan, Eliad Eliahu	10 Dec. 2009
Billig, Miriam	15 Dec. 2009
Brasher, Brenda	5 Sept. 2000
Caplan, Kimmy	10 Sept. 2009
Cohen, Bezalel	3 Sept. 2009
Cohen, Liat	10 Dec. 2009
Cohen, Nachshon	9 Dec. 2009
Cohen, Stuart	20 Mar. 2009
Dabit, Busayna	20 Dec. 2009
Dahan, Sharon	9 Dec. 2009
de Hartog, Amnon	6 Dec. 2009
Drori , Ze'ev	26 Apr. 2009
Eisenstadt, David	21 Jan. 2003
Ehrlich, Yifat	24 Feb. 2003
Eliahu, Ariel	4 Nov. 2009
Eliraz, Kobi	28 July 2010
Etkes, Dror	3 Mar. 2009, 16 Oct. 2009, 12 July 2010
Ezrahi, Yaron	11 May 2009, 16 Aug. 2009

Fine, Jonathan	13 Dec. 2009
Fischer, Shlomo	4 Oct. 2009
Friedman, Menachem	29 Mar. 2009, 11 Oct. 2010
Genad, Roni	17 Mar. 2009
Golani, Motti	9 July 2007
Goldschmidt, Ronny	22 Aug. 2010
Gottlieb, Daniel	25 Nov. 2009
Gouri, Haim	6 Aug. 2003, 12 Sept. 2003, 28 Oct. 2003, 9 July 2004
Grinberg, Lev	11 Sept. 2009
Hagar, Moshe	26 Oct. 2009
Harel, Itay	17 Mar. 2009
Harel, Yehudah	4 Nov. 2003
Harel, Yisrael	23 Mar. 2004
Haviv, Itai	12 June 2002
Hawary, Sami	8 Dec. 2009
Horovitz, Pnina	18 July 2010
Hurvitz, Einat	3 Jan. 2011
Ilany, Yudit	12 Aug. 2010
Jabareen, Tawfiq	2 June 2003
Jabarin, Shawan	8 Aug. 2010
Jbarah, Hussein	29 July 2010
Karlinsky, Nahum	1 Nov. 2009
Karp, Yehudit	8 Aug. 2010
Khalil, Suheila	8 Dec. 2009
Kirshenbaum, Fania	15 Oct. 2006
Krebs, Ronald	25 July 2010
Kretzmer, David	2 Feb. 2006, 29 June 2006, 21 Sept. 2010
Kuttab, Jonathan	16 July 2010
Lahat, Shlomo	26 Aug. 2003
Lein, Yehezkel	23 Feb. 2003
Levy, Yagil	8 Mar. 2009, 15 Mar. 2009
Lieberman, Avigdor	15 Nov. 2006
Mahameed, Hashem	2 June 2003
Mali, Eliyahu	12 Aug. 2010
Maswari, Abd al-Aziz Abu Isba	29 July 2010
Meinrat, Gershon	4 Nov. 2003
Melchior, Michael	16 Mar. 2009
Meron, Theodor	12 June 2007
Mirsky, Yehudah	23 Aug. 2009, 14 Sept. 2009
Moskovic, Moshe	24 Dec. 2003, 31 Dec. 2003, 12 Jan. 2004
Naeh, Eli	27 Oct. 2009
Naor, Arye	21 Dec. 2009
Negbi, Moshe	11 Nov. 2005, 7 July 2010
Nevo, Galit	10 Dec. 2009

Nissim, Yitzhak	25 Mar. 2009
Odeh, Ahmed	8 Dec. 2009
Ofran, Hagit	24 Nov. 2010
Omari, Suheil	8 Dec. 2009
Paparin, Sara	8 Dec. 2009
Paz, Ilan	16 Sept. 2010
Perry, Yaakov	9 July 2007
Peters, Gretchen	24 Mar. 2009
Porat, Hanan	3 Sept. 2003, 30 Oct. 2003, 27 May 2004
Raz, Avi	31 Aug. 2009
Reznikovich, Naftali	9 Dec. 2009
Rozovsky, Yosef	27 Oct. 2009
Rubin, Yishai	9 Dec. 2009
Rubinstein, Meir	27 Oct. 2009
Saifi, Johayna	10 Dec. 2009
Sasson, Talia	17 Mar. 2009
Sat, Eytan	5 Nov. 2003
Sfard, Michael	20 Dec. 2009
Shalev, Nir	15 Sept. 2010
Shamgar, Meir	13 July 2010
Shbaytah, Fadi	8 July 2010
Shehadeh, Raja	14 July 2010
Shilhav, Yosseph	19 Nov. 2009
Shoval, Ronen	4 Feb. 2010
Shushan, Itzik	5 July 2010
Siksek, Omar	11 July 2010, 21 July 2010
Skali, Cheftziba	29 Oct. 2010
Sklar, Lea	28 Feb. 2003
Spiegel, Dror	4 Nov. 2009
Sullaiman, Mohammed	12 July 2010
Tikochinski, Shlomo	27 Oct. 2009
Tirza, Dany	7 Apr. 7, 2003
Tzaban, Dror	5 Feb. 2003
Wallerstein, Pinchas	22 June 2010, 9 Aug. 2010
Wreshner, Noam	8 Dec. 2009
Yinon, Avigail	15 Dec. 2009
Zabari, Menachem	23 Aug. 2010
Zar, Itai	28 Oct. 2009
Zecharia, Shlomy	20 Dec. 2009, 7 Nov. 2010
Zohar, Zvi	15 May 2008

Students at Elisha and Beit Yatir academies and Akko *hesder* yeshivah; soldiers of the Netzah Yehudah brigade; and residents of outposts, Akko, and *haredi* locales—names withheld.

INDEX

abortion law, 175

Absentees' Property Law (1950), 52–53, 80–81, 205

Adam settlement, 132

Adei Ad, 100

Adva Center, 112

Agranat, Shimon, 33–35

Agudat Yisrael, 31, 38, 40–41, 167–68, 170, 173–75, 180

Ahdut Ha'avodah, 28, 54, 63, 66

Ahmed, Abdulkarim Ayoub, 115

Akko (Akka, Acre), 49, 195–201, 203
    riots of 2008, 199–201, 203

Al-Aqsa Mosque
    Sharon visit of 2000, 112–13

Albeck, Plia, 69, 83–85

Alexandroni Brigade, 20

Al-Ittihad (newspaper), 32

Allon, Yigal
    Altalena and, 22, 27–28, 30
    maps and, 66–67
    settlements and, 69–71
    Six-Day War and, 62–63, 65

Allon Plan, 65, 68–69

Altalena crisis, 16–28, 162, 235

Amana, 88, 102, 121, 128

American Jews, 70–71, 247

Amir, Yigal, 107–8

Amital, Yehudah, 149

Amonah, 118, 126–31

anti-Semitism, 36, 38, 211, 216, 243–44

Arab (Palestinian) citizens of Israel, 246
    civil service and, 205, 214
    disenfranchised, 219

early policies toward, 7, 45, 49–50, 52–54

East Jerusalem Palestinians vs., 64

education and, 205–6

elected leadership, 8–9, 184

equality and, 43, 204–6, 222–24, 226, 235–38

High Court of Justice on rights of, 111

housing discrimination vs., 205, 207–9, 217–18

Jaffa and, 202

Jewish settlers in mixed cities and, 10, 195–205

Knesset and, 30, 206

land and, 52–53, 208–9, 217

military and, 138, 145, 238

military government of, 53–54, 205

policing of, 219

population and, 28

schools plan, 47–48

security fence and, 206–7

seen as enemy, 10, 53, 195–98, 204, 207–8, 210–15

voting and, 54

West Bank Palestinians vs., 65, 206–7

Arabic language, 237

Arab intellectuals, 55, 206

Arab Legion, 49

Arab parties, 183–85, 206, 226

Arafat, Yasser, 125–26

Ariel, Uri, 203

Ariel, Yisrael, 233

armistice of 1949, 27–28, 49, 61

Association for Civil Rights in Israel, 208, 215

Index

Atarot, 64
Ateret Kohanim yeshivah, 153
Aviner, Shlomo, 150–51, 153–55
Azaryahu, Sini, 61–63
Azzun Atma, 114–15

Bamahaneh (magazine), 144
Bani Na'im, 86
Bank of Israel, 109
Baqa al-Gharbiyah, 208
Barak, Aharon, 147
Barak, Ehud, 108, 113, 128, 161
Bar-Ilan University, 90, 107
Bar-Lev, Haim, 82
Bar-Yehudah, Yisrael, 41
basic laws, 31, 111, 239
Beduin
    expulsion from northern Sinai (1972), 146
Be'eri, Dan, 106–7
Begin, Menachem
    Altalena and, 16–21, 23, 25
    Ben-Gurion vs., 28
    coalition with ultra-Orthodox and, 174–78
    constitution and, 41, 43
    German reparations and, 55
    settlements and, 68–69, 80, 82–83
    Six-Day War and, 63, 65
Beinisch, Dorit, 133, 137
Beitar Illit, 185–88
Beit Dajan, 121–22
Beit El, 86, 133, 150, 201, 202
Beit Shean, 47, 49
Beit Ya'akov seminaries, 167
Beit Yatir academy, 150
Believe and Plant fund, 116
Bemuna company, 202
Ben-David, Ariel, 202
Ben-Eliezer, Binyamin, 102
Ben-Gurion, David, 184, 194
    Altalena and, 15–16, 18–20, 22–24
    Arabs and, 45, 47–49, 51, 54
    armistice and, 27–28
    coalition with United Religious Front
        and, 30–31, 38–40
    constitution and, 41–43
    Kol Ha'am case and, 32–35, 112
    mamlakhtiut and, 30–31
    resignation of, 54
    Whole Land and, 28

Ben-Porat, Eran, 187
Benziman, Uzi, 64
Besheva (newspaper), 136, 151, 160, 199
Bethlehem, 43, 63, 65
Bet Zouri, Eliahu, 197
Bialik, Haim Nahman, 55
Bible, 12, 36–37, 63, 97–101, 118. *See also*
    Torah
Bilin
    land dispute, 85
Birkat Moshe yeshivah, 106
Bnei Akiva, 90, 94
Bnei David academy, 141–42, 144, 159–60
borders. *See also* Green Line
    Allon and, 67
    birth of state and, 26–28
    democracy and, 89
    future Palestinian state and, 229
    Oslo and, 126
    partition plan and, 44
    reestablishing, 226, 232, 235, 238–39, 247
    West Bank fence and, 114
Botavia, Moshe, 135–37
Bozaya, Ibthisam, 118
Brasher, Brenda, 239–40
Breaking the Silence, 155–56, 215
Britain, 27, 46, 83
British Mandate, 16–18, 24, 27, 32–33, 38,
    47, 51, 53, 76–77, 91
B'Tselem, 215
Bush, George W., 115

cabinet, Israeli, 104
    illegal outposts and, 124–28
    settlements and, 68–69, 73–76, 102
    Six-Day War and, 64–67
Camp David summit of 2000, 108, 113
Cast Lead. *See* Gaza Strip, invasion of 2009
Central Bureau of Statistics, 109
Central Command, 142
Chazan, Naomi, 216
Chetboun, Yehonatan, 219
children
    freedom of religion and, 190
    stipends for, 175–77
cinema industry, 214–15
citizenship. *See also* Arab (Palestinian)
    citizens of Israel
    loyalty oath and, 214–15

military service and, 138–39
naturalization and, 246
citizenship law (1952), 50
Civil Administration (West Bank), 56, 101–2, 127, 130
civil service, 214
Clinton, Bill, 125
Cohen, Bezalel, 177–78, 188–89
Cohen, Nachshon, 198–99
Collapse (Diamond), 58
Committee of Rabbis in Judea, Samaria, and Gaza, 106
Communist Party, 29–30, 32–34, 41, 53–54, 184
community settlements, 93–96. *See also specific settlements*
inside Israel, 207–9, 218
Constituent Assembly, 28
constitution
basic laws as, 111–12, 239
debate over, 28, 30–31, 34, 41–43
conversion, 182–83, 245–46
Council of Settlements in Judea, Samaria, and Gaza, 57, 102, 116, 121, 128, 130, 132
Custodian for Governmental and Abandoned Property, 83–85

Danon, Danny, 216
Dayan, Moshe, 20–21, 62, 65–66, 69, 75, 77–78, 146
declaration of independence, Israeli, 7, 16, 18, 27, 34
Defense Ministry, Israeli, 30, 128, 132–33, 207
Deganyah, 60
Deir Nidham, 4
Deir Yassin massacre, 48
democracy
Allon map and, 67
Arab citizenship and, 13, 43–44, 50–52, 96, 111–12
constitution and, 41–43
depoliticizing army and, 235
development of, in Israel, 7–11, 26, 32, 35–36
education and, 95–96, 241
elections of 1949 and, 7, 28–29
equality and, 43, 222–24
individual rights and, 32

Jewish state and, 28, 43–44, 64, 77, 103, 222–23, 235–36
Kol Ha'am case and, 32–36
military government over Arabs and, 54
non-Jewish citizenry and, 51
occupation and settlements and, 4–5, 70, 77, 89–90, 103–4, 111–12, 133, 194, 208–9, 220
reestablishing ideals of, 13, 221–23, 226, 241, 248
Six-Day War and, 64
ultra-Orthodox and, 7, 167, 172–73, 190–91
Democratic List of Nazareth, 30
Development Authority, 52
Diamond, Jared, 58–49
Diaspora, 51, 177, 236–37, 247–38
Diskin, Yehoshua Leib, 187
divorce laws, 181–83
Dome of the Rock, 88
Drori, Ze'ev, 193–94
Druckman, Haim, 161–62

Eastern European Jews, 6, 36, 38, 172, 174
East Jerusalem, 9, 88, 105, 109, 203
annexation of, 64, 67, 229
Eban, Abba, 32
Eckstein, Shlomo, 107
economy, 5, 9, 177, 224–25, 241–42
education
Allon and, 67
Arab schools and, 47, 111, 205–6, 236
core curriculum and, 189, 240–41
free, compulsory, 31, 167
funding for, 94–95, 111–12
national system created, 168
parental choice and, 237
party control of, 31
religion and, 240–41
state secular and religious schools established, 29, 36–37, 39–41
ultra-Orthodox, 94–95, 110–12, 167–69, 173–76, 178–80, 186–91
Education Ministry, Israeli, 4, 95, 120, 189
Egypt, 27, 62–65
peace treaty of 1979 and, 79, 88
Ein Yabrud, 72
Eitam, Effie, 127–28
Elazar, General, 62, 70

Index

elections
 of 1949, 28–29
 of 1951, 31
 of 1969, 78
 of 1977, 8
 of 1992, 183–84
 of 1996, 107, 211
 of 1999, 211–12
 of 2003, 177
 of 2006, 183–84, 212–13
 of 2009, 212, 213–14
Eliahu, Ariel, 193
Eliahu, Mordechai, 116, 193, 198
Eliahu, Schmuel, 198, 217–18
Eli, 141
Elisha academy, 1–5, 151, 218
Elitzur, Yosef, 119–20
Elon Moreh, 82–83, 152, 198, 202
Emergency Regulations (1945), 53
employment
 Arabs vs. Jews and, 53
 ultra-Orthodox and, 169, 178–81, 186–91,
  241
Eshkol, Levi, 55, 61, 64–65, 73, 75
ethnocracy, 5, 11
Ethnocracy (Yiftachel), 5
Etzion, Yehudah, 58, 88
Europe, 6, 17, 26, 36–37, 44–45, 91

fertility, 110, 166, 169, 174–77
Fighters List, 29
Filber, Yaakov, 91, 92
Finance Ministry, Israeli, 109, 112
Foreign Ministry, Israeli, 76
Friedman, Menachem, 38, 165, 169, 189
Fund for Redemption of the Land, 84–85
Fur'ata, 100–101

Gal, Reuven, 145
Galilee, 27, 70
Galili, Yisrael, 15–16, 18–20, 23, 61, 63, 65,
  69, 80
Ganim evacuation, 136
Gans, Chaim, 222, 238
Gaza Strip, 5
 evacuation of 2005, 103, 109, 115–18, 130,
  135–36, 148–53, 157–60, 212, 231, 233
 invasion of 2009, 154–58, 216
 one- vs. two-state solution and, 224–25

Palestinian Authority and, 105
Palestinian self-rule and, 9, 79
settlements and, 78–79, 108
Six-Day War and, 8, 63, 65
Gazit, Shlomo, 74–75
General Zionist Party, 29
Geneva Accord (2003), 229
Geneva Convention, Fourth, 73–77
Germany, 17, 38, 43
Gilad's Farm, 97–98, 100–104, 131, 156–57
Ginsburg, Yitzhak, 118–20, 129
Glick, Moshe, 84–85
God of Vengeance (Asch), 203–4
Golan Heights
 annexation of, 79
 settlements and, 70–72, 76, 81
 Six-Day War and, 8, 63
Golani, Motti, 138
Goldstein, Baruch, 107, 119
Goldstone Report, 216
Gordon, A. D., 60
Gouri, Haim, 28
gray refusal, 139, 150–51
Grays vs. Greens, 128–29, 132–33
Green Line, 28, 67, 78, 80, 84, 89, 91, 93, 94,
  110, 113–14, 158–59, 179, 186, 203, 206,
  207, 220, 228–29
Gush Emunim, 57, 71–72, 82, 93, 94
Gutoff, Joshua, 191

Ha'aretz (newspaper), 32, 128, 166
Haganah, 16–18, 23–24, 48, 197
Hagar, Moshe, 150
Hague Regulations (1907), 80–81
Haifa, 47, 49
Hakim, Eliahu, 197
halakhah. See Jewish religious law
Halutz, Dan, 148, 153
Hapoel Hamizrahi, 23, 29
Har Brakhah, 160
haredim. See ultra-Orthodox
Harel, Itay, 132
Harel, Yisrael, 57, 132
Har Etzion yeshivah, 149
Harlap, Ya'akov Moshe, 100
Haviv, Itai, 146
Hazon Ish. *See* Karlitz, Avraham
  Yeshayahu
Hebrew University, 67

Hebron, 43, 71, 198
  crimes vs. Palestinians in, 86–88, 107, 119
  Six-Day War and, 63, 65, 67
Herut, 28, 41, 42, 54, 55
hesder yeshivot, 140–42, 148–49, 153, 159–62, 183, 193, 195–200, 202, 233–34
Hever, Ze'ev, 88, 102, 128
Histadrut, 29, 47
Hneini, Aziz, 121–22
Holocaust, 24, 38, 55, 116, 138, 172, 244
housing
  discrimination and, 217–18, 236
  settlements and, 76, 110, 124, 185–86
Housing Ministry, Israeli, 2, 84, 108, 121, 127–28
  2003 report on, 109
human rights, 103, 111–12,
human rights organizations, 90, 100, 111, 122, 131, 209, 215–17, 248

Ibrahimi Mosque (Tomb of the Patriarchs)
  murders of 1994, 107
immigration, 242–46
  early Jewish, 6, 19–20, 24, 31, 45, 59–60, 197
  future of Jewish, 242–47
  Jews and right of, 50–51, 215, 244–45
  non-Jewish, 215, 242–46
  Soviet Jewish, 196, 198, 211
Im Tirtzu, 215–16
Independent on Sunday, The (newspaper), 74
Interior Ministry, Israeli, 27, 32–33, 47, 110, 124
International Criminal Tribunal
  for the former Yugoslavia, 74
international law, 58, 64, 72–75, 80–81, 84, 89
Intifada
  First (1987), 104, 139, 187–88
  Second (2000), 95–96, 101, 113, 136, 139, 144, 177
Irgun Tzva'i Le'umi, 16–25, 48
Islamic Movement, 112
Israel, state of
  as Accidental Empire, 8–9, 63
  Arab lands and property, 49, 51–52
  declaration of independence, 7, 16, 18, 27, 34
  dismantling of, 2, 10, 89–90

founded, 6–7, 16–30, 38, 44–52, 226
  future of, 4–5, 10, 222–48
  historical parallels with, 10–12
  Jewish identity and, 31
  Jewish majority and, 45–46, 64
  as sacred, 12–13, 31
Israel Broadcasting Authority, 57
Israel Defense Forces (IDF), 1–2, 9, 13, 213, 144–62
  71st Battalion, 20
  89th Battalion, 20
  Arab service in, 238
  Beduin expulsion and, 146
  communal nature of, 145
  crimes by settlers and, 88–89
  depoliticization of, 233–35
  early Israel and, 18–23, 27, 30
  evacuation of settlements and, 9, 115–16, 135–38, 148–52, 158–62
  Gaza evacuation of 2005 and, 148–52
  Gaza invasion of 2009 and, 154–57
  Givati Brigade, 151, 157
  Golani Brigade, 143–44, 151
  human rights groups and, 215–17
  illegal outposts and, 126–27
  Kfir Brigade, 160–61, 194
  Manpower Branch, 192
  Nahal unit, 74–75
  Netzah Yehuda Battalion, 191–94, 234
  noncombatants and, 119, 154–58
  Northern Command, 70
  Orthodox influence in, 3–4, 23, 134–44, 148–56, 161–62, 233–35
  refusals and, 13, 135–39, 144–53, 155–62, 233–35
  settlers' antipathy to, 101, 156–58
  Shimshon Battalion, 161
  ultra-Orthodox avoidance of service, 169
  West Bank fence and, 114–15
  West Bank governments and, 78–79, 233–35
  Yom Kippur War and, 81
Israel Is Our Home, 211–16
Israel Religious Action Center, 120
Itamar, 128, 153

Jabareen, Tawfiq, 207
Jabotinsky, Ze'ev, 17
Jaffa, 49, 202–3, 205

Jenin, 136
Jericho, 114
Jerusalem, 38–39, 44–45, 48–49, 63–64, 72,
    114, 130–31, 153, 163–65. *See also* East
    Jerusalem
Jewish Agency, 16–18, 24, 45, 47, 70–71,
    204–5, 208–9, 236
    Settlement Department, 60–61, 70
Jewish Leadership, 213–14
Jewish National Fund (JNF), 51–53, 59,
    204–5, 236
Jewish religious law (*halakhah*), 98, 102,
    154–55, 166–67, 170–72, 244–45
Jewish state, ideal of, 28, 38–39, 43–44, 64,
    77, 103, 222–23, 235–36
Jewish terror underground of 1980s, 58, 88,
    101
Jews
    defining who qualifies as, 181–82, 244–45
    as nationality, 36–37
Jordan, 17, 62, 69, 81, 83. *See also* Transjordan
    dan
judicial review, 35, 112, 239

Ka'adan, Aadel, 208–9, 218
Ka'adan, Iman, 208–9, 218
Kadimah, 183–84, 213–14, 218
Kadim, 136
Kahane, Meir, 129, 157
Kaplan, Eliezer, 47
Kaplan, Lawrence, 171
Karlitz, Avraham Yeshayahu (Hazon Ish),
    168, 170–72
Karp Report, 86–89, 122
Katif Bloc, 135, 162, 186
Katzir, 208–9
Kfar Darom, 117, 135–36
Kfar Etzion, 71, 73–75, 140
    battle of, 49, 73
Kfar Maimon, 116–18, 130
Kfar Vitkin, 15–16, 19–21, 162
Khalidi, Rashid, 44
kibbutzim, 59–61, 90, 93, 138, 145
Kifl Harith, 118
Kiryat Arba, 86–87, 106–7, 121, 135, 137,
    140, 152, 157
Kiryati Brigade, 21, 22
Knesset, 28–31, 41–43, 50, 52, 55, 77–78,
    113, 168, 183, 211–17

Akko report and, 200
Arab citizens and, 206–7
Education Committee, 167
Finance Committee, 175
Israel Is Our Home and, 211–14
Law Committee, 214
ultra-Orthodox and, 175–76, 189
Kol Ha'am case, 32–35, 112
kollel students, 164, 168–69, 172–74, 177–80,
    188–89
Kook, Avraham Yitzhak Hacohen (elder),
    91, 100
Kook, Tzvi Yehudah (younger), 91–93,
    99–100, 141
Kretzmer, David, 82

Labor Party, 92, 142
    coalition of 2009, 214
    election of 1992, 183, 184
    Kadimah and, 213
    Mapai coalition and, 66
    settlements and, 66, 68–69, 72
Labor Zionism, 59–60, 68, 92
Lahav, Pnina, 33–35
Lam, Yosef, 42–43
land
    Arab citizens and, 207–9, 236
    ownership rights and, 51–53, 58, 80–86,
        110, 121, 122, 126–27, 132–33, 205,
        236
land-swap proposal, 229
land-use laws, 58, 205
Law of Return (1950), 50, 224, 244–45
Law of the King, The (Shapira and Elitzur),
    119–20
League of Nations, 17, 76
Lebanon, 5, 27, 142, 157, 235
    invasion of 1982, 139, 146
left Zionists, 16, 51
Lehi, 17, 20, 29, 48, 197
Leibowitz, Yeshayahu, 12–13, 40, 66, 220,
    239, 240
Levac, Alex, 166
Levenstein, Meir David, 41
Levi, Keren, 158
Levinger, Moshe, 71–72, 87–88, 91
Levinstein, Yigal, 141–42
Levy, Yagil, 152
Levy, Yitzhak, 108

Liberal Party, 55
Lieberman, Avigdor, 124, 210–15, 217
Likud, 8, 210–14, 216, 219
    coalition with Agudat Yisrael, 174–76
    settlements and, 69, 79, 86, 92, 94, 207–8
Livni, Tzipi, 114, 214
Lod, 49, 219, 201–2

Ma'aleh Adumim, 81, 106, 108–9, 229
Ma'aleh Mikhmas, 86
Mahmeed, Hashem, 207
Maimonides, Moses, 171
Mali, Eliyahu, 202
mamlakhtiut policy, 30–31, 149, 159
Mapai
    Arab policy and, 53–54
    birth of Israel and, 16, 29–30
    coalition with United Religious Front,
        30–31, 38–39
    constitution and, 41–43
    Labor Party and, 66
    Six-Day War and, 63
Mapam, 22, 23, 28–30
    Arab policy and, 54
    constitution and, 41–43
    Six-Day War and, 63
Margalit, Avishai, 11, 117
marriage
    arranged, 180–81
    civil, 183, 240
    religious control of, 39, 181–83, 239, 240
Mateh Binyamin Regional Council, 105,
    122, 126, 132
Mazuz, Meni, 131
Meir, Golda, 47, 146
Melamed, Eliezer, 160–62
Meron, Theodor, 73–75
Middle Eastern Jews, 138, 176, 208
Migron, 131–33
military draft, 3–4, 18, 138, 145–46, 158, 241
    deferments 3, 39, 169, 175
    exemptions for Arabs, 238
    exemptions for Orthodox women, 175
military government
    Arab population within Israel and, 53–54,
        204
    occupied territories and 89
Ministerial Settlement Committee, 69
Mintz, Adi, 128

Mitzna, Amram, 142
Mizrahi, 29, 37–38
Modi'in Illit, 185
Mofaz, Shaul, 124, 128
moshavim (cooperative villages), 60–61, 93,
    138
Moyne, Lord, assassination of, 197
municipal governments, 57, 110
mystical nationalism, 91–92

Nablus
    olive grove attacks near, 97–100
    settlements near, 118–19, 128, 158, 160
    West Bank fence and, 114
Nahal Brigade, 140
Nahal outposts, 75
Nahariyah, 27
Nakba (the Catastrophe), 7, 246
Naor, Arye, 176
Nasser, Gamal Abdel, 62
National Insurance Institute, 78, 178
national priority areas, 110, 111
National Religious Party, 93, 127, 176
    coalition of 1999 and, 108
    coalition with Mapai, 90
    state religious schools and, 39–40
National Union, 203, 212, 214
Neeman, Yaakov, 214
Nekuda (magazine), 106, 201, 202
Netanyahu, Benjamin, 9
    child stipends and, 177
    elections of 1996 and, 107, 124, 211
    elections of 1999 and, 108
    elections of 2009 and, 213–15
    illegal outposts and, 124–26
    Oslo and, 106, 107
    Wye summit and, 125–26
Neveh Dekalim, 116, 135–36
Neveh Tzuf, 4
Neveh Ya'akov, 64
New Israel Fund (NIF), 215–16
Nissim, Yitzhak, 151
Nitei Meir school, 186–88
Nokdim, 211

occupied territories. *See* Palestinian Arabs;
    settlements and settlers; *and specific*
    territories
Od Yosef Hai yeshivah, 118–20, 153, 233

Ofrah, 56–58, 72, 85–86, 93–96, 105, 108–9, 118, 126, 128, 132, 152, 208
Olam Katan, 218–19
Olmert, Ehud, 183, 212
one-state solution, 223–25, 232
Orthodox Judaism, 8, 69, 71, 73, 87, 102, 149, 231. *See also* ultra-Orthodox Judaism
  birth of Israel and, 30–31, 36–38, 40–41
  illegal outposts and, 129–30
  military and, 2–4, 23, 140–44, 148–53, 156–62
  Oslo and, 106
  police recruitment and, 218–19
  premilitary academies and, 141–43, 150–51
  schools and, 29, 39–40, 95–96
  settlements and, 232–33
  transformed by occupation, 90–95
Orthodox parties, 30–31, 38–39, 41–43
Orthodox Zionism. *See* Orthodox Judaism, religious Zionism
Oslo Accord (1993), 2, 9, 103–8
  illegal outposts and, 123–25
  Wye summit and, 125–26
Ottoman rule, 39, 83, 84
Oz, Amos, 40, 163–65

Palestine, pre-partition
  Bible and, 98–100
  population of, 6
Palestine Liberation Organization, 103
Palestinian Arabs. *See also* Arab (Palestinian) citizens of Israel
  crimes vs., 86–89, 122, 129
  disenfranchisement of, 8, 96
  family reunification and, 54
  High Court of Justice and, 81–82
  land of, 57, 79, 81–85, 132–33
  Law of Return and, 224, 246
  military government over, 88–89
  nationalism and, 55, 104
  as noncombatants, 154–58
  one-state solution and, 224–25, 232
  partition and, 6–7
  peoplehood of, 103
  population of, 49, 64, 66
  pre-Israeli statehood, 24
  reconciliation and, 246
  self-governing authority and, 79
  settlements and fragmentation of, 2, 69

two-state solution and, 103, 246
war of 1948 and, 5–7, 26, 44–53
West Bank fence and, 114–15
Palestinian Authority, 26, 105, 126
Palestinian citizens of Israel. *See* Arab (Palestinian) citizens of Israel
Palestinian state, proposed, 9, 228, 231–32, 246. *See also* two-state proposal
Palmah, 21–23, 60, 71
Paparin, Sara, 199
partition, 18, 26–28, 44–49
Peace Now, 90, 112, 130
Peel Commission, 46, 60
Peres, Shimon, 58, 69, 72, 107
Perry, Yaakov, 104
planning process, 122–26, 205
Pnei Hever, 203
Poland, 17, 38, 43
police, 53, 86–89, 101, 122, 130–31, 151–52, 218–19
Porat, Hanan, 71–73, 91, 117
premilitary academies, 3–4, 141–44, 150–51, 156, 159, 202, 218–19, 234
Press Ordinance (1933), 32–34
pro-democracy groups, 111–12

Raananim, 219
rabbinic courts, 181–83
Rabin, Yitzhak
  Altalena and, 25
  assassination of, 107–8, 185, 233
  election of 1992 and, 184–85
  Ofrah and, 58, 72, 105–6
  Oslo and, 104–8
  Palmah and, 22
  settlement frozen by, 124–25
Rabinovitch, Nachum, 106, 233
Rafi, 66
Ramallah, 57
Ramleh, 49, 202, 219
redemptive Zionism, 3, 91–92, 99, 106, 118, 140, 152, 159–60, 198, 231
Reform Judaism, 36, 120
regional councils, 124, 127
Registrar of NPOs, 217
Religious Front, 41–42
religious Zionism (Orthodox Zionism), 90–93, 96, 106, 158, 164, 173–74, 231–33. *See also* redemptive Zionism

Revisionist Zionists, 16–17, 24, 28
right of return, 73, 224, 246
rights
  bill of, 239
  freedom of religion, 190
  freedom of speech, 33–35
  individual and minority, 41–42, 222–23
  of non-Jewish citizens, 223
right to human dignity and freedom, basic
    law (1992), 111
right to pursue livelihood, basic law (1992),
    111
Roadmap to a Permanent Two-State
    Solution (2003), 115–16, 123, 131
Robinson, Shira Nomi, 54
Ronski, Avihai, 149, 153–56
Rotem, David, 214
Rozovsky, Yosef, 187
Rubin, Yishai, 198, 201
Rufeisen, Oswald (Brother Daniel),
    244–45
rule of law, 24, 77–80, 82–90, 103, 123–26,
    133, 147–48, 226
Russia, 46, 210. *See also* Soviet Union

Sadan, Eli, 141, 159–60
Sadat, Anwar al-, 90
Safed, 47, 49, 217–18
Sapir, Pinhas, 66
Sasson, Talia, 123, 131, 134
Sasson Report, 123, 125, 127–28, 131, 153
Scheinfeld, Moshe, 170
secular Jews, 36, 40, 68, 102, 106, 117–18,
    138–39, 143
secular Zionism, 36, 92, 154–55, 164
separation of religion and state, 9, 12–13, 40,
    43, 183, 222, 226–27, 234, 236–37,
    239–40, 248
settlements and settlers
  Allon and, 67–68
  crimes vs. Palestinians and, 86–89,
      97–102, 121–22
  early Zionist values and, 58–61, 68–69,
      72, 227
  established, post-1967, 8, 56–58, 61,
      67–75
  first- vs. second-generation, 97–104, 118,
      121, 129–31
  Geneva Convention and, 73–75

  government funding for, 69–70, 72–73,
      76, 78, 94–95, 103–4, 109–12, 118–20,
      122–31
  housing problems and, 185–86
  illegal outposts, 101, 104–34, 153, 160,
      218–19
  Israeli law extended to, 77–80
  Israeli-Palestinian talks of 2000 and,
      108–9
  Jewish Leadership and, 213
  land and property rights and, 58, 80–86,
      224
  military refusals and, 115–18, 134–36,
      139, 144, 146–52, 158–62
  move deep into West Bank, 93–94
  move into mixed cities within Israel, 10,
      195–203
  need to evacuate, 10–11, 222, 226–30, 232,
      238–39
  Oslo Accords and, 104–8
  planning procedure and, 122–25
  post-Oslo, 9, 108–9, 123–25, 128
  process for evacuating, 224, 228, 230–35
  religious Zionism and, 8–9, 12, 91–104,
      129–30
  rule of law and, 71, 89
  security and, 81
  Sharon and, 69, 128
  West Bank fence and, 114–15
Shamgar, Meir, 82
Shapira, Avraham, 148, 150
Shapira, Ya'akov Shimshon, 66, 77
Shapira, Yitzhak, 119–20
Sharansky, Natan, 127
Sharett, Moshe (*formerly* Shertok), 45,
    48–49, 54
Sharon, Ariel, 9, 35, 142
  Beduin expulsion and, 146
  coalition of 2003 and, 177
  Gaza evacuations and, 115–16
  Gilad's Farm and, 102
  illegal outposts and, 124–28, 131
  map of settlements by, 69, 105
  Oslo and, 106
  as prime minister after 2001, 113
  Sasson Report and, 123
  Temple Mount visit of 2000, 113
  West Bank fence and, 113–14, 206–7
  Wye summit and, 125–26, 128

Shas, 176, 184–85
Shebab (*haredi* youth), 188
Shechner, Ron, 124
Shertok, Moshe. *See* Sharett, Moshe
Shilhav, Yosseph, 186
Shin Bet security service, 53, 101, 104
Shlaim, Avi, 62
Shoval, Ronen, 216
Shvut Ami, 100
Sinai Peninsula
  Beduin expulsion and, 146
  settlements in, 76
  Six-Day War and, 8, 62, 63, 65
  withdrawal of 1982, 79, 88
Sing Unto the Lord Yeshivah, 97
Situation Committee, 46–49
Six-Day War (1967), 3, 5, 8, 13, 35, 61–65,
  90–92, 140–41, 226
Skali, Cheftziba, 121, 131, 233
Skali, Yitzhak, 121
Skali's Farm, 120–21
Sklar, Lea, 95
Sklar, Moti, 57, 95
socialism, 16, 25, 59–60, 165
Sofer, Moshe, 37
Soviet Union, 22, 32, 54, 210
Spiegel Report, 57, 86
Stalin, Joseph, 210
State Attorney's Office, 123
  Civil Division, 69, 83
  Department for Special Assignments,
    123
state budget, Israeli, 112, 127, 230
State Education Law, 168, 189
state religious bureaucracy, 39, 166–67,
  173–74, 181–82, 245
state religious schools, 3, 9, 39–41, 94, 96,
  141, 168, 173, 175, 186–87, 189–91, 237,
  239–41
state school system, 37, 39–41, 239–41
Sternberg, Eren, 157
Suez Canal, 62
Supreme Court, Israeli, 8, 137, 239, 244–45
  basic laws decision and, 111–12
  as High Court of Justice, 33, 81–83, 111,
    120, 130–33, 183, 189, 208–9, 218
  Kol Ha'am case and, 32–35
  military refusals and, 146–47
  settlement cases and, 133

Swirski, Shlomo, 112
Syria, 27, 62–65, 70, 81

Tabenkin, Yitzhak, 22, 70
Tale of Love and Darkness, A (Oz), 40, 164
Talmon, 100
Talmud, 12, 191, 226
talmudei torah schools, 180
Tchernichovsky, Shaul, 55
Tel Aviv, 16, 21–23, 67, 202, 205
Tell, 100
Temple, destruction of ancient, 157
Temple Mount, 63
  Sharon visit of 2000, 113
Tiberias, 47, 49
Tikochinski, Shlomo, 188
Tirza, Dany, 114
Tolstoy, Alexey, 210
Tomb of the Patriarchs (Ibrahimi Mosque)
  murders, 107
Torah, 41, 37, 106, 154, 157
Torah jobs, 173–74, 178–80
Toubi, Tawfik, 30
Transjordan, 27, 28, 49, 52. *See also* Jordan
Tsur, Yaacov, 109
Turmusayya, 100
two-state solution, 9, 104, 214, 220, 223–26
Tzaban, Dror, 112
Tzvi, Shabtai, 99

ultra-Orthodox Judaism (*haredi*), 3, 7
  child stipends and, 177–79
  development of, 163–66
  early state assumptions about, 40–41
  education and, 9, 31, 39–41
  education of, and employment problems,
    164–82, 186–91, 241–42
  government funding and, 9, 12, 40–41,
    165–68, 173–80, 186, 189, 239–42
  historical origins of, 36–38
  housing and, 185–86
  isolation of, 164–65
  Jewish law and, 170–73
  marriage and, 168–70, 173–74, 178
  military and, 38–39, 138, 191–94
  population of, 38, 177
  secular world and, 170–73, 179–81
  state rabbinate and, 181–82
ultra-Orthodox parties, 9, 176, 183–85, 226

Umm al-Fahm, 206–7
Underground Railroad, 147
United Kibbutz Movement, 22–23, 60, 70
United Nations, 213
  cease-fire of 1948 and, 16, 21
  Goldstone Report and, 216
  partition and, 6–7, 17–18, 26–27, 44, 46–48
United Religious Front, 30–31, 38
United States
  constitutionalism and, 42
  Eban and, 32
  ethnocracy and, 11, 46
  religion and state and, 239–40
  settlements and, 73, 123
  Six-Day War and, 64
U.S. Constitution, 11, 34, 43
Upper Galilee Regional Council, 70

Va'ad Le'umi, 16, 24, 47

Wallerstein, Pinchas, 57, 105, 117
War of 1948, 6–7, 15–16, 26, 28, 39, 47–49,
  53, 60, 69, 138
Weinstock, Yossi, 142–43
Weisglas, Dov, 115
Welfare Ministry, Israeli, 120
West Bank, 1–2, 4–5, 56–58. See also specific
    locations
  Allon and, 65, 71
  Civil Administration and, 56
  constitution debate and, 43
  court-ordered demolitions in, 132–34
  crimes against Arabs in, 86–89, 97–100,
    107, 122
  disengagement of 2009 and, 161
  education funding and, 95
  ending occupation of, 9, 226–29, 231–32
  evacuation of, and military refusals,
    115–16, 136, 152–53, 161–62
  international law and, 72–75
  land laws and, 80, 83–84
  municipal governments in, 78–79
  Olmert proposals on, 212
  one- vs. two-state solution and, 224–25
  Palestinian Authority and, 79, 105
  Palestinian self-rule and, 9

policing, 122, 162, 194
post-Oslo settlements in, 2, 9
Rabin road building in, 105, 108
renamed Judea and Samaria, 67
security fence and, 113–15, 206–7
Six-Day War and, 8, 62–63, 65–66
state aid for settlements in, 93, 95, 103–4,
    124–25, 127–28, 185–86
war of 1948 and, 28
Wye agreement on, 126
West Germany, 55
Whole Land of Israel ideal, 17, 28, 63,
    69–70, 90–92, 98–100, 106–8, 136–38,
    140, 152, 155, 159, 162, 212, 234
women
  rabbinic court and, 181
  as soldiers, 152
  ultra-Orthodox, 173, 175, 186–87
World War II, 17, 26, 46, 60
World Zionist Organization, 236
  Settlement Division, 71, 84, 124, 127
Wye summit (1998), 125–26, 128

Ya'ari, Meir, 42
Yad Vashem, 243
Yesh Din, 122, 133, 215
Yesh Gvul, 139
Yevsektsia, 42
Yiftachel, Oren, 5, 11
Yitzhar, 118–20, 152, 156, 202, 233
Yom Kippur War (1973), 69, 81, 146

Zamir, Yitzhak, 86
Zar, Gilad, 101
Zar, Itai, 101–3, 131, 157
Zar, Moshe, 101
Zionism. See also Labor Zionism;
    redemptive Zionism; religious Zionism;
    Revisionist Zionism; secular Zionism;
    and specific political parties
  birth of Israel and, 5–7, 22, 24–25, 29,
    44–46
  early history of, 36–38, 51, 59–60
  settlements not serving, 89–90, 96, 227
Zionist Organization, 16–17, 24, 51
Zohar, Zvi, 182

GERSHOM GORENBERG has written for *The New York Review of Books*, *The New York Times Magazine*, *The Atlantic*, and in Hebrew for *Ha'aretz*. He is a senior correspondent for *The American Prospect* and blogs at SouthJerusa lem.com. Gorenberg is the author of *The Accidental Empire: Israel and the Birth of the Settlements, 1967–1977* and *The End of Days: Fundamentalism and the Struggle for the Temple Mount*. He lives in Jerusalem with his wife and their three children.